HOW TO FIX ALMOST EVERYTHING

HOW TO FIX ALMOST EVERYTHING

BY STANLEY SCHULER

Illustrations by Sigman • Ward

Published by
M. EVANS AND COMPANY, INC., New York
and distributed in association with
J. B. LIPPINCOTT COMPANY,
Philadelphia and New York

Library of Congress Catalog Card Number 63–19655
Manufactured in the United States of America

Designed by James Darby

CONTENTS

HOW TO USE THIS BOOK

A couple of years ago, I was playing bridge at the home of a close friend. At one point during the evening, when I was dummy, I went to the kitchen for a glass of water. The flow from the faucet was little better than a trickle. Being something of a busybody, I guess, and because I had designed the kitchen, I unscrewed the aerator on the faucet snout, found it clogged and rinsed it out. It took me about two minutes. Later, it turned out that my host had been wondering for weeks what was wrong with his kitchen plumbing.

Another friend, leaving home with his family for a week end, found gasoline dribbling from a stone-cut in the bottom of his gasoline tank. It was Saturday, and the repair shop couldn't have it welded that morning. They *could* get a new tank—perhaps on Monday. That would be about thirty-five dollars. Or if he could leave the car on Monday they could have the tank welded by Tuesday afternoon.

My friend is a choleric man. He fixed the tank himself, at a cost of less than a dollar. His week end started an hour later than he had planned, of course, but he had the pleasure of driving the car for another year without further trouble, and when he sold it, his gas-tank patch was still intact.

These are random samples. There are dozens of fix-it jobs that need to be done around the house—anybody's house. Half of them are left as lingering nuisances—not because they are difficult, but simply because so many people are afraid that they will botch the job, or that they don't know what kind of glue to use, or think they have to have special tools, or don't realize that a few minutes' time and a few cents worth of material may be all that is needed.

We live surrounded by thousands of *things*. And sooner or later, most of them break, rip, rust, chip, tear, stain, leak, or get out of whack in some other way. Something has to be done about them—and to find the somebody to do that something often turns out to be either agonizingly slow or astonishingly expensive. Or both.

Not everything in and around the house that breaks down or is broken can be fixed. But hundreds of things *can* be, and fixed well and handily by anybody who can read simple directions and has the normal use of his hands. *How To Fix Almost Everything* is intended to tell you what you can use to fix what, and how to use it in the best and easiest way.

What do we mean by fixing? To most people, the word "fixing" implies making a relatively *simple* repair. And that's the way the word is used here. You *replace* a roof, but you may *fix* a leak; you *remodel* a kitchen, but you *fix* a zipper; you *repave* a driveway, but you *fix* a crack in the walk. This, then, is a book about fix-it-sized problems—the hundreds of them which you can handle even though you are not a mechanic. It does *not* include major repairs that are too big or too complicated for the average person. Unless you have special skills, you will find it cheaper and safer and better to let a professional handle these big jobs for you.

How To Fix Almost Everything has been arranged to make it as easy as possible to find the specific information you need at the moment.

The first and main section of the book is an alphabetical listing of *things* you may want to know how to fix and also of the *materials* they are made of. You will find such entries as *fluorescent lamp, bird bath, galoshes, umbrella, zipper.* You will also find entries such as *aluminum, brass, concrete,* and *leather.* And sometimes, when there are many related things in one large category, you may find them grouped under such general headings as *toys* or *clothing.* Where there was more than one likely place to list something, we have used cross references. And finally, there is the index which covers everything in the book. If the information you need is in the book, you will be able to find it with very little difficulty.

The second and smaller part of the book will help you if you are a little uncertain about some of the common *techniques* that are used in many repairs. If you are replacing an odd-shaped pane in a window, you will need to know how to cut glass. There are instructions about that in the second part of the book. There too you will find sections on soldering, on making basic stitches, on methods of painting, on mixing and handling concrete, on selecting a right glue for a particular job.

Experienced "fixers" will need to refer to this section less frequently than those who are less proficient, but products and practices change over the years, and even the old hands may find some useful hints in these chapters on basic methods.

A word about *brand names:* You will find several used throughout the book. They are used simply because there seemed to be no other convenient way to specify certain specific types of material in an understandable manner. A long scientific name—if there *were* one—would mean nothing to most readers, and indeed to many experts. The products mentioned are certainly not the *only* ones of their kind on the market. But they *are* widely known, they are available almost anywhere in the country, and when you ask for them by name, the men in the hardware store will know what you are talking about.

No book could conceivably cover all the things that every reader might want to mend. This one is intended to provide usable advice on ways to handle the common fix-it jobs that the average person can tackle with some assurance of good results. If, in looking through the list, you find some problem that is not covered, it is probably either because the job is too complicated for most householders—or because it is so simple that the procedures are obvious.

So here—for those who have been as baffled as my friends and I when faced with necessary chores—are some handy hints on ways to handle the one thousand and one pesky little jobs that all too often remain undone.

Cos Cob, Conn. *Stanley Schuler*

Section 1

HOW TO FIX ALMOST EVERYTHING

ACOUSTICAL TILE

Loose, bulging. If tile is applied to wood furring strips, nail back to the strips with flat-headed nails. If applied on plaster, use cement-coated nails. Countersink the nail heads and cover with spackle.

Stained by a leak. Stop the leak. Tile can be painted with any interior paint without damaging its acoustical qualities. But if you prefer to replace the tile, cut it out with a knife. Trim off flanges on new tile as necessary so that it can be fitted into the hole (most acoustical tiles have interlocking edges). Nail tile in place or glue it down with acoustical tile mastic.

AIR CONDITIONER, CENTRAL

Note: Like many other major pieces of equipment in the house, a central air conditioner is too complicated for the average person to fool with. Of course, if it doesn't work, you should check whether the fuse has blown; and you should see that the filters are clean at all times. Beyond that, leave repairs to an expert.

AIR CONDITIONER, ROOM

Note. Call a serviceman if machine doesn't work properly, but before doing so, check and correct points noted below.

Doesn't work. Check: Is it plugged in? Has fuse blown?

Labors. Clean filters. Your problem may also be a voltage drop. Such drops are often temporary but sometimes continue. If conditioner labors only briefly, don't worry. But if laboring continues, call serviceman.

Freezes. Turn off unit at once. Restart after a few hours.

Compressor cycling—turning on and off at short intervals. Move thermostat up two points.

Noisy. Check whether grille or window is loose. Shim up conditioner with wedges if it is not level. Oil fan motor.

Cooling efficiency drops. This can happen if sun shines on conditioner for any length of time. Hang an awning over it.

Heat from heat-pump model drops. Temperature outside has dropped and coils on weather side have iced up. Defrost conditioner by turning it to cooling cycle for a few minutes. Then switch to heating.

ALABASTER

Broken. Clean and coat both broken edges with a film of Duco cement. Let dry. Then apply a second coat to one edge and press together for several hours.

ALUMINUM

Small holes, tears. Clean metal with steel wool. Apply plastic aluminum.

Large holes, tears. If edges are more than 3/16″ apart, cut a patch out of sheet aluminum. Clean patch and area around hole with steel wool. Spread plastic aluminum or epoxy glue on patch and press down. Patch can also be soldered (see Basic Methods: How to Solder Metal).

Seam between two pieces of aluminum open. If previously soldered, heat metal with torch and apply new solder. Otherwise, glue pieces together with plastic aluminum.

Note. If there is strain on a patch or seam, riveting is advisable (see Basic Methods: How to Fasten Metal).

Heavy aluminum broken. Solder or apply epoxy glue to the broken edges and press together.

Aluminum separated from other materials, such as felt, glass, etc. See household decorative accessories (metal).

Dents. Hold a block of wood over concave side of dent. Hammer out carefully (use light taps, not heavy blows) with a rubber mallet. Hammer from edges of dent toward the center.

Stains. Scrub with fine steel wool and a prepared heavy-duty aluminum cleaner.

AQUARIUM

Leaks. Dry and clean the leaking seam on the inside. Remove loose or crumbly caulking. Then squeeze in asphaltic aquarium sealer available from pet stores or the Five and Ten. Let dry for at least two hours.

Glass broken. Break it out and pick out all splinters. Scrape cement completely from the slate and frame. Clean thoroughly and let dry. Have piece of glass cut to size. Mix 100% Portland cement with linseed oil to a thick consistency; roll into a rope and press firmly into the track at bottom and on sides. Slip glass through top of frame and press securely into the cement. Press cement into track at top. Let cement dry one or two days and then trim off excess.

ARROW

Feathers off or damaged. Remove all feathers, whether damaged or not, and scrape off glue and any thread bindings. Select three feathers from a turkey wing or, if not available, from a large chicken wing. (Arrow feathers are also available from outstanding sporting-goods stores.) Be sure feathers come from the same side of the turkey's body or arrows won't fly straight. Split the feathers down the midrib and smooth the ribs on fine sandpaper. Trim feathers roughly to size and allow 1" of midrib to extend beyond either end. Arrange feathers at 120° angles around the arrow and glue midribs to the wood with Duco cement. Then wrap fine thread around the exposed midribs and coat with Duco cement.

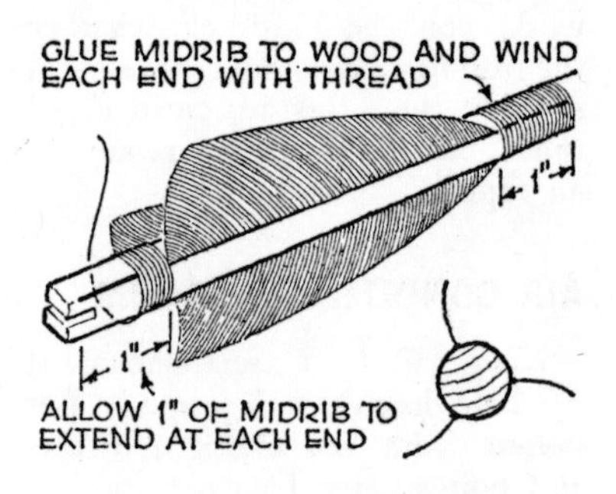

ASBESTOS-CEMENT SHINGLE OR BOARD

See roof, asbestos-cement shingle.

ASPHALT ROLL ROOFING

See roof—asphalt roll roofing; or exterior wall—asphalt roll siding.

ASPHALT SHINGLE

See roof, asphalt shingle.

ASPHALT TILE

See floor, asphalt tile.

ATTIC FAN

See fan, attic.

AUTOMOBILE

This is probably the one piece of mechanical equipment that people understand reasonably well. But unless you're a real mechanic, leave repairs to the so-called experts. However, if your car fails to start, check the following points before sending out an SOS:

Is battery dead? If lights don't go on, it probably is.

Are cables to battery broken? You can buy and easily install new ones yourself.

Are you out of gas?

Are the spark plugs and carburetor dry? If not, wipe off carefully with a rag.

AUTOMOBILE BODY

Holes in panels under doors. Make sure drainage holes in bottom of panel are clear. With your vacuum cleaner blow air through rusted-out hole into the panel. This will help to drive out moisture. Then let metal dry for 24 hours or longer if possible. Then spray two coats of Rust-Oleum 769 Red Primer into the panel with Snorkel kit sold by the paint manufacturer. When paint dries, thoroughly clean metal around rusted-out hole and wad metal screen wire into hole until wire is reasonably secure. Exposed surface of wire should not protrude beyond surface metal. Cover wire with auto body solder and build this up in thin layers until they finally overlap surrounding metal. Let dry completely. Then file and sand smooth and paint.

If screen wire cannot be readily wadded into hole, spread body solder around the outside edges, embed in it a patch of flat screen wire, and cover with more body solder. When dry, apply additional body solder to make a smooth surface.

Tears in fenders. Scrape off paint, clean metal with coarse steel wool, and roughen with a file. If edges of metal are not in line, bend straight and clamp. (In the case of very bad tears, it may be advisable to drill holes through the metal and bolt a steel mending plate or piece of galvanized flashing underneath.) Cover the tear with auto body solder. File and sand smooth when and paint.

Dents. If you can get at the back side of the metal, hammer out the dent with a rubber mallet. Otherwise, fill with auto-body solder. File and sand smooth when dry, then paint.

Paint scratched, chipped. Clean metal with the point of a knife and emery cloth. Be sure to get off the rust. Then paint with touch-up enamel.

Chromium rusted. See chromium plate.

Chrome strips off or loose. Place the strip over the little clips in the body and snap into place. If clips do not hold, it is advisable to have strip properly installed by a body shop. However, you can stick it in place yourself with several dabs of plastic steel.

Door rattles, doesn't close all the way. Check whether it is possible to loosen strike plate of the latch and move it slightly inward.

Rattles and leaks can also be stopped by installing new door gaskets available at auto supply stores.

Leaks around windshield. Clean sealing strip and squeeze in Duro windshield sealer.

Side windows leak, rattle. Replace old weather stripping with new. Strips are available at auto supply stores.

Rubber strips around fenders pulled out. Clean the crack between fender and body with a thin spatula and emery cloth. Clean rubber strip with gasoline. Squeeze plastic rubber into crack and push strip back into place.

Holes in convertible tops. Out of matching fabric cut a patch 1" larger in all dimensions than the hole. Cut with pinking shears. Coat with Devcon Patch glue and smooth over hole. On vinyl tops use a vinyl patch and plastic-mending adhesive.

Door or luggage compartment lock stiff. Squirt into keyhole a little auto-lock lubricant. Let it penetrate for an instant, then work lock back and forth.

AUTOMOBILE EXHAUST

Note. Fix holes in a muffler or exhaust pipe immediately. The danger of being killed by carbon monoxide is too great to take chances.

Small holes in exhaust pipe. Clean metal with a knife and steel wool. Spread plastic steel over holes.

Small holes in muffler. Clean metal thoroughly and cover hole with plastic steel. Pinholes can also be plugged with short self-tapping screws.

Large holes in exhaust pipe. As a temporary repair, cut off the top, bottom, and rims of a tin can. Cut can down the seam, then wrap the metal around the exhaust pipe over the hole. Bind tightly in place with strong flexible wire.

Large holes in muffler. For a temporary repair, cut a steel or aluminum patch large enough to overlap the hole ½" on all sides. Clean metal around hole thoroughly and apply a continuous strip of plastic steel. Set patch in place and bind with string until adhesive sets. You can then, if you wish, drill small holes through the two sheets of metal and secure the patch further with self-tapping screws.

Exhaust pipe loose, dangling. If brackets have rusted out, loop bailing wire twice around the pipe and then secure the ends to the body frame.

AUTOMOBILE INTERIOR

See also automobile seat cover.

Seats torn. Seat fabrics are stretched too tight for you to sew a rip with any assurance that the stitches will not pull out. The only thing you can do is cut a patch out of matching fabric or out of the excess material tucked behind the back seat, coat lightly with appropriate glue and smooth over the tear. A better solution is to get seat covers.

Fabric on doors, side panels torn. Spread a light coat of Devcon Patch glue under the tear with a spatula; then immediately pull edges of tear together neatly, and smooth down. If the tear is very large, glue one section at a time.

Fabric on armrests worn. Remove screws under armrest. Rip out seams in fabric carefully and use the old covering as a pattern for a new one. Sew new covering out of matching or contrasting material, wrap around armrest, and screw armrest to door again.

Rubber floor mats torn. Clean mat with gasoline or benzine. Roughen surface with sandpaper. Apply plastic rubber to small holes and tears. For large holes, cut a patch from a tire tube or old rubber mat. Clean the back. Apply plastic rubber to the patch and to the mat, and smooth patch down.

Stains on carpet. See rug.

Stains on seats. See clothing—fabrics.

Stains on plastic surfaces. Wash with detergent. Remove grease and oil with benzine.

AUTOMOBILE RADIATOR

Leaks. If hole is visible and accessible, drain radiator to below that point, clean and dry metal, and spread on a thick coat of plastic steel. If hole is invisible or inaccessible, pour in radiator-sealer available from service stations or auto supply stores.

Frozen. Fill with water. Replace cap but leave it slightly loose. Cover radiator with a blanket. Start engine and let it idle until steaming stops.

AUTOMOBILE SEAT COVER

Holes in plastic. Cut a patch from matching material (if you can't buy this, cut a small piece from the seat cover where it is tucked behind the back seat). Coat with plastic-mending adhesive and glue in place over or under the hole (whichever looks better).

Holes in fabric. Glue a patch of matching material in place with Devcon Patch glue.

Holes in fiber. Trim off raw edges. Cut a patch out of matching fiber at least 2″ wider and longer than the hole. Coat bottom of seat cover with Elmer's Glue-All and press down on patch. When dry, spread a little more glue around top edges of hole.

Seams split. Take off cover. Baste edges of material together. Then baste twill tape to both sides of seam and stitch on sewing machine.

AUTOMOBILE TIRE

See tire.

AWNING

See canvas or aluminum as case may be.

AXE

Blade badly nicked. Remove nicks with metal file. File toward sharp edge. When nicks are gone, hone blade on a carborundum stone.

Handle broken. See hammer.

BABY CARRIAGE

Fabric torn. Cut a patch out of matching material and glue over tear with Devcon Patch glue.

Seams in fabric split. If the fabric is not too dried out, rip old seams open and cut off edges at thread line. Turn new edges out and baste. Then cover with cloth mending tape or leatherette and restitch.

Mildew stains on fabric. Wash with household detergent.

Wheel off. Pry off hubcap by opening the split metal tabs that clamp around the spokes. Slip wheel on axle and insert new cotter pin in end of axle.

Wheel wobbly. Take off hubcap, pull out cotter pin in axle and remove wheel. Slip tight-fitting steel washers over the axle, replace wheel and insert cotter pin.

Brake doesn't hold. Remove rust from brake joint with emery cloth and apply oil. If brake still doesn't hold, bend ends of brake rod slightly toward the wheels so they will grip tighter against the tires.

Joints in frame stiff. Rub off rust with liquid rust remover. Polish metal lightly with very fine steel wool. Apply oil.

BADMINTON RACKET

Handle or frame split. Spread Elmer's waterproof glue on both split edges and clamp together for 24 hours or longer with C-clamps.

Strings broken. Better have an expert restring the racket. However, you can buy lengths of racket string from sporting-goods or mail-order stores. Pull broken string ends out through holes in frame and knot them tightly against the frame. Cut replacement string longer than is needed and knot it at one end. Pull unknotted end through hole in top of frame and weave it through the sound strings. At bottom of frame, thread string through hole and knot it against the frame.

BAKELITE

See plastics—general.

BALL, INFLATED LEATHER

Leak in bladder. Unlace ball, remove bladder, and patch like a tire. See tire.

Leak in laceless leather ball. Send it back to the factory.

Leather dried out. Inflate ball. Rub a damp cloth in saddle soap and rub soap vigorously into leather. Remove excess soap with a cloth dampened in water.

Seams torn. If the ball is laced, you may be able to get inside with your fingers and resew seams with strong cotton thread. A curved needle will help. But don't count on success. If seams in a laceless ball are torn, send the ball back to the manufacturer.

BALL, INFLATED PLASTIC

Holes, tears. Deflate ball. Patch with matching material or patch that comes with plastic-mending adhesive kit. Spread adhesive on back of patch, smooth over hole and let dry 24 hours before inflating ball.

BALL, INFLATED RUBBER

Holes, tears. Deflate ball. If rubber is heavy and appearance is not important, see tire (tube punctured). For lightweight, colored rubber, try to secure a scrap of similar material. Clean and roughen surface of ball around tear, and back of patch with sandpaper. Apply thin coat of rubber cement to both surfaces and let dry. Apply a second coat to patch and press to ball surface immediately.

BAMBOO

Breaks, splits. Glue with Elmer's Glue-All and hold in place with clamps, or wrap with thread or light cord until glue sets. For further reinforcement, when glue is dry, wrap neatly with heavy cotton thread (see fishing rod) and brush on varnish.

Another way you can sometimes reinforce bamboo is to insert in the hole in the bamboo a wood dowel of approximately the same diameter as the hole. Coat the dowel first with glue.

BASEBALL

Seams split. With heavy cotton thread, sew leather together in same manner as sound seams: Insert needle under the edge and through leather on one side of seam. Then insert it under the edge and through the leather on the other side of the seam. Continue in this manner to the end of rip, then tack thread securely and draw end of thread back under stitches.

BASEBALL MITT

Seams split. Sew together with strong cotton thread. Match stitches with surrounding seams.

Holes. Out of strong, soft leather cut a patch at least ½″ wider on all sides than the hole. Feather the edges slightly with a sharp razor blade. Coat back of patch and area around hole with Pliobond cement. Let dry until tacky, then press patch over hole.

BASEMENT AREAWAY (WINDOW WELL)

Floods. Dig out ground within areaway 6″ to 8″ below window sill. Fill with 4″ to 6″ of gravel. Level off gravel 2″ below sill.

BASEMENT BULKHEAD (OUTSIDE STAIRS)

Badly split, rotten. Replace with a steel bulkhead.

Door hinges loose. See door, garage.

Floods in heavy rains. Tack wood batten strips over open cracks. Tack wide strips of tire tube around edges of doors. To divert water from cracks at the top of the doors, nail 1″ by 1″ strips of wood to the bulkhead just above the doors. The strips should form a V pointing upward toward wall of house.

If water is coming through around the bottom edges of bulkhead, pull soil away from it so that the top of the masonry opening is at least 2″ above ground level.

BASEMENT FLOOR

Rough, irregular. See floor, concrete.

Leaks around edges. Chip out cracked, soft, and crumbly concrete with a cold chisel. Blow out crumbs with a vacuum cleaner hose. Fill crack with asphalt roofing cement or hot waterproofing pitch.

Leaks all over floor. This is a

big job. Individual cracks can be filled as above, but an entirely new surface is probably indicated. Call in a masonry contractor.

Concrete floor dusty. See floor, concrete.

Floor drain clogged. See drains, plumbing.

BASEMENT WALL

Wall weeps. Remove all paint and wash wall thoroughly. Let dry for an hour. Mix cement paint according to manufacturer's directions and scrub it into walls with a scrubbing brush, using a circular motion. After paint has dried for a couple of hours, spray with a fine mist of water. Repeat misting several times during the next 24 hours. Then apply second coat of cement paint in same way and repeat water-misting for 48 hours.

Wall drips in many places. Call in a masonry contractor. Only certain cure is to cover outside of walls with asphalt and cement.

Isolated cracks that leak. Chip out crack as deeply as possible with a cold chisel. Blow out crumbs with a vacuum cleaner and wet edges with water. Cram a stiff mortar of 1 part cement and 2 parts sand into opening. Cover with damp burlap for several days.

If crack leaks continually, ordinary mortar cannot be used successfully. Use quick-setting plugging cement instead. Open up crack and make it wider at the back than in front if possible. Blow out crumbs. Mix with water just enough plugging cement to fill hole, and mold it in your hand until it feels warm and begins to stiffen. Then cram it into crack and hold in place for several minutes.

BASKET

Woven wood or fiber basket broken. See wicker. Baskets made of wide wood strips are easily repaired in the same way.

Joints in steel wire basket broken. Clean wires with steel wool. Bring them together and, if necessary, clamp with a C-clamp or with a loop of wire. Heat with a soldering iron or torch and apply solder (see Basic Methods: How to Solder Metal).

BATHROOM ACCESSORIES (towel rod, soap dish, paper holder, etc.)

Accessory mounted on wall surface insecure. Anchor with long spring-wing toggle bolts or shorter expansion bolts, depending on wall thickness (see Basic Methods: How to Support, etc.).

Base of surface-mounted accessory secure, but leg holding towel rod, soap dish, etc., loose. In this old type of accessory, the leg is held in place by a short screw on the underside of the base. If simple tightening of screw does not correct problem, pull off leg and, with a file, notch or flatten the spindle on the end of the leg at the point where the screw touches it.

BATHROOM FIXTURES

See also bathtub, faucet, drains—plumbing, shower head, shower stall, toilet.

Chipped surfaces. Clean and dry the scarred area. With a tiny brush, apply epoxy resin or porcelain glaze made for the purpose.

Surfaces stained. Do not use abrasives or abrasive scouring powders. First, try washing with household ammonia and water, or a solution of 3 tbsp. Javelle water to 1 qt. water. If this doesn't work, scrub with a special non-abrasive cleanser such as Zud.

BATHTUB

Crack around rim. Clean out old plaster, tile cement, etc. Let wall edge and tub rim dry thoroughly. Then squeeze in tub-caulking compound and smooth off with a small spatula or knife.

Drain clogged. See drains, plumbing.

Chipped surface. See bathroom fixtures.

Stained surface. See bathroom fixtures.

BATTERY

Wearing out. Automobile batteries can be recharged if you buy a recharging unit that plugs into the house electrical system. The small batteries for cameras, toys, etc. can also be recharged, provided they have any life left in them, with a gadget made by Dynamic Instrument Corp. of Long Island. Follow the directions for use.

BEADS

String broken. Remove string entirely and arrange beads on a soft cloth surface so they won't roll away from you. Start with largest bead and arrange others on either side in graduated sizes. Knot end of new cord and lace it through the row of beads. After each bead, make a knot in the cord. Before tightening the knot, stick a pin through it and draw it up against the bead; then tighten knot and withdraw pin.

BEAM, EXPOSED INTERIOR

Cracks in wood. Clean out dust and cobwebs with a vacuum cleaner. Stain plastic wood to match beam and press into crack. If beam is painted, use plastic wood as it comes from the can, and repaint after 12 hours.

Shrunken away from ceiling or wall. Clean out crack with a vacuum cleaner, then fill with spackle. Sand smooth when dry and refinish.

BEDSPREAD

See clothing—fabrics.

BELT

See clothing—belt.

BELT, MACHINE

Slips. Belt is too loose. It should have some play, but not too much. Loosen motor from its base, move further away from machine and retighten.

Motor not running right. Belt may be too tight. There should be some slack in it but not so much that it slips. Loosen motor from its base, move toward machine and retighten.

Runs off pulley, frayed. Pulleys on motor and machine are not in line. Check with a straight edge laid across the ends of pulleys. Then loosen pulley on machine (not motor) and move into line.

Squeals. If belt is not frayed, turn off motor and rub belt with a wet cake of soap.

BICYCLE

Tire punctured. If location of hole is obvious (for instance, if there's a tack in the tire), wheel does not have to be removed from bicycle. First take out tire valve. Squeeze tire to unstick it from the rim. Balloon tires can now be pushed part way off the rim by hand; but with regular tires you need a tire iron. When tire is thus pushed to one side, pull out tube and patch like an automobile tire (see tire).

If location of hole is not evident, remove wheel from bicycle. Take off tire. Test tube for a leak in a tub of water and repair like an automobile tire.

Handle grips loose. Remove from handle bar and roughen bar with emery cloth. Coat with rubber cement and apply cement inside grip. Push grip back on.

Handle bar loose—easily pushed down so that grips point toward pavement. If tightening of nut at middle of handle bar doesn't correct matters, loosen the nut and shift the bar to one side. Wrap the middle of the bar with friction tape or two strips of emery cloth glued back to back. Then center bar and tighten nut.

Pedal treads split, worn. Remove nut at back end of tread, knock out bolt, install new tread.

Pedals stiff. If oiling doesn't improve matters, remove both treads as above. Unscrew lock nut on end of center spindle, take out washer and unscrew nut behind it. Take out ball-bearing sleeve and pull off the entire housing. Clean in kerosene. Fill ball-bearing sleeves with vaseline. Reassemble housing on spindle. Screw on nut that bears against outer ball-bearing sleeve. Screw it tight, then give it a quarter turn in opposite direction to allow for bearing clearance. Then install washer and spindle nut and reassemble treads.

Pedal crank loose. Take off left pedal and the crank nut (it has a left-hand thread). Then proceed as if you were fixing a stiff pedal, as above.

Rim brakes don't hold. Loosen cable controlling brakes and pull it back until brakes are 3/16″ from rim. Then retighten cable.

Coaster brakes don't hold. Leave repair to an expert.

Wheel wobbles sidewise. At point where rim is bent outward, loosen spokes on bulging side of rim and tighten those on the opposite side. Loosen spokes one turn at a time and tighten one turn at a time. If wheel cannot be straightened this way, you can remove it from bicycle and try bending it over your knee.

Wheel out of round—is flat at one point, has a bump at another. Remove wheel from bicycle and take off tire and tube. With a spoke wrench and screwdriver loosen the spokes at the flat point, tighten them at the bump. To check roundness of wheel, tie a string to a nail; hold nail in center of axle hole, and sweep string around the rim.

Note. A number of bolts on bicycles have left-hand threads, so if you come up against one that is difficult to loosen, try screwing it in opposite direction.

BIRD BATH

Concrete basin broken. Clean broken edges with a spray of water and let dry for several days. Apply Miracle Adhesive to one edge and firmly press broken pieces together. Remove excessive adhesive that oozes out from break. Let dry for 24 hours.

BLANKET

Bindings worn, torn. Rip off. Buy new binding material, turn edges under, fold around blanket and stitch down.

Edges frayed. Trim off. Put in two parallel lines of machine stitches close to the edge. Then, if you wish, finish by blanket stitching.

Other problems. See clothing—fabrics.

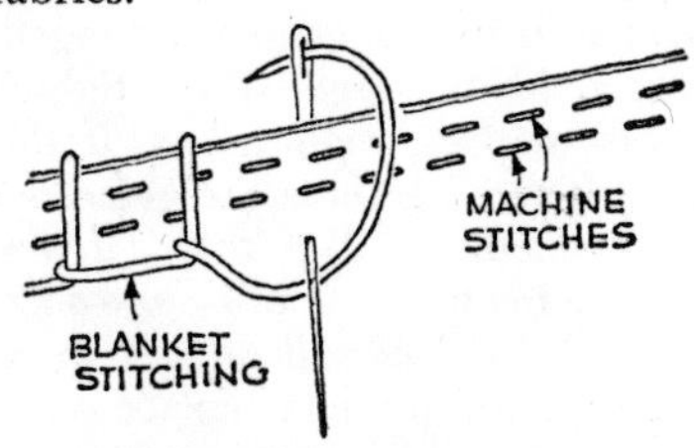

BLANKET, ELECTRIC

Doesn't heat. Check whether blanket is connected to cord and cord is plugged into house current. Check whether fuse on house circuit has blown and whether outlet used for blanket is okay (just plug in a light). Examine cord for breaks and replace if necessary. If these measures fail, you need a new blanket.

Hot spots or cold spots in blanket. Buy a new one.

Plastic control case broken. If control is still operative, disconnect it and coat broken edges with plastic-mending adhesive. Press together overnight.

Bindings worn, edges frayed. See blanket.

BLENDER, ELECTRIC

Doesn't work. Check whether fuse on house circuit has blown. Plug a light into outlet used for blender to see whether outlet is defective. Disconnect blender and examine cord for a break. Replace if necessary. If these measures fail, take blender to a service shop.

BOAT, ALUMINUM

Small holes. Clean metal with steel wool and fill hole from both sides with plastic aluminum.

Large holes, tears. Steel-wool metal on the inside and reshape it if it is bent or distorted. Cut a patch out of heavy aluminum flashing, hold over hole, and drill a series of small holes around the edges through both pieces of metal. Then coat underside of patch heavily with plastic aluminum and rivet it over hole with aluminum rivets driven from the outside. Make sure that plastic fills rivet holes. When plastic has dried, smooth off rough edges and spots with a file.

Dents. See aluminum.

BOAT—FASTENINGS AND FITTINGS

Corroded. Leave corroded screws in the hull. Drill beside them and put in new screws of Everdur or Monel. Replace bolts with new Everdur or Monel bolts. Above deck, fastenings can be removed and replaced with brass fastenings, although Everdur and Monel are far preferable on salt water.

In steel and aluminum boats use steel and aluminum fastenings respectively.

Replace corroded fittings—preferably with Everdur or Monel.

Fastenings loose. If wood through which bolts pass is rotten, brush on Calignum until surface looks slick; then let harden for ten days. If bolt holes are slightly enlarged but wood is sound, flow in Elmer's waterproof glue. To prevent bolts from pulling all the way through fiberglass, install large washers or plates under the nuts.

BOAT, FIBERGLASS-COVERED

Scratches, gouges. See boat, molded fiberglass.

Holes in fiberglass. Make sure wood is dry. Sand smooth. Sand fiberglass covering around hole to remove paint and marine growth. Brush polyester resin used in fiberglass boat construction on wood and cleaned area of fiberglass. Let it stand for 15 minutes. Then apply a second coat and let stand another 15 minutes. Meanwhile, cut a patch out of fiberglass cloth. Lay this over the tacky resin and smooth down. Brush more resin over patch and let dry. Then sand and apply one or two more coats of resin.

Small leaks. If source of leak is hard to find, pull the boat out of the water and fill it part way with a hose. Watch where the water flows out. Then dry the surface thoroughly and clean. Open the hole slightly with a knife or beer can opener. Fill with a polysulfide caulking compound such as Alroy 707. Work fast because the stuff hardens rapidly. Then sand smooth.

BOAT—INBOARD ENGINE

Note. Roughly the same things that happen to an automobile engine can happen to a marine engine. Problems can be avoided by taking care of engine as directed in instruction manual. Let an expert make repairs, but before calling on him, check points noted below:

Hard to start. Check: Is battery dead or low? Are you out of gas? Is ignition system wet?

Stops. How is the fuel supply? Is fuel system clogged? Is there a broken wire in ignition circuit? Is propeller fouled?

Runs badly. Any number of things can cause this. Get an expert.

Propeller nicked. See boat–outboard motor.

Propeller shaft stuffing box leaks. If leak occurs only when engine is running and it is not severe, there is nothing to worry about; but if leak occurs when engine is stopped, it should be fixed. First tighten grease cup on stuffing box. If this doesn't work, tighten the gland nut just enough to stop drip (if you tighten too much, it will cause shaft to bind). If this still doesn't work, loosen gland nut and replace packing inside.

BOAT, MOLDED FIBERGLASS

Shallow scratches. Clean with sandpaper. Brush on polyester resin available from boat dealers.

Deep scratches, gouges. Sand thoroughly. Mix ⅛" clippings of fiberglass mat with polyester resin to form a putty. Trowel into scratches, allow to dry and then sand smooth.

Small breaks. Open the hole slightly with a file. Then with a disc sander, grind down the inside surface of the hull around the hole. The sanded area should extend about 3" on all sides of the break and should be deeper at the center (i.e., more or less saucer-shaped).

Out of fiberglass mat available from a boat dealer, cut a patch to fill the sanded area. Lay this on a sheet of cellophane and spread polyester resin evenly over the patch. Cover with another piece of cellophane, and with your fingers or a stick of wood squeeze the resin into the fiberglass until it is thoroughly saturated. Paint the sanded area inside the hull with resin. Then remove top sheet of cellophane from the patch, press patch over hole and smooth it on hull. Let the resin set, then remove cellophane. Sand the patch and then apply additional layers of fiberglass mat in the same way until the patch is the thickness of the hull. Then sand and finish.

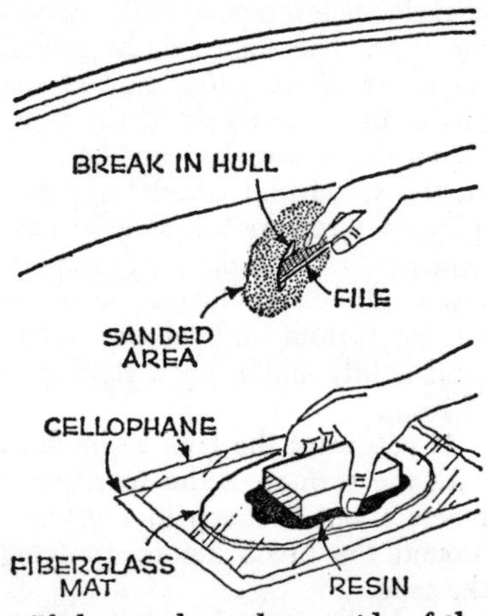

If the crack on the outside of the hull is not completely filled, you can then mix ⅛″ clippings of fiberglass mat with the polyester resin to form a putty. Spread this into the crack.

Large or compound breaks. With a small metal-cutting saw, cut out the damaged area entirely. Then feather back the edges of the hole on the inside of the hull for 3″ or more. Cover one side of a piece of shirt cardboard with cellophane and lay this over the hole on the outside of the hull (the cellophane should face inward). Tape in place with strong pressure-sensitive tape. Then build up layers of fiberglass mat on the inside of the hull in the manner described above for small breaks. Remove cardboard backing when job is completed and fill any imperfections in the outside surface of the patch with the fiberglass "putty" used to fill small breaks.

Lightweight aluminum sheet can be used instead of cardboard as a backing material. It is easier to handle if the hole is in an area of complex curves or bends. It does not have to be covered with cellophane.

Note. It is preferable to apply patches on the inside of the hull because they are less obvious and need little, if any, finishing. Outside patches are equally serviceable, but require more careful finishing.

BOAT—OUTBOARD MOTOR

Note. Follow instruction-manual directions for care and adjustment of motor. Let an expert make repairs, but before calling on him, check and correct points noted below:

Doesn't start. Check: Are you out of gas? Is gas-line valve closed? Is carburetor flooded? Is there water or dirt in fuel system? Is spark plug fouled or cracked? Are electrical connections loose?

Loses power. Check: Is there dirt in fuel system? Is carburetor adjustment too rich or too lean? Have you correct amount of oil in fuel?

Idles roughly. Check spark plugs, carburetor adjustment. Is a gasket blown?

Vibrates. Check spark plug and carburetor adjustment. Is motor properly mounted on boat? Is propeller damaged or fouled?

Motor runs, boat doesn't go. Propeller shear pin is broken. Drive it out and replace with new one.

Motor runs, boat sluggish. Propeller may be fouled or damaged. Motor may not be deep enough in water.

Propeller nicked. If nicks are not serious, smooth them with a fine-toothed file. To maintain propeller balance, try to remove the same amount of metal from each blade. Do this even if only one blade is damaged. If propeller has been dressed in this way several times, have it reconditioned by an expert.

BOAT, PLYWOOD

Seams open. See boat, wood.

Holes in plywood. Brace on the inside with a piece of exterior-grade plywood that is secured to the hull with Elmer's waterproof glue and brass or bronze screws. Then clean paint out of hole on the outside. Prime with new paint. When dry, fill with a plywood patch, or trowel in cement or glazing compound (marine grade). Sand smooth when dry and apply finish paint.

If plywood is also so badly dented that it bulges inward, drill a hole through center of dent and run a bolt through it and through blocks of wood on both sides. Draw up tight for 24 hours or longer. Then patch as above.

Another way to repair a hole is to cut away the splintered edges with a saw. With a disc sander, feather back the edges of the hole on the inside of the hull for about 3". Then fill hole with fiberglass mat (see boat, molded fiberglass).

BOAT, SAIL

Spars broken, cracked. If the break is at right angles to the spar, better have a professional repair it. But if the break runs with the grain, coat the broken edges with epoxy glue and clamp together for 24 hours. Then sand the spar in the area of the break to remove the finish. Coat the bare wood with polyester resin used in repairing fiberglass boats. Allow it to stand for 15 minutes, then apply a second coat and allow this to stand for another 15 minutes. Then wrap fiberglass cloth tape spirally around the spar. The tape should extend for about 3" on either side of the break. Butt the edges of the tape. When this has soaked up the resin on the wood and cured for a few minutes, wrap another strip of tape over the first, spiraling it in the opposite direction. Brush on more polyester resin and let dry. Then sand lightly and apply a third coat of resin.

If you want the tape to be flush with the surface of the spar, cut a recess about ⅛" deep in the wood around the break before applying the tape.

Leaks in centerboard trunk. If these cannot be stopped by caulking with glazing compound or any of the newer caulking compounds available from marine dealers, pull the boat from the water and overturn. Let wood dry thoroughly. Sand off any marine growth in the trunk. Then wrap a piece of wood with felt, dip in Seaprene or Vinylon, and thoroughly coat the trunk on the inside. The coating will dry to form a watertight, flexible seal.

Hull problems. See boat, molded fiberglass; boat, plywood; or boat, wood.

Sails torn. See boat–sails.

BOAT—SAILS

Holes, tears in canvas. Dry sail. Cut patch of canvas, making cuts parallel with weave of cloth. The patch should overlap the hole in all directions at least 1″. Allow ¼″ extra to compensate for shrinkage. Place patch in position on sail parallel to sail weave, turn under edges and draw line on sail around patch. Then baste patch in place, allowing some give in the fabric around the edges. Then stitch around the patch close to the edges. Use linen or cotton thread. Turn sail over and trim out edges of hole, but leave a margin. Turn under the sail edges. Then sew these down with zigzag stitches.

Holes, tears, rips in nylon or Dacron. Dry sail. Cut a piece out of adhesive-coated nylon or Dacron sold by marine dealers, smooth over hole, and let dry.

Rips in canvas sail. With doubled cotton or linen thread, stitch together with herringbone stitch. Do not knot the thread at start or finish, but cut it off 3″ or more beyond the ends of the stitching. This will permit sail to shrink without puckering.

Stitching in batten pockets worn. Remove batten. Stitch pocket to sail with doubled cotton, linen, or synthetic thread.

BOAT, STEEL

Small holes. Clean metal thoroughly with steel wool. Smear on plastic steel and trowel smooth on both sides of hole.

Large holes. Have these welded.

Seams split. Clean thoroughly with steel wool. Press together (if necessary, have someone bear down on the seam with a piece of pipe). Then heat with torch and run in solder (see Basic Methods: How to Solder Metal). Don't release tension on seam until solder has hardened.

BOAT, WOOD

Topside seams open. Scrape out old caulking with a beer can opener and prime seams with paint. Smooth on glazing compound or marine-grade trowel cement. Let dry. Sand and apply a second coat of paint. Fill in any remaining cracks or depressions with more glazing compound. Sand when dry and apply final coat of paint.

Bottom seams open. If it is a racing boat, treat seams as above. Otherwise, after scraping seams open and priming, fill with glazing compound and groove it inward slightly to allow for swelling of the planks. Let dry. Then sand and apply finish coat of paint.

Instead of using conventional marine paint for the final coat, you may apply Seaprene or Vinylon. These coatings, and others similar to them, form continuous hides that completely seal the hull and flex under impact rather than cracking.

Seams expand and contract excessively. Fill with Alroy 707 or Polypoxy caulking.

Breaks, splits in wood. Fill with epoxy or resorcinol glue. For emergency repairs, use 3-Ton Adhesive, which sets in about five minutes.

Wood rotting. Apply a special wood toughener called Calignum.

If affected wood is thin, sand thoroughly and then simply apply Calignum with a brush. On thick wood, drill ⅜″ holes approximately 3½″ apart into wood and funnel in Calignum until wood surface is slick. Then plug holes with wood dowels.

Marine borers in wood. Cut or bore holes to expose the insects' tunnels. Then treat with Calignum as above.

Seams in wood deck open. See topside seams.

Canvas deck torn. See canvas deck.

Deck too slippery. Clean thoroughly. Brush on a coat of Vinylon coating and embed in it Vinyl Weve flexible mesh. When surface is dry, brush on a second coating of Vinylon.

BOILER, HEATING

See furnace. See also coal stoker, gas burner, or oil burner.

Water level in gauge glass on steam boiler too low. Open valve on water inlet pipe and let in water until it reaches middle of gauge or point marked on boiler.

Water level in gauge glass on steam boiler too high. Washer on inlet valve may be worn and needs replacement.

BOLTS

Rusted tight. Squirt on Liquid Wrench penetrating oil and let it soak into the joint for a while. Then loosen with wrenches. In severe cases, soak the nut in a bath of penetrating oil for a day.

Head of machine bolt battered so that wrench won't hold. Turn with a tooth-jawed Stillson wrench.

Head of stove bolt battered so that screwdriver won't hold. Cut new slot in head with a hacksaw.

Threads stripped, won't hold nut. If bolt cannot be replaced, smear plastic steel on threads and tighten nut. Put a dab of plastic steel on the exposed side of the nut.

Threads battered so that you can't screw on nut. Clean out threads with a small triangular metal file.

BONE

Broken. Coat both edges with Duco cement and clamp together for six hours. If the broken object is exposed to weather, use epoxy glue instead.

Separated from metal. Coat with epoxy glue and press together.

BOOK

Page torn. Place a sheet of wax paper under the tear. Put a little white paste on the torn edges and bring them together. Then rub a strip of white tissue paper into the paste so that it sticks the entire length of the tear. Weight down until paste dries. Then tear off excess tissue, pulling toward the tear from both sides. This repair is easy to make and does not become soiled or discolored like a repair made with cellulose tape.

Page loose. Apply a ⅛″ strip of white paste to the inside margin of the leaf. Insert in book so that it sticks to adjacent page. To prevent paste from spreading over the two pages, place wax paper between them. Press down loose page until paste dries.

Page corner torn off. Place a piece of matching paper under the torn page and trace missing corner on it with a pencil. Cut the right angle with scissors or a razor blade, and tear along the hypotenuse parallel with the pencil line but ⅛″ further from the corner. The tear should have a feathered edge. Paste new corner to page with Elmer's Glue-All.

Back, or spine, of book torn. If appearance is not important, cover with adhesive-backed cloth tape. Fold tape over top and bottom of back and tuck it in between the cover and the back of the pages.

Cover torn from book. Remove cloth and glue from the back of the pages. Cut a piece of muslin 2″ wider than the back and as long as the book is tall. Center this on the back of the pages and glue with Elmer's Glue-All. Rub down smooth and let dry. Then lay the book in its covers and glue the flaps of muslin to the covers. Insert wax paper between the covers and the pages. Close book, lay flat and weight down. To improve appearance, paste end-sheets on inside of covers to hide the cloth ends.

Book warped. Set book on a flat surface in the kitchen, bathroom or other humid atmosphere. Place a board on top and weight down for several days.

Leather bindings powdery, scuffed. Rub smooth with very fine emery cloth. Heat 2 parts lanolin in a double boiler until it melts; then mix in 3 parts neat's-foot oil. Rub this rapidly and evenly over entire leather surface. Rub in well. Let stand overnight. Then polish with a soft cloth. If you wish, leather can be further protected by brushing on bookbinder's lacquer 48 hours after oil treatment described.

Ink stains on cloth covers. If you can't wipe them off with a damp cloth, leave well enough alone.

Ink stains on pages. Remove with ink eradicator.

Grease stains on cloth covers. Rub lightly with carbon tetrachloride; but don't count on success.

Grease stains on pages. Place a piece of aluminum foil under the page. Moisten Fuller's Earth with carbon tetrachloride and spread the paste over the stain. When dry, remove with a cloth. Don't count on success, however.

Mildew stains on cloth covers. Wipe off with a dry cloth. Then wipe with a cloth dampened in soapy water.

BOOKSHELF

Shelf sags. The alternatives are these: (1) Nail a 1″ x 2″ wood cleat to the wall under the shelf. The cleat should be at least 16″ long so that it can be nailed to the studs at the middle of the shelf. It is preferable, however, for the cleat to extend the full length of the shelf. (2) If there are several shelves and the bottom one is well supported, insert a length of 6″ board vertically between each shelf. Center these supports on the shelves and push them back against the wall where they won't be noticeable. Nail in place. (3) If shelves rest on adjustable metal wall brackets, insert a third bracket midway between the end two. (4) Replace sagging shelf with a new one of thicker wood.

Free-standing shelves wobble. Cover the back of the bookcase with hardboard or ¼″ fir plywood. Screw this securely to sides, top and bottom of frame.

Free-standing shelves tip for-

ward. Drive shingles under the bottom at the sides. Cut off flush with bookcase when it stands straight. Then if you wish, glue the wedges to bottom with Elmer's glue. If bookcase is heavily loaded, an alternative (or additional) method is to drive one or two small screw eyes into wall in back of bookcase. Insert corresponding screw eyes in back of case. Then wire together.

BOOT, RUBBER

Holes, tears. See tire (tube punctured).

BOOT, WOMAN'S PLASTIC

See galoshes.

BOWL

See wood bowl. For any other type of bowl, see appropriate material.

BRASS

Small holes, cracks. Heat metal and run in solder (see Basic Methods: How to Solder Metal). Fill from reverse side if possible. Touch up visible solder line with metallic paint.

Dents. Hold a block of wood over concave side. Gently tap out dent with a rubber or plastic mallet. Work from sides of dent toward the center.

Brass broken. It is best to have it welded. However, you can do a pretty good job by coating the broken edges with epoxy glue and pressing together.

Brass separated from other materials. See household decorative accessories.

Lacquer worn from brass. Rub off remaining lacquer with lacquer thinner. Then clean brass thoroughly with a brass polish, rinse in water and dry. Apply one or two thin coats of spray lacquer.

Brass plate worn off base metal. Have piece replated by a metal-working shop.

Tarnished. Rub on brass polish. Then rinse in hot soapsuds.

BRIC-A-BRAC

See household decorative accessories.

BRICK

Broken. If brick is in a masonry wall, floor, walk, or steps, crack it out with a hammer and cold chisel. Chip off mortar on surrounding bricks. Soak new replacement brick in water for a half hour and thoroughly wet bricks surrounding cavity. Then set in new brick with mortar as below.

Mortar joints around brick cracked or eroded. Chip out loose and weak mortar. Blow out dust with vacuum cleaner. Wet cracks with water. Mix 1 part cement, 1 part hydrated lime and 6 parts sand with just enough water to hold mixture together. Pack this into joint and smooth to match nearby joints.

For very small cracks, simply brush in a soupy grout made of 3 parts cement, 1 part lime, and 4 parts fine sand.

Efflorescence on brick. Check wall or floor for leaks and stop these. To get rid of efflorescence, scrub with a wire brush. If this is ineffective, mix 1 part hydrochloric acid with 10 parts water and scrub on stains with a fiber brush. Wear gloves. Avoid getting too much of the solution into mortar joints. Rinse thoroughly with clear water.

Mortar stains. Scrape off mortar chunks with a chisel or putty knife. Soak brick with water. Then treat as for efflorescence.

Paint stains. Remove fresh paint with paint-remover and wash with water. Scrape off old paint with putty knife and clean with steel wool. If necessary, use paint-remover, too.

Oil stains. Dissolve 1 lb. trisodium phosphate in 1 gal. water, then mix with whiting to form a paste. Spread ½" layer over stain, let dry thoroughly, then scrape off and wash with clear water.

Smoke stains. See fireplace, masonry.

BRIEFCASE

Seams split. If possible, re-stitch with heavy cotton thread and a blunt needle. Run needle in and out of old thread holes. For a quicker but less neat repair, coat facing leather surfaces with Pliobond cement. Let dry until tacky and then press seams together.

Other problems. See suitcase.

BROILER, ELECTRIC

Doesn't heat. Check whether fuse on house circuit has blown. Plug a light into outlet used for broiler to see whether outlet is defective. Examine cord for a break and replace if necessary. Check whether heating element is broken. If it is, buy a replacement and install in same way. If these measures fail, take broiler to a service shop.

BRONZE

Small holes, cracks. Heat metal and apply solder (see Basic Methods: How to Solder Metal). Work on reverse side of metal if possible. If not, visible solder can later be touched up with bronze paint.

Bronze broken. Have it welded for best results. Or apply epoxy glue to the broken edges and press together.

Bronze separated from other materials. See household decorative accessories.

Lacquer worn from metal. Remove remaining lacquer with lacquer thinner. Clean metal with a good brass polish. Wash and dry. Spray on several coats of new lacquer.

Tarnished. Clean with brass polish and rinse in hot soapsuds.

BRUSH, HAIR

Brush head loose from metal handle. Clean back of head and handle cavity. Stick together with four or five dabs of Duco cement. Then carefully bend or tap the metal edges down around sides of brush head.

BRUSH, SINK

Metal wires holding bristles come loose from wood or plastic handle. Dry the wires. Let the handle dry thoroughly (this may take several days if it is wood). Fill hole in handle with Miracle Adhesive and insert wires. Let glue dry 48 hours or more.

BUCKET

Holes in metal. Clean metal thoroughly with steel wool. Smooth plastic steel over hole.

Holes in rubber. Wash surface, dry, and roughen with sandpaper. Spread on plastic rubber. If hole is very large, spread plastic rubber on bucket and on a patch of rubber, and hold together until adhesive sets.

Holes, cracks in plastic. Wash surface. Apply plastic-mending adhesive.

Holes in porcelain. Chip away a little of the porcelain from around the hole and clean metal with steel wool. Spread plastic steel over hole.

Ear loose on metal bucket. Drill a hole through the ear and the bucket and rivet together.

Wood handle on bail broken. If it is split, glue it together with Elmer's Glue-All. If it is too badly damaged to be saved, slit a short length of rubber hose down one side, wrap around bail and apply rubber cement to both edges of slit. Let this dry, then apply a second coat of cement to one edge and press the two together.

BUREAU SCARF

See clothing–fabrics, or clothing –hems.

BURLAP

Holes, tears. To make a neat repair in a wall covering or drapery, unravel strands from a scrap piece of burlap and weave into place with a needle. If appearance is not important, cut a burlap patch, slather with Devcon Patch glue and press over hole.

CABINET, FILE

Drawers move stiffly. Remove drawer. Clean runners and oil lightly. Oil wheels. If drawer is still sluggish, check whether cabinet is resting on a flat surface. Shim up corners with wood shingles if it is not.

Wood front of drawer split. Remove drawer and drawer handle but don't bother to take front off drawer. Coat split edges with Weldwood plastic resin glue. Set drawer front down on wax paper over plywood and force sections together. See furniture–table (joined boards in top separated). As further reinforcement, screw small steel mending plates across split on inside of drawer.

Wood drawers broken. See furniture–chest of drawers.

CABINET, KITCHEN

Paint on metal cabinets chipped. See painted surface.

Doors bind. See door, cabinet.

Doors bang when closed. Metal cabinets are equipped with small rubber bumpers. If these are flattened or broken, try to find replacements. Or out of a tire tube, cut small round patches and glue to frame of cabinet with Pliobond cement.

On wood cabinets glue rubber patches to frame as above. It may then be necessary to readjust catches so they will close and hold properly.

Spring catches jammed. Remove from cabinet and soak in paint-remover; then clean and reinstall. If old catches are broken, replace them entirely with new magnetic catches.

Open space between top of cabinets and ceiling or between sides and walls. If crack remains open at all times of year, fill it with spackle; sand and paint. If crack opens and closes, tack strips of quarter round to the ceiling.

CABINET, MEDICINE

Enameled surface inside cabinet damaged by medicines. Wash thoroughly and dry. Cut thin vinyl to proper shape. Coat back of vinyl with Pliobond cement, and apply cement to cabinet surface. Let dry until tacky, then smooth vinyl down.

Sliding doors stiff. Clean out channels with an old toothbrush and vacuum cleaner. Make sure all gummy residues are removed. Put a few drops of light oil in channel and slide doors back and forth.

Light diffusers broken. See electric light.

CAN OPENER—WALL TYPE

Doesn't work properly. Scrub cutting mechanism thoroughly under hot water to remove gummy food residue, grease, etc. This usually solves the problem. If it doesn't, check whether space between cutting wheel and cogged wheel is too wide for cans to be held securely. This space can be reduced by tightening nut found either on the front of the cutting wheel or on the shaft behind it.

CANDLE

Bent. Place in a barely warm oven until wax softens slightly and candle can be bent straight again.

Colored surface broken off white wax base. Hold chip about an inch over the hole and hold a lighted match underneath so that you soften both the bottom of the chip and the base at the same time. Immediately drop chip into hole. This is a tricky little job, however, because it is difficult to get the chip placed properly in the very short time that the wax surfaces are soft.

CANE (the material)

See furniture—caned seat or back.

CANE (walking stick)

Broken. See entry for the material of which cane is made.

Different materials separated. See household decorative accessories.

CANOE, ALUMINUM

See boat, aluminum.

CANOE, CANVAS

Canvas ripped. Trim away loose threads. Then carefully pry canvas from wood for about 1″ on either side of tear and ½″ at the ends. Cut canvas patch the size of the loosened canvas. Spread Elmer's waterproof glue on one side of patch and slip patch through hole and smooth down. Then coat top of patch with more glue and press down loose canvas. This patch is adequate but is improved by applying a second, slightly larger patch over the tear when the first patch dries.

To make a hurry-up patch, scrape some of the paint from the area around the hole. Cut a canvas or balloon-cloth patch to cover. Spread Duco cement under torn canvas if it is loose. Then coat patch liberally with cement and spread a thin layer on canvas. Smooth down patch. You'll be ready to go again as soon as cement dries in 30 to 60 minutes.

Ribs, planks cracked or broken. If breaks are not serious, coat them with Elmer's waterproof glue. Ribs can be clamped, in a fashion, with

C-clamps. Splits in planks may possibly be brought together somewhat if you turn the canoe over and weight down the broken area with a 50-pound sack of sand. If ribs are separated from planks, cover with wax paper and weight down with sand (or weight from the outside).

If the bottom is buckled or badly broken, get an expert to repair it.

Holes, tears in caned seats. See furniture–caned seat or back. Use waterproof glue. You can also cover the seat with canvas, tacking it to the frame underneath.

CANOE, FIBERGLASS

See boat, molded fiberglass.

CANOE PADDLE

Cracked. Dry wood thoroughly. Spread epoxy glue or Elmer's waterproof glue on broken edges. Clamp together for 24 hours.

Blade splintered, cracked slightly at tip. Smooth off splinters with sandpaper. Force glue into splits. To prevent further damage, bend a strip of lightweight copper or aluminum around tip and tack in place with copper or aluminum tacks respectively.

CANVAS

Holes, tears. With pinking shears, cut a canvas patch that overlaps hole about ½″ on all sides. Apply Devcon Patch glue to reverse side of damaged material. Stick on patch and smooth down. For greater strength, stitch around hole–preferably on sewing machine–with heavy cotton thread.

Leaks. See tent.

Stains. See clothing–fabrics.

Canvas straps frayed at the ends. Cut off frayed portion. Coat strap for 1″ back from end with Devcon Patch glue.

CANVAS DECK

Holes, tears. Out of new canvas cut a patch ¾″ to 1″ larger on all sides than the hole. Spread white lead or white lead paint on deck under hole. Lay patch under hole and cover with more white lead. Tack down old canvas over patch with copper tacks spaced ½″ to 1″ apart. Apply deck paint when white lead dries.

CARDBOARD

Torn. Cut a patch out of cardboard (shirt cardboard will usually do) and apply rubber cement to patch and to area around tear. Let dry. Then apply a second coat of cement to the patch and smooth it down.

Pieces of heavy cardboard separated. Glue together with rubber cement or, better, with Elmer's Glue-All.

Separated from another material. Reglue with rubber cement or Pliobond cement.

CARPET

See rug.

CARPET SWEEPER

Pulley slips, brushes don't revolve. Wrap adhesive tape around the center pulley wheel.

CAST IRON

Cracked, broken. Clean metal thoroughly with steel wool. Coat edges of break liberally with plastic steel or epoxy glue and clamp together. Applying a coat of plastic steel on the outside of the break will add strength. Nevertheless, don't count on this mend's ability to withstand hard abuse.

Pitted. Clean pits with steel wool and smooth on plastic steel.

Rusted. Clean metal with a wire brush, steel wool, and liquid rust remover. Apply a rust-inhibiting primer and finish paint.

Cast iron separated from other materials. See household decorative accessories.

CATALIN

See plastics—general.

CELLOPHANE

Tears, open seams. Overlap edges of cellophane and press with a medium-warm iron until edges stick together.

CELOTEX

See interior wall, composition board.

CERAMICS

See earthenware or tile, ceramic, as case may be.

CHAIN

Broken. Repair links of various sizes are available at hardware or mail-order stores. If you can obtain one of the right size, simply insert it in the chain and hammer it closed.

If chain is not subject to great strain (the chain in a toilet tank or a dog leash, for example), you can also cut out the broken link and twist wire of appropriate size through the adjacent links. Twist ends of wire together and tuck into the chain so that they will not snag on anything the chain touches.

Chains subject to strain, such as an anchor chain, can be mended temporarily with repair links but should be welded.

Watch chains can be mended satisfactorily by looping tiny copper wire from the ends of an electric cord through the links several times. But for best results, see a jeweler.

Tangles, knots in watch chain. Don't pull. Drop loosely on a flat surface and pick out the knot with two pins.

Swivel snap on end of chain broken. Buy a replacement at hardware store, slip the bottom loop through the last link of the chain and hammer it closed.

CHAIN, TIRE

Links broken. Insert a monkey link, available from service station, through adjacent links. It will tighten when you get on the road again.

Entire cross link broken. You can cut it out with a hammer and chisel and put in a replacement, but it's easier to let a service station do the job.

CHARCOAL GRILL, METAL

Hole in firebox. Scrub metal with detergent, rinse and dry. Then clean with steel wool and coat hole heavily with plastic steel. Henceforth, don't build fire directly on the metal. Put in a layer of gravel or vermiculite.

Grid post stuck in slot. Soak in detergent solution to remove grease. Dry. Then saturate crack between post and slot with Liquid Wrench penetrating oil and try to tap post out with a hammer and blunt chisel. Don't pound too hard. If post doesn't loosen, apply more penetrating oil and let it soak in for several hours. Then use your hammer again. When post finally comes out, clean it and the slot with steel wool. In the future, remove and clean the post periodically. Sprinkling with powdered graphite will help.

CHIMNEY

Note. If you see smoke curling out of the sides of a chimney or if a chimney feels uncomfortably hot to the touch, damp the fire and call in a masonry contractor immediately. You have a real fire hazard. If you suspect that a chimney is leaking, you can test it by building a smoky fire in the fireplace and blocking the outlet at the top of the chimney with a wet blanket. Smoke escaping through the masonry shows the location of leaks.

Leaks water. Check as follows: 1. Is flashing sound and secured to chimney? For repairs, see flashing, copper. 2. Are mortar joints cracked or eroded? For repairs, see brick. 3. Is top of chimney cracked? It's best to have a mason replace the cap. But if cracking is not severe, chip out the cracks, blow out crumbs with vacuum cleaner, and pack in latex cement. Then cover entire cap with two ⅛″ layers of latex cement. Slope cement away from flue toward edges of cap.

Throws sparks. Have spark-arresters installed.

Fireplace smokes, draft is faulty. Have chimney cleaned and examined by a professional. If cleaning does not improve condition, call in a mason.

Crack between chimney and siding. Clean out crack and pack in caulking compound. Smooth it off flush with siding.

CHINA

Broken. Wash broken edges and dry thoroughly. If broken piece is used and washed frequently, spread epoxy glue on the edges and press together for 24 hours. If piece is rarely used or washed, you can use Duco cement. Spread this on both edges and press together. In either case, to hold the pieces together while the glue dries, stick strips of cellophane tape or adhesive tape across the crack.

Separated from another material. See household decorative accessories.

CHIP BOARD

See particle board.

CHISEL

Top of handle splintered by hammering. Glue down largest splinters with Weldwood plastic resin glue. Sand top smooth and fill cracks with plastic wood. Then tap a round metal furniture glide on to top of handle to protect it in future.

Dull. Sharpen only on the beveled side. Hold at about a 25° angle to a grinding wheel or a flat carborundum stone (in the latter case, hold chisel firmly against a triangular block of wood). Make sure you do not sharpen more at one edge of blade than the other and thus get edge out of square. Sharpen first on rough side of carborundum, then on smooth side. Then turn blade over so that beveled side is up; hold flat against smooth side of stone, and remove any burrs by stroking blade sidewise several times.

CHRISTMAS TREE LIGHTS

Note. Repairs to Christmas tree light strings, if not made properly, can start a fire.

Cord broken. Remove ½″ of insulation from each end of broken wire. Bend wires around each other, twist tight and always solder them together. Cover with cellophane electrical tape.

Cord pulled out of socket. This happens on series strings, especially those using miniature bulbs. Pull plastic socket cover away from metal socket. You will find that one wire is soldered to the outside of the screw shell, the other into a small hole in the end of the socket. If wire attached to screw shell is loose, simply hold it in place over the solder blob and heat with a soldering iron. If wire in end of socket has broken, as is more often the case, carefully drill out the hole in the socket a little. Cut end of broken wire cleanly and remove ⅛″ of insulation. Twist strands tight, then melt a tiny bit of solder on to the strands. Insert the wire in the socket hole and with the point of your soldering iron heat the edge of the metal around the hole until wire is secure. Make sure bare ends of wires do not touch. Then replace plastic cover. For safety, fill hole in the back of the plastic cover with plastic rubber.

If this repair proves difficult (it is not always possible to separate the plastic cover from the copper socket, for instance), you can simply cut the socket out of the string entirely and splice the two wires.

Wires rarely break at the sockets in parallel strings. But if they do, don't try to repair them. Simply cut the socket out of the string and splice together the wires of the same color (see cord broken).

CHRISTMAS TREE ORNAMENT

Neck broken off glass ornament so that wire loop slips out. Close prongs of loop and wrap tightly with paper to size of hole. Apply light coat of Elmer's Glue-All to paper and insert roll part way through hole.

CHROMIUM PLATE

Scratched, rusted. Clean with a chrome cleaner available from auto supply stores. If rust remains in deep scratches, carefully scratch it out with the point of a knife. Do not use steel wool or emery cloth. To improve the appearance and protect the chrome against further damage, spray on a chrome protector, also available from auto supply stores. Fill deep scratches with Duro plastic chrome.

CLAY TILE

See tile, ceramic.

CLOCK

Glass broken. If glass or plastic is flat and rectangular, you can easily remove it (usually by taking out the bolts in the base of the case) and replace it with a new glass cut to size. But if glass is curved, round, oval, etc., return clock to maker for repairs.

Plastic case broken. Clean cracked edges and coat with plastic-mending adhesive. Clamp edges together for 24 hours.

Electric clock doesn't run. Examine cord for a break. Because clocks are rarely moved, their cords seem to get stiff with age; and then the insulation on them sometimes breaks when the clock's position is changed.

CLOSET, CLOTHES

Rod sags. Replace with a new one. Or twist a strong wire around the center of the rod and attach to a screw eye in the ceiling.

Rod loose. Drill a small hole diagonally through the end and nail rod to the wall with a long finishing nail.

Shelf sags. Nail a wood cleat to the wall under the middle of the shelf. The cleat should be long enough to be nailed into at least two studs. If shelf not only sags but is also warped, support it on a large angle iron screwed to the wall or on a right-angled metal shelf support.

CLOTHING—BELT

Leather belt delaminated. Spread a thin coat of Pliobond cement on both surfaces. Let dry. Apply a second coat to one surface and press layers together.

Belt loop worn, broken. Remove from belt and open material to its full size. Use as a pattern for a new loop.

On most men's belts, buckle and belt loop are held in place by metal snaps. Open these. Stitch new loop closed (so it is a complete loop). Slip over end of belt and close snaps.

On women's belts, buckle and belt loop are not usually removable. In this case, before closing the loop, slip one end of the loop material through fold of belt behind buckle and bring it around in front. Dab Pliobond cement on ends of loop and squeeze ends together. While glue is still wet, stitch ends of loop with thread. When glue is dry, twist stitched ends around under belt.

Tongue of belt buckle on wrong side of buckle. If buckle can be removed from belt, remove it and swing tongue around to top of buckle. Otherwise, with pliers, bend tongue until it can be forced back through buckle; then straighten tongue. To protect finish on tongue wrap it with adhesive tape.

Snap fasteners behind buckle loose. Open fasteners and with pliers squeeze down on fastener prongs to flatten them slightly. See snap fastener.

CLOTHING—BUTTONHOLES

Split at end. Stitch back and forth across the end on sewing machine.

Frayed around edges. If buttonhole is not badly frayed, whip the edges with thread. If hole is badly frayed and appearance is not too important, make two closely spaced rows of machine stitches all the way around hole. Then whip the edges by hand, or machine stitch back and forth across the parallel rows of stitches.

CLOTHING—BUTTONS

Button off. Remove old threads. Double new thread and knot it at end. Make a small stitch through material, then bring thread up through one hole and down through another in the button. To make button stand away from the material, slip a pin through the threads on the front of the button; then continue sewing through button, running the thread over the pin. When button is secure, remove pin, pull button out as far as possible, run thread down through hole in button between the button and the fabric and loop thread several times around the button stitches. Finally, take thread down through fabric and make several overcasting stitches through the threads.

Button torn out. Place a small patch of material under hole and stitch it in place securely. Then sew on button as above.

CLOTHING—COAT

Corners of cuffs frayed. Either leave them alone, because the holes are not likely to enlarge very much, or carefully darn them with threads raveled from an inner seam.

Buttonholes frayed or torn. See clothing–buttonholes.

Buttons off or torn out. See clothing–buttons.

Holes in pockets. See clothing–pockets.

CLOTHING—FABRICS

Specific entries are given for burlap, canvas, clothing–stretch fabric, felt, fiberglass, lace, lastex, leatherette, oilcloth, vinyl.

Light material worn thin. Turn wrong side out. Hold a sheet of white cardboard or paper underneath to determine size of reinforcement needed. Cut a patch out of lightweight material that has some give and that is approximately the same color as material to be mended. Place reinforcement on wrong side of material and pin and baste in place. With thread of proper color, make straight rows of stitches lengthwise of fabric and about ¼″ apart. Make stitches on right side of material so small as to be invisible; on the wrong side, up to ¼″ long. Do not draw up each row of stitches; leave them slightly loose.

Heavy material worn thin. Same as above, but use diagonal basting stitch (see Basic Methods: How to Make Basic Sewing Stitches). Rows of stitches can be spaced slightly further apart. The alternative to reinforcing in this way is to darn the weak spot.

Holes. If material can be darned, pull threads from a side seam or ravel those that run lengthwise of a scrap of the same material. Use short threads and a fine needle and imitate as closely as possible the sound fabric. Darn on the right side of the fabric. First make stitches lengthwise across the hole; then weave thread at right angles, going over and under. To help conceal the darn, extend the stitches at different distances into the sound material. Do not pull stitches too tight, especially when you make a turn. Ends of threads should be on the wrong side of the fabric. Do not cut them off too close.

If material cannot be darned, cut a square or rectangular hole around the hole. Make small diagonal cuts in the four corners and turn the raw edges under. Cut a matching patch

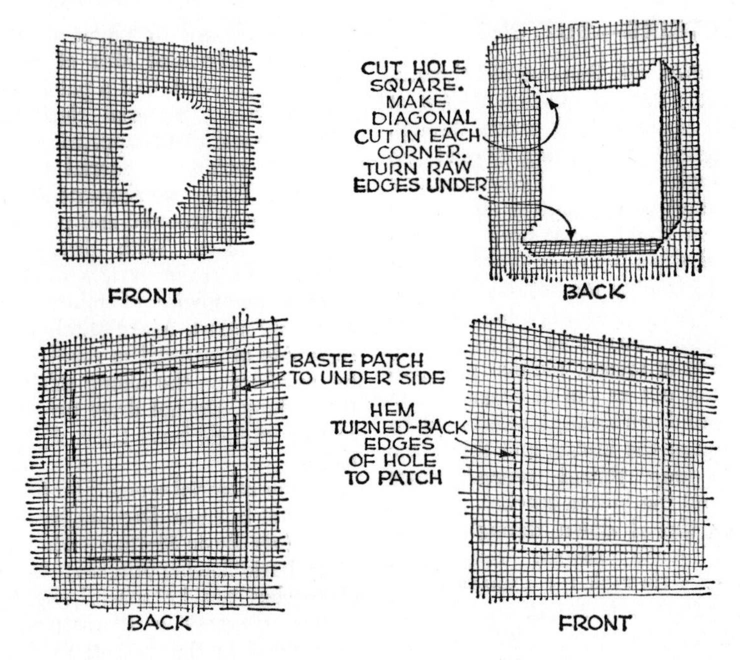

1″ to 1½″ larger than the new hole and center it underneath. Baste in place. Then, working on the right side of the fabric, hem the edges of the hole to the patch. Remove bastings. Turn fabric wrong side up and turn under raw edges of patch. Hem them down.

If appearance of patched material is unimportant (as in sheets and men's shorts), cut the hole out cleanly in a square or circle. Place a patch underneath. Pin in place. Then make long, closely spaced zigzag stitches on your sewing machine across the edges of the hole.

Instead of sewed-on patches, you can in some cases mend holes with press-on patches—provided the article is not dried in a dryer. Or you can glue any patch material to the original material with Devcon Patch glue.

Tears, slashes. Darn a straight tear like a hole (see above). If it's a right-angle tear, darn each side like a straight tear and overlap the two darns at the corner for extra strength at that point.

Diagonal slashes should be basted first to hold them in place (baste on a reinforcement if necessary). Then darn.

Stains. See chart on pages 39–43. Note well the following points:

1. Carbon tetrachloride is highly toxic. Use only in a well-ventilated room. Keep container closed. Wear rubber gloves.

2. When sponging a stain, always place a pad of clean absorbent cloth under it. Sponge from the edges of the stain toward the center. "Feather out" the edges to avoid leaving a ring.

3. Before bleaching a colored fabric, always test it in an inconspicuous spot.

Stain	White cottons, linens	Washable colored fabrics	Non-washable fabrics
Alcohol New	Sponge with cool water.		
Persistent	Soak for 30 min. in solution of 1 tbsp. hydrogen peroxide to 2 qt. water. Rinse in water.		Dry clean.
Blood New	Soak in cool water till stain turns brown. Wash in warm suds and rinse.		Sponge with cool water.
Persistent	Soak in cool water till stain turns brown. Soak for 15 min. in solution 1 tbsp. hydrogen peroxide to 2 qt. water. Wash in warm suds and rinse.		Dry clean.
Candle wax	Scrape with dull knife. For white wax, place clean white blotters over and under stain and press with warm iron. Sponge with carbon tetrachloride.		
Chewing gum	Pick off as much as possible. Sponge with carbon tetrachloride.		
Chocolate New	Scrape with dull knife. Wash in warm suds and rinse.		Scrape with dull knife. Sponge with cool water. Dry. Sponge with carbon tetrachloride.
Persistent	Soak for 30 min. in solution of 1 tbsp. hydrogen peroxide to 2 qt. water. Rinse.	Sponge with solution of 1 tbsp. hydrogen peroxide to 2 qt. water. Wash in warm suds and rinse.	Dry clean.
Cod-liver oil New	Sponge with carbon tetrachloride. Wash in warm suds and rinse.		Sponge with carbon tetrachloride.
Persistent	Soak for 30 min. in solution of 1 tbsp. hydrogen peroxide to 2 qt. water. Rinse.		Dry clean.

Stain	White cottons, linens	Washable colored fabrics	Non-washable fabrics
Coffee New	If there was cream in coffee, first sponge with carbon tetrachloride. Soak in cool water. Wash in warm suds and rinse.		Sponge with cool water. Dry. Sponge with carbon tetrachloride.
Persistent	Soak for 30 min. in solution of 1 tbsp. hydrogen peroxide to 2 qt. water. Rinse.		Dry clean.
Fruits New	Soak in cool water. Wash in warm suds and rinse.		Sponge with cool water, then with solution of 1 part white vinegar to 10 parts water.
Persistent	Soak for 30 min. in solution of 1 tbsp. hydrogen peroxide to 2 qt. water. Rinse.		Dry clean.
Grass New	Wash in hot suds and rinse.	Wash in warm suds.	Sponge with carbon tetrachloride.
Persistent	Soak for 15 min. in solution of 1 tbsp. household bleach to 1 qt. water. Rinse.	Soak for 15 min. in solution of 1 tsp. sodium perborate to 1 pt. hydrogen peroxide. Rinse.	Sponge with solution of 1 cup denatured alcohol to 1 pt. water. Then sponge with water.
Grease, oil	Wash in very hot suds. Then sponge with carbon tetrachloride if necessary.	Sponge with carbon tetrachloride. Wash in warm suds. Rinse.	Sponge with carbon tetrachloride.
Ice cream—vanilla	Soak in cool water. Wash in warm suds and rinse.		Sponge with cool water. Dry. Sponge with carbon tetrachloride.

Stain	White cottons, linens	Washable colored fabrics	Non-washable fabrics
Ice cream—chocolate			
New	Sponge with carbon tetrachloride. Wash in warm suds and rinse.		Treat as for vanilla ice cream.
Persistent	Soak for 30 min. in solution of 1 tbsp. hydrogen peroxide to 2 qt. water. Rinse.		Dry clean.
Ice cream—fruit			
New	Soak in cool water. Wash in warm suds and rinse.		Treat as for vanilla ice cream.
Persistent	Treat as for chocolate ice cream.		Dry clean.
Ink			
New	Run cool water through stain. Wash in warm suds with a very little household ammonia added. Rinse.		Dry clean.
Persistent	Soak in hot suds for 15 min. Rinse. Soak for 15 min. in 5 per cent solution of oxalic acid (available from drugstore). Rinse.	Soak for 15 min. in 5 per cent solution of oxalic acid. Rinse.	Dry clean.
Lipstick	Sponge with carbon tetrachloride. Wash in warm suds and rinse.		Sponge with carbon tetrachloride.
Mascara	Wash in warm suds and rinse.		Sponge with carbon tetrachloride, then with a solution of 1 part denatured alcohol and 2 parts water, then with cool water.
Meat juice	Sponge with cool water. Wash in warm suds and rinse.		Sponge with cool water. Dry. Sponge with carbon tetrachloride.

Stain	White cottons, linens	Washable colored fabrics	Non-washable fabrics
Medicines	Sponge with cool water. Take to dry cleaner.		
Mildew New	Brush off. Wash in warm suds. Rinse.		Dry clean.
Persistent	Soak for 30 min. in solution of 1 tbsp. hydrogen peroxide to 2 qt. water. Rinse.		Dry clean.
Nail polish	Sponge with nail polish remover (but use carbon tetrachloride on acetates). Soak for 30 min. in solution of 1 tbsp. hydrogen peroxide to 2 qt. water. Rinse.		
Paint—oil base	Scrape off. Soak in turpentine. Wash in warm suds. Rinse.		Sponge with turpentine. Dry clean.
Paint—water base	Scrape off. Soak in cool water. Wash in warm suds. Rinse.		Sponge with water. Dry clean.
Perspiration New	Wash in warm suds and rinse.	Hold over an open ammonia bottle. Wash in warm suds and rinse.	Dry clean.
Persistent	Soak for 30 min. in solution of 1 tbsp. hydrogen peroxide to 2 qt. water. Rinse.		Dry clean.
Rubber cement	Rub off as much as possible with your finger or with a dry ball of rubber cement. Then sponge with rubber cement thinner.		
Rust New	Wash in warm suds and rinse.		Dry clean.
Persistent	Soak for 15 min. in 5 per cent solution of oxalic acid (from drugstore). Rinse.		Dry clean.
Scorch New	Wash in warm suds and rinse.		Dry clean.
Persistent	Soak for 30 min. in solution of 1 tbsp. hydrogen peroxide to 2 qt. water. Rinse.		Dry clean.
Shoe polish	Sponge with carbon tetrachloride.		

Stain	White cottons, linens	Washable colored fabrics	Non-washable fabrics
Tar	Scrape off as much as possible. Soften with Vaseline. Sponge with carbon tetrachloride. Wash in warm suds. Rinse.		Same as for other fabrics but don't wash.
Tea	See coffee.		
Urine	Wash in warm suds. Rinse.	If fabric color is changed, soak in solution of 2 tbsp. household ammonia to 1 cup water. Then wash in warm suds. Rinse.	Dry clean.

CLOTHING—FOUNDATION GARMENT

Garters or elastic torn. Buy replacements at notion counter and sew into garment.

Girdle seams split. Stitch together on sewing machine with zigzagger. If seam needs reinforcement, sew twill tape over seam on wrong side of garment.

Elastic fabric torn. Reinforce with twill tape and stitch as above.

CLOTHING—GLOVE

Seams split. With a fine needle, restitch to match original stitches.

Hole in fabric glove. See clothing—fabrics.

Hole in knitted glove. See clothing—knitwear.

CLOTHING—HEMS

Plain hem out. Turn in the hem about ⅛", then turn in again about ¼" and hem to body of fabric. Or you can attach hem by machine stitching.

Rolled hem out. Roll edge tight and hem down. Take tiny stitches.

Note. These are the two simplest and most common hems. If other types are out, resew like the sound hem.

CLOTHING—HOOKS AND EYES

Metal hook or eye off. Position on fabric. Then attach with overcasting stitches.

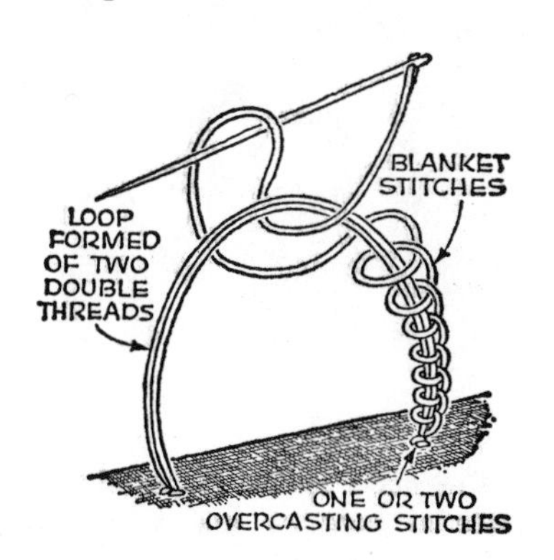

Thread eye broken. Snip out old eye. Knot a doubled thread at the end. Start with one or two overcasting stitches on wrong side of material. Then bring needle through to right side of material and form a loop of the proper size. Secure in material and make a second loop of the same size. Then whip the four strands of the loop together with a blanket stitch.

CLOTHING—KNITWEAR

Runs. To stop a run, dab clear nail polish at top and bottom and extend it three or four strands to either side of run.

To mend a run, if appearance is not important, simply whip together the threads on each side of run. If appearance is important, pick up the free loop at the bottom of the run with a crochet hook. Then pull through the loop, one after the other, each of the threads in the run. Secure the top loop on the wrong side with needle and thread.

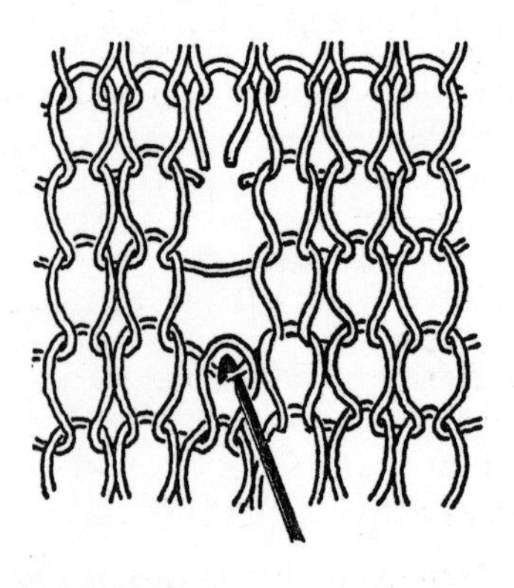

Crosswise splits. Place edges of material together and whip with matching thread.

Holes. Use a long length of matching yarn. Catch it in the material at the bottom right corner of the hole, then weave it through the loops across the bottom of the hole to the left side of the hole. Reverse thread and catch it in loop in next row at right of hole. Reverse again to left, then to right until entire hole is covered. Then, starting at a top corner of the hole, make a series of chain stitches down across the hole. When you reach the bottom, thread the yarn straight back up through the first crosswise stitches to the top of the hole. Then make the next series of chain stitches down. Continue in this way until hole is closed.

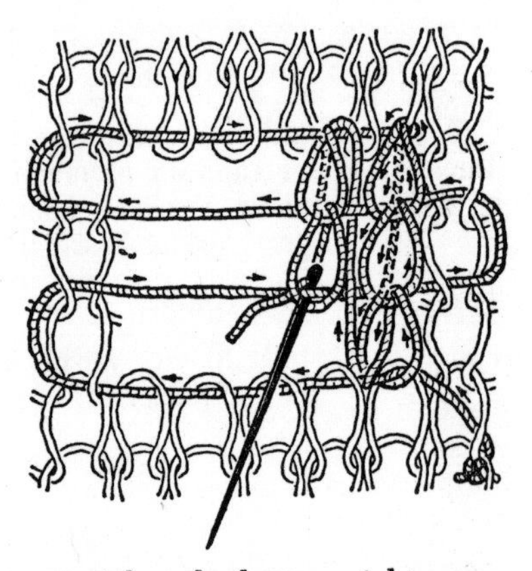

CLOTHING—PAJAMAS

Drawstring in pants pulled out. Pull string all the way out of casing. Put a large safety pin through one end. Then work pin through casing. To prevent string from pulling out again, center it at back of pants and stitch in place.

Buttons off or torn out. See clothing–buttons.

Placket torn. See clothing–plackets.

Holes, tears. See clothing–fabrics.

CLOTHING—PLACKETS

Torn at end. Baste a piece of twill or bias tape under tear. Lap edges of placket and stitch to tape on sewing machine.

CLOTHING—POCKETS

Holes worn in fabric. Apply a press-on patch on the inside of the pocket. Or machine stitch across the pocket just above the hole.

A better repair is made by ripping out the old pocket and replacing it with a new one purchased at a notions counter.

Garment fabric torn at corner of patch pocket. Rip the pocket to below the tear. Reverse garment and, with running stitches, sew a strip of tape along the length of the tear. Then darn across the tear on the right side of the garment. Stitch the pocket corner down.

CLOTHING—SEAMS

Split. Iron edges of fabric flat together. Pin if split is a long one. Sew with a straight running stitch on a machine or by hand.

Seam edges fray. If material does not fray badly, notch edges with pinking shears. If material is heavy and frays easily, protect edges with deep, closely spaced overcasting stitches. If material is light and frays easily, turn raw edge of each seam under and sew with a straight running stitch.

Hemstitched seam broken. Mending is a painstaking job. It's easier to separate hem edge entirely and rejoin to the body of the fabric with a strip of straight-edged lace. Or if appearance is not important, simply sew the hem edge over the edge of the fabric on your sewing machine or by whipping.

CLOTHING—SHIRT

Collar frayed. You can turn over the collar if it does not have pockets for stays on the underside. But it is better to buy a new collar at a notions counter. Carefully rip the collar from the neckband (tiny stitches are easily cut with a razor blade). Do not open seam beyond ends of collar. Fold new collar in half and mark center with a pin. Fold neckband in half and mark center with a pin. Insert collar in band, making sure pins are in line. Pin ends of collar to band. Then put in a whole row of pins from one end of collar to the other, and then baste. Make sure that basting stitches go through both sides of neckband as well as collar. Remove pins and carefully stitch collar to band on a sewing machine.

Cuffs frayed. You can turn French cuffs, but it is better to replace all cuffs with new ones from a notions counter. Rip off old cuff. Insert sleeve end into top of cuff. Pin, baste, then stitch on sewing machine like a collar.

Holes. Patch with press-on mending tape.

Buttons off or torn out. See clothing–buttons.

CLOTHING—STRAPS

Torn loose. Simply stitch in place again. If material is badly frayed or weak, replace strap entirely or cut off damaged end, stitch on new material and sew in place. Fabric to which strap is sewn may also need to be reinforced.

CLOTHING—STRETCH FABRIC

Holes, tears. Darn with nylon thread (which has some elasticity). Use regular darning technique (see clothing–fabrics).

Seams split. Stitch with nylon thread.

CLOTHING—TROUSERS

Bottom edges of cuffs frayed. Easiest solution is to cut stitches at side seams and rip stitches that tack down end of fabric inside of trouser leg. Cut about ¼″ from end of fabric. Now make a new cuff that is about ¼″ narrower than the original one by pulling down the outside layer of fabric ¼″, pressing top of cuff flat, then pulling fabric up on inside of trouser leg and stitching in place. Frayed edge is now inside trouser leg. Cover the tear with press-on mending tape.

If you have the scrap material cut from the trouser legs when trousers were purchased, a better solution is to cut stitches holding frayed cuff at seams and to rip out stitches inside of trouser leg. Open material, flatten it, and cut it off somewhere between the bottom of the trouser leg and the top of the cuff (in other words, on the inside layer of the cuff). Stitch the new fabric to old on a sewing machine. Then form new cuff. Press. Stitch end of material inside of trouser leg and stitch cuff to outside seams.

Belt loops off. Restitch at top or bottom as necessary. If ends of loops are badly frayed, remove loop. Make new one from scrap material or from excess material in cuffs or seams.

Buttonholes frayed or split. See clothing–buttonholes.

Buttons off or torn out. See clothing–buttons.

Holes in pockets. See clothing–pockets.

COAL STOKER

Doesn't start. Check for blown fuse. Turn off stoker and check for obstruction. Follow manufacturer's directions for removing any obstruction. If you still have trouble, call heating contractor.

Jams. Turn off stoker and remove obstruction according to manufacturer's directions.

Note. Don't lose manufacturer's instructions for operating stoker. Keep them available near stoker. Follow directions for oiling.

COFFEE MAKER, ELECTRIC

Doesn't work. Try another cord; the original may be broken. Check whether fuse on house circuit has blown. Plug a light into outlet used for coffee maker to see whether it is defective. If these measures don't work, take coffee maker to a service shop.

Stains on inside. Dissolve a kitchen detergent in enough hot water to cover the stain. Pour into coffee maker bowl (from which any other parts have been removed). Turn on coffee maker until water is very hot. Then empty and rinse with clear water.

COLUMN, WOOD

Rotting at top. If rot has not progressed too far, cut out soft spots and fill with plastic wood. Saturate entire top of column with pentachlorophenol wood preservative. Slip a sheet of aluminum or copper flashing over top, bend it down around the edges and tack.

Base rotting. Cut out base entirely and make a new one to fit. Cut a cross-shaped groove in bottom, ½ inch deep by half the width of base so that air can circulate under it. Soak for 24 hours in pentachlorophenol and set in position.

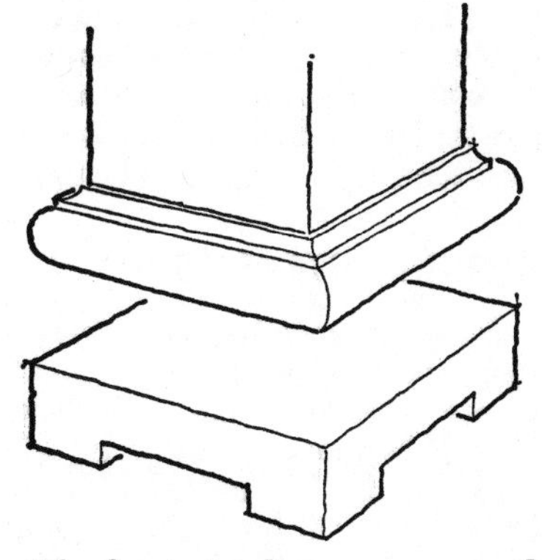

If column stands on masonry and has no base, cut rotten part off square. Purchase box-like metal base made for the purpose. With a carbide drill, make a hole in the masonry under the column. Set in bolt, threads up, and anchor it with concrete mortar or plastic steel. Set box over bolt and fasten down with nut. Nail or screw other half of box to bottom of post and set it in bottom half of box.

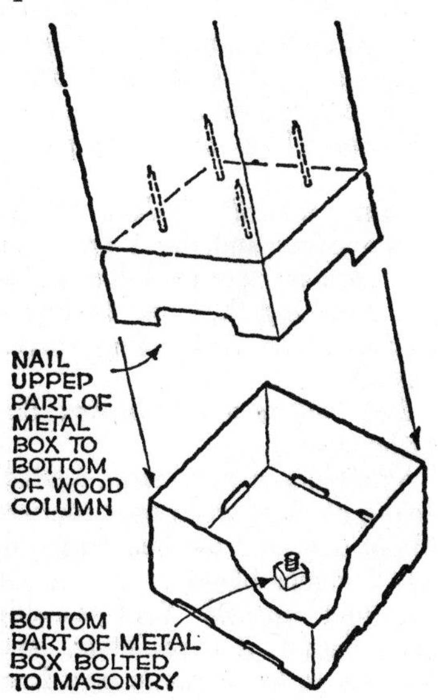

COMB

Comb loose from metal back. Clean top edge of comb and inside the metal channel. Apply a light coat of Duco cement to both surfaces and reset comb in channel. Crimp metal edges along sides of comb if they are loose.

COMBINATION WASHER-DRYER

See washing machine.

COMPOSITION BOARD

See interior wall, composition board.

CONCRETE

For how to use concrete, see Basic Methods: How to Mix and Handle Concrete.

Cracks. Chip open as deeply as possible with a cold chisel. Blow out crumbs with vacuum cleaner. Wet the edges with clear water. Fill with mortar—usually 1 part cement to 2 parts sand mixed with just enough water to make a mixture that holds together when squeezed. Be sure that mortar is packed in solidly. Trowel smooth.

Holes. Break out all loose and broken concrete. Then handle as above. If hole is very large, use a mortar of 1 part cement, 1 part sand and 1½ parts coarse aggregate. When this is placed in the hole, work it well in order to fill voids around the aggregate. Trowel off smooth a fraction of an inch above the surrounding surface. Keep covered with damp burlap for 48 hours or longer.

Surface pitted, rough, uneven. Clean thoroughly and wash with water. Let dry. Spread on latex cement and trowel smooth. If surface has deep depressions, cement must be built up in ⅛″ layers. Allow each to dry before applying the next.

Thin sections of ornamental concrete broken (as in a bird bath or jardiniere). Clean broken edges thoroughly. Let dry several days. Apply Miracle Adhesive to one edge and press other into this firmly. Clamp if necessary. Let dry for 48 hours.

Surface dusty. See floor, concrete.

Oil stains. Wipe up newly spilled oil at once and cover with hydrated lime or dry Portland cement. For old stains on rough concrete, pour on Rust-Oleum Surfa-Etch and agitate with a bristle brush for five minutes. Then rinse with water, agitating as you do so. For old stains on terrazzo, scrub with benzine and a bristle brush.

Rust stains. Treat with Rust-Oleum Surfa-Etch as above. If stain lingers, mix 1 part sodium citrate crystals in 6 parts water, then mix with whiting to form a thick paste. Spread a heavy layer on stain. Remove when dry and repeat process as necessary.

Smoke stains. Scour with powdered pumice or gritty scrubbing powder. Then dissolve 2 lb. trisodium phosphate in 1 gal. hot water. In a separate enamel vessel make a smooth stiff paste of 12 oz. of chlorinated lime in water. Pour the two mixtures into a 2-gal. stoneware jar and add water until full. Stir well, cover and allow to settle. Then saturate a 3- or 4-layer pad of white flannel with the liquid, paste over stain and cover with a pane of glass. Make sure cloth is pressed tight against stained surface. Resaturate cloth as often as necessary until stain disappears.

Paint stains. Apply paint-remover; let stand until paint is soft, then scrape off. Rinse with benzine.

COOKING UTENSILS

Holes in metal. Scour surface thoroughly, rinse, and dry. Spread plastic steel into and over hole. This withstands up to 600° F., will therefore not be affected by oven heat; but it will break down under high direct heat. However, even under these circumstances the patch will hold as long as the utensil has liquid in it.

Holes in porcelain enamel. Scour surface and dry. Chip off a bit of the porcelain from around the hole. Then cover bare metal with plastic steel.

Glass utensil broken. Wash broken edges and dry thoroughly. Coat both surfaces with epoxy glue and press together for 24 hours. Utensil can be used again for oven cooking.

Earthenware utensil broken. See earthenware.

Aluminum, copper, steel, dented. Hold a block of wood over concave side of dent and tap out dent with light hammer blows.

Bottom warped. You probably can't flatten it completely, and don't try to because you may fracture the metal. However, you can flatten it enough to sit steadily on a burner by turning the utensil upside down and pressing down on the bottom with the palm of your hand. Do not use a hammer.

Handles broken. If made of plastic, coat the broken edges with plastic-mending adhesive and press together overnight. If handle is wood, use Elmer's waterproof glue.

Handle broken from utensil. You can drill holes (if none exist) through the handle and the utensil and rivet the pieces together with steel or aluminum rivets. But it is preferable to take utensil to a metal-working shop and have handle spot-welded on.

Cap on whistling teakettle spout doesn't spring closed. Unscrew the bolts holding the handle to the kettle. Lift up trigger that controls the cap. Remove the coiled spring and replace with a new one purchased at hardware store.

Cast iron rusted, pitted. Remove rust with liquid rust-remover and fine steel wool. Smooth plastic steel into pits. Henceforth, do not wash cast-iron utensils with scouring powders or steel wool; a slight coating of grease on the surface prevents rusting.

Copper discolored. Sprinkle with salt and then rub with vinegar.

Aluminum darkened. Scour with fine steel wool. If necessary, wash the stain with vinegar or mix 2 tsp. cream of tartar in 1 qt. water and bring to a boil in the utensil.

Enamelware stained. Scrub with a household cleanser. If stains remain, fill with a solution of laundry bleach and let stand overnight.

Brown stains on stainless steel. Scour with a household cleanser.

Tinware rusted. Remove rust with liquid rust-remover. (Do not use steel wool because it will remove the tin coating as well as the rust, and rust will then spread.) If tinware is painted (a breadbox or canister, for example), prime cleaned metal with a rust-inhibiting paint. Then apply gloss enamel.

Food burned on utensil. Soak overnight in a strong solution of household ammonia. Then scrub off.

COPPER

Note. The best way to mend copper is by soldering. Use an acid flux except for electrical work, which requires a rosin flux (see Basic Methods: How to Solder Metal). It is perfectly feasible, however, to make many repairs with plastic steel. See galvanized iron. Copper color can be given the plastic by rubbing with a penny.

Small holes, tears. Clean metal thoroughly, apply flux and heat with a torch. Then run in solder.

Large holes, tears. If edges are more than 3/16" apart, cut a patch out of copper flashing. Steel wool patch and area around hole thoroughly. Apply flux. Then heat patch and apply a thin layer of solder on one side. Do same thing to metal around hole. Lay patch over hole, tinned surface to tinned surface. Heat until solder flows together.

Seam between two pieces open. Clean with steel wool. Heat and press together. If old solder is not sufficient, apply a little more.

Scratches. Rub with very fine steel wool.

Dents. Hold a block of wood over concave side. Hammer reverse side lightly with a rubber mallet. Work from edges of dent toward the center.

Green oxide stains. Try a brass polish first. If this doesn't work, rub with very fine steel wool, then buff vigorously with a soft cloth. Spray on one or two coats of lacquer to prevent further staining.

Tarnished. Rub on a brass polish. Rinse in hot soapsuds.

CORK

Holes, dents. Cut a piece of waste cork or even a bottle cork into tiny slivers (use a kitchen grater if you wish), mix with white shellac or clear lacquer and immediately spread into hole. Sand smooth when dry.

Burns. If stain cannot be removed by sanding, cut it out and fill hole as above.

Loose from base. Scrape out old adhesive and stick down with linoleum cement.

Pieces of cork separated. Coat both surfaces with Pliobond cement and let dry until tacky, then press together.

Cork separated from other materials. See household decorative accessories.

Stains. Wash with soap and lukewarm water. If stains persist, sand lightly with No. ½ sandpaper.

COUNTER TOP

See plastics, laminated; linoleum, tile, etc. as the case may be.

CROCKERY

See earthenware.

CROQUET MALLET

Head loose from handle. Remove handle and clean dirt from end and from the hole in the head. Let wood dry completely if damp. Spread Elmer's waterproof glue in the hole and on end of handle. Tap together and let dry for 24 hours.

Handle broken. If the break parallels the grain, coat both surfaces with Elmer's waterproof glue and clamp together with C-clamps or by overwrapping with wax paper and string. If break is across grain, make a new handle out of a broomstick.

CURTAIN

See draperies.

CURTAIN ROD

Cord on traverse rod loose, dangling. If cord is looped through a spring pulley on the wall or floor, close curtains, pull out knot in one end of the center carrier until cord is taut. Then reknot. If cord is in two pieces (not looped through a pulley), attach weights to the pulling ends.

Curtains on traverse rods do not close at center of window. Open curtains wide. On the back of one of the center carriers you will find a hook around which the cord is looped. Loosen cord. Push carrier as far to the side of the window as possible. Tighten cord by pulling on the end, then loop it around the hook again.

CUSHION, BENCH

Holes, burns. Cut small round patch of matching material. Glue down with Devcon Patch glue if cover is a fabric; plastic-mending adhesive if it is plastic; rubber cement if is leather.

Buttons off. See mattress.

CUTLERY, KITCHEN

Tang loose in handle. Remove handle and clean tang with steel wool. Make sure hole in handle is dry. Coat tang and hole with epoxy glue and reset tang in handle. Allow glue to dry 48 hours.

Handle split. If it is wood, dry thoroughly and force epoxy glue in the split. If plastic, use plastic-mending adhesive. Clamp the handle in either case until glue dries.

Wood handle roughened, bleached by hot water. Smooth with fine sandpaper and steel wool. Then saturate wood with linseed oil and rub it in well.

Metal rusted. This happens only to very old cutlery, not to stainless steel. Rub liquid rust-remover on the metal. Then go over it with fine steel wool or emery cloth.

Knife dull. Use a flat carborundum stone (the bigger, the better). Hold blade almost flat on this and sharpen with a circular motion.

CUTLERY, TABLE

Knife blade loose in handle. Remove blade and clean tang with fine emery cloth. Apply epoxy glue and reset in handle.

If hole in handle is much larger than the tang of the blade, take knife to a jeweler for repair. Hollow-handled knives are filled with a white cement which occasionally erodes and needs to be replaced entirely if blade is to hold tight.

Fork tines bent. Wrap with paper or cloth and bend them straight with pliers.

Tips of silver spoons bent. You can usually straighten these with your fingers, but don't try anything more violent.

Ceramic or bone handle broken. Apply Duco cement to both edges and clamp together for six hours.

Silver tarnished. See silver.

Carving knife dull. See cutlery, kitchen.

DECK

See canvas deck.

DISHWASHER, ELECTRIC

Note. Call a serviceman if machine doesn't work properly, but before doing so check and correct points noted below.

Doesn't work. Check: Has fuse blown? Is anything interfering with tight closing of door or lid?

Hums but doesn't work. Check: Is anything jamming impeller? Is strainer in outlet clogged?

Doesn't fill with water. Your water pressure may have dropped too low. If this condition doesn't quickly correct itself, call a serviceman. You may then have to call in a plumber.

Soap dispenser doesn't open. Clean thoroughly. Make sure that catch which holds dispenser closed has not been bent.

Dishes don't wash clean. Check: Have you changed detergents? Try it. Is water hot enough? Maybe you should move up thermostat setting on water heater.

Dishes don't dry thoroughly, or are water spotted. Try changing detergent.

Stains, film on dishes and sides of dishwasher tub. Try changing detergents. If this doesn't correct situation, there's something wrong with your water. Call in a plumber. You may need a water softener or water conditioner of some kind.

DISPOSER, GARBAGE

Doesn't work. Check whether fuse on house circuit has blown. Then call a serviceman.

Grinding wheel jammed. Turn off. With a stick of wood, such as a broomstick, reach down to grinder and push it to the right to loosen obstruction. Then turn on motor. If disposer still doesn't work, call a serviceman.

Other problems. Let a serviceman cope with them.

DOG COLLAR

See clothing—belt.

DOG LEASH

Swivel snap broken. With a hacksaw, cut the loop that fastens the snap to the leash. Buy a replacement snap at hardware store. Slip the loop through the end of the leash and hammer it closed.

Leather handle broken. Cut the broken ends off cleanly. Apply Pliobond cement to one side of one end and the other side of the other end. Let dry until tacky. Then overlap the ends about 1″ and press together. When glue has dried, punch a hole through the overlap and insert a steel rivet.

Leather leash damaged. If badly weakened, cut out the bad leather, overlap the cut ends and glue and rivet together as above. If leash is simply delaminated, spread Pliobond cement on the laminations and press together.

Chain broken. See chain.

DOLL

See also stuffed animal.

Note. Some doll repairs are very easy, others quite difficult. Before attempting to fix a broken head or a torn body it is well to find out—if you can—what material you are dealing with. This can save you time in selecting the right glue and/or patching material. But don't worry too much if the answer escapes you. If the first things you try don't work, you can always try something else.

If the doll has pulled apart, the first thing to determine is how it was put together. Then, can you get inside the body to fix it? And do you have the materials you need?

Finally, before mending a doll, decide how much you value it. If it is just an ordinary doll and repairs seem relatively easy, go ahead and make them. But if repairs look difficult for one reason or another or if doll is an antique with real or sentimental value, then it is better to take it to a doll hospital.

Head, limbs, body made of solid material broken. Coat broken edges lightly with Duco cement and let dry. Then apply a second coat and press pieces together. If the broken part is known to be made of a modern plastic (other than polyethylene), use plastic-mending adhesive instead of Duco.

Holes, cracks in soft rubber body. Cut a patch out of thin flesh-colored rubber or any thin, flesh-colored fabric. Coat patch and area around hole with rubber cement. Let dry. Apply a second coat of cement to both surfaces and smooth patch down. Be sure not to stretch or bend the body from its normal position when applying patch, because if you do, patch will be permanently wrinkled.

Holes, cracks in soft plastic. Use plastic-mending adhesive kit. Apply patch from kit or cut a patch out of any thin, flesh-colored vinyl. Spread adhesive on patch and smooth over hole when body is in normal position (not bent or stretched).

Holes, tears in cloth. Cut a patch out of matching material and glue over hole with Devcon Patch glue.

Limb off jointed doll. Jointed dolls made during the past several generations are held together with wire hooks connected to one or more thick rubber bands. A single limb may come off when the hook to which it is attached becomes disengaged either from the rubber band or from the mount inside the limb. In either case, bend a stiff wire into a hook, reach through limb socket, slip hook around rubber band, pull band out and hook the doll wire around the rubber band or the limb mount as the case may be. Pinch the hooks in the doll wire closed, then let limb snap back into socket.

Four limbs and head off jointed doll. The rubber band connecting the head and limbs has probably broken. If you can buy a replacement from the doll manufacturer or a doll hospital, do so. Otherwise use the ⅛″ wide elastic used in dressmaking. Cut this into a length slightly longer than the broken rubber band, or if the band has disappeared, cut a length about double the length of the doll's body. Tie a square knot in the ends. Insert the elastic loop into the body through the neck; stick a long nail through it at the neck end (where the knot should be), and lay the nail across the neck opening so that the loop won't get away from you. Then hook the legs, arms, and finally the head on to the elastic. Remove the nail from across the neck opening and let the head snap into place. If the limbs and head are held tight to the body, fine. If not, pull out head and retie the knot to shorten the loop. When you are satisfied with the adjustment, sew down the ends of the knot in the elastic to prevent it from loosening.

Limbs off jointed wood dolls. The limbs on many wood dolls are constructed with a tongue that fits into a slot in the piece above it. The two pieces are held together by wire or pegs. The easiest way to repair these is to insert a piece of small wire through the holes in the slot and tongue and bend or twist the ends so the wire can't come out.

Limbs off a soft body which does not have rubber bands inside. These are attached in various ways and you will just have to investigate the proper repair. Limbs that are ordinarily sewn on should be resewn. Molded-on rubber or plastic limbs are most easily attached with material wrapped around and glued to them and then to the body (see holes, cracks). In some cases, excess material at the top of a limb is simply wedged under a cardboard disc which is held tight to the body by a spring inside.

Limbs off floppy rag doll. Add stuffing to limb if needed. Stitch opening closed. Then sew limb on body.

Stuffing out of body. Fill with cotton, soft rags, whatever seems appropriate. If the doll head is easily removed, it is best first to close the hole in the body by sewing or gluing on a patch, and then to stuff the body through the neck opening.

Rag doll too floppy. Additional stuffing will correct matters. Or open body and insert a stick of wood or, for greater flexibility, a strip of aluminum sheet. In arms and legs use semi-flexible wire. Be sure to bend ends of wire into closed hooks so that they can't poke through the "skin" of the doll.

Eyes out of sockets. The eyes and balancing weight are mounted in a metal bracket that is clamped on a projection inside the head. You can pull back head and try to squeeze the bracket on the projection from which it sometimes comes loose, but the odds are against you. Better let someone who specializes in repairing dolls take over.

Eyes bang when they open. Pull off head and glue a patch of red flannel, about ¾" square, behind the mouth. Use Elmer's Glue-All.

Shoes keep coming off. If your child doesn't object, spread rubber cement on sole of foot and in the bottom of the shoe. Let dry. Apply a second coat of cement and put on shoe. If doll has socks, first glue these to foot; then glue on shoe.

Hair off. Reglue with Duco cement.

DOOR, ACCORDION

Works stiffly. Clean the overhead track and coat it very lightly with vaseline.

Touches latch jamb at top but not at bottom. Unscrew door from opposite jamb. Loosen all the screws in the overhead track except the last one before the latch jamb. Starting at the opposite jamb, insert wood shims under the track until door hangs parallel with the latch jamb. Then screw track tight. For appearance's sake, the long wedge-shaped crack between the track and the top jamb should be filled with a continuous strip of wood.

Touches latch jamb at bottom but not at top. Loosen all the screws in the overhead track except the last one before the opposite jamb. Shim the track down, as above, until door hangs parallel with latch jamb.

Holes in vinyl covering. Cut a patch out of matching vinyl and glue over hole with plastic-mending adhesive. Let dry about six hours before moving door.

Damage to wood doors. See wood.

DOOR, CABINET

Door sticks. Rub paraffin on all edges. If this doesn't work, sand down the edges that bind.

Other problems. Adjustment of hinges solves most of these. See door, hinged; see also hinges.

DOOR, GARAGE

Overhead door operates stiffly. Lubricate moving parts of hardware with oil or powdered graphite. Spread a little heavy grease in tracks. If this doesn't improve operation, call in carpenter.

Lower panels of overhead door rotten. This may happen to doors with inset panels. First, carefully cut out panels with a saber saw or jig saw. Cut new panels from ¼" exterior-grade plywood or hardboard. Hold in place in frame with ¼" quarter-round strips nailed around opening on front and back of panels.

Hinges on out-swinging door loose. If screws cannot be tightened because wood has rotted or hinges have rusted, remove them entirely. Drill through hinge holes to other side of door. Secure hinge with nuts and bolts.

Out-swinging door sags, but hinges tight. Drive wedges under dropped corner of door until it hangs straight. Strengthen corners with right-angle steel mending plates. Then install metal door brace with turnbuckle (see door, screen).

Top edge of out-swinging door rotting. If rot has not progressed too far, cut out soft wood and fill with plastic wood. Saturate with pentachlorophenol wood preservative. Out of aluminum flashing, cut a narrow strip 2″ wider than thickness of door. Fold this over top edge of door and nail along both sides with aluminum nails.

DOOR, HINGED

Warped door won't latch. If warped on the hinge side, install a third hinge midway between those at top and bottom. If warped on the latch side, pry up the stop bead on the latch side of the frame. Close door and draw a pencil line on the frame along the inside edge of the door. Nail the stop bead along this line.

Door closes with a bang. Chances are the top slants in toward the jamb. Check with a spirit level. Then remove top hinge from jamb and reset it further away from the stop bead, or move bottom hinge further in toward the stop bead.

Door won't close because it strikes jamb on latch side. Check if there is a wide crack on hinge side. If there is, screw hinges down tighter. If this doesn't produce results,

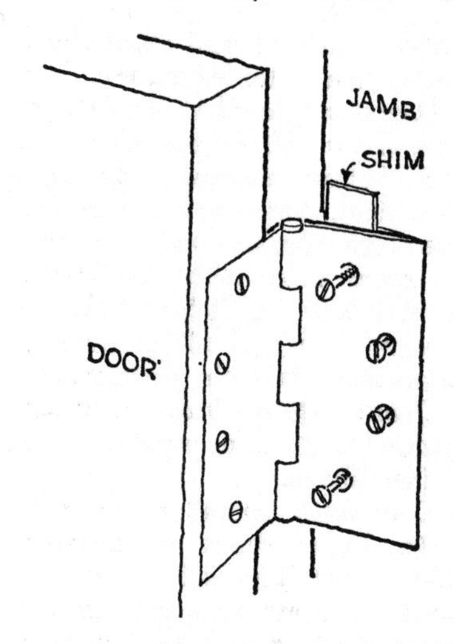

loosen hinges from jamb and insert under their inner edges thin strips of cardboard (shims). If there isn't a crack on the hinge side, door has swelled and to make it close you must shave down the hinge-side edge.

Door won't close because it binds against hinge jamb. If there is a wide crack on the latch side, loosen

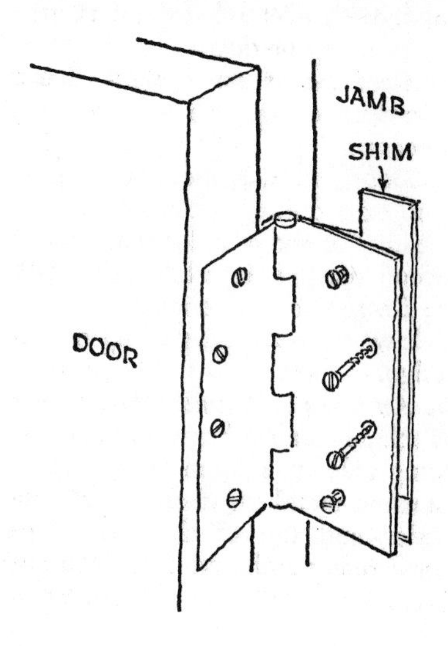

hinges from jamb and insert shims under their outer edges.

Door won't close because it strikes jamb at top. If there is a wide crack at the bottom, unscrew hinges from jamb and, with a sharp chisel, extend the mortises downward. Plug old screw holes with wood plugs or plastic wood. Rehang door in new position and fill in exposed hinge mortises with plastic wood.

Door won't close because it strikes threshold. Reverse procedure described above.

Door latch doesn't reach strike plate. Insert shims under outer edges of both hinges. If this doesn't work, remove hinges entirely and insert thick cardboard or wood shims the full size of the hinges in the mortises.

Door won't latch because latch and strike plate are not in line. If difference in alignment is not great, unscrew strike plate, clamp it in a vise and, with a file, extend the hole in the plate up or down as necessary. If difference in alignment is considerable, unscrew strike plate and, with a chisel, extend mortise in jamb up or down.

Door hangs on a slant. Insert shims under top or bottom hinge as necessary.

Door rattles. Remove strike plate and extend mortise toward the stop bead. Fill screw holes with plastic wood and then reinstall strike plate.

Draft under interior door. Tack felt weather stripping along bottom edge.

Air leaks in around exterior door. Tack felt or rubber weather stripping along bottom edge. Tack flexible metal weather stripping to sides and top of the jamb. The tacked edge should face the door when it is open.

DOOR, SCREEN

Screening corroded, torn, etc. See screen, window.

Door sags. Buy a long metal door brace with screw eyes in each end and a turnbuckle in the middle. Extend the brace to its greatest length. Screw one end of brace to the rail at the center of the sagging corner. Screw the other end as far up on the hinge-side stile as possible. Then tighten turnbuckle until corner of door is raised.

Bangs shut. Replace door spring with a pneumatic closer.

DOOR, SLIDING

Warped. There is no positive cure, but you may be able to prevent door from binding against frame or other doors by screwing door guides to floor.

Door jumps track. If this happens repeatedly and door appears to be straight and hanging properly, the cause may be the size of the wheels in the track. If these are less than 1″ diameter, install new track with larger wheels.

Hangs on a slant. Remove hanger arms from back of door. Line up door with door frame. Then attach hangers in the proper position.

DOOR, SLIDING GLASS

Moves stiffly. Clean out tracks with a vacuum cleaner, then scrape out hardened paint, wax, etc. Polish lightly with steel wool. Then rub a light film of oil on the track.

Leaks at the bottom. If water enters under the track, force caulking compound under it. Otherwise call in dealer.

DOOR, SWINGING

Works stiffly. Remove cover plates from both sides of hinge at bottom of door. Clean dust, lint, etc. from mechanism. Squirt powdered graphite into pivot and spring. Work door back and forth.

Strikes jamb. Check whether hinge and pivot at top of door can be moved closer to the hinge jamb. If they can't be, the swinging edge of door will have to be planed down slightly. You can do this if you have a good plane and are a good workman; but it may be better to call in a carpenter. Planing a door edge evenly is not easy.

DOOR—THRESHOLD

Worn, splintered, scuffed. Saw in two, pry out in two pieces, take to lumber dealer and buy a matching threshold. At home again, use old threshold as a pattern for the cuts that have to be made in the new one. Use fine-toothed saw for cutting. Place in position in doorway and nail down with 3″ finishing nails (drill holes for the nails first so as not to split the wood). Countersink nail heads and cover with plastic wood.

DOORBELL

Won't ring. Tighten nuts that hold small bell wires to low-voltage side of transformer. Have someone push the door button. If you hear a hum, the wiring is okay. If you don't, attach short wires to another bell and hold these to the low-voltage terminals of the transformer. Bell should ring if transformer is all right. If it doesn't ring, shut off house current and tighten connections on high-voltage side.

If bell still doesn't ring when power is restored, check whether bell clapper strikes bell. Bend it if it doesn't. Clean contact points inside bell box with emery cloth or fine sandpaper. Bend contact tab on one side of bell to correct vibration speed of clapper rod (some bells have a screw to make this adjustment). If bell still doesn't ring, remove door button and check wire connections. If they appear to be okay, lay a knife blade across the two terminals. If this makes bell ring, clean contact points in button with emery cloth. If bell doesn't ring, however, buy a new button.

If bell still doesn't ring, examine exposed wires running through the house for a break. If you can't see any, attach short wires to a test bell. Then, starting at the transformer, scrape a bit of insulation from the wires at 3′ intervals, and touch exposed wires with test bell wires. When test bell stops ringing, you are near break and can easily find it by feel. Then splice broken wires together.

DOOR CHIME

Won't ring. Follow procedure for mending doorbell. When checking whether chime is clean, remove it and slide out rod and spring you will find inside. Clean these in gasoline before replacing.

DOOR KNOB

Loose. Loosen set screw in shank of knob. Turn knob to right until it is firm, and reset screw (make sure it seats against flat side of spindle). If knob is still loose, loosen set screw again and turn knob to left until it pulls free of spindle. Pull out other knob with the spindle. Replace spindle.

Glass or porcelain knob loose from metal shank. Better get a new one. But if you must save the old one, try drilling a hole through the metal behind the knob and squeeze in as much Duco cement as possible. If you're lucky, it may hold for a while.

DOOR LOCK OR LATCH

Latch or lock tongue stiff. Scrape off any paint that may be binding it. Squirt powdered graphite on the tongue and into keyhole. Work door knob back and forth. If this doesn't do the trick, remove lock by unscrewing set screw in one of the door knobs and pulling out both knobs. Then remove screws holding lock in edge of door and pull out lock assembly. Take to a locksmith for repair.

Latch or lock broken. If it is a modern lock or latch set, remove as above and take to a locksmith. Note, however, that so much inferior hardware is being used in postwar houses that it may be better in the long run to replace the unit entirely. If you suspect this to be the case, take the lock or latch set to a builder's hardware dealer and ask for his advice.

If lock or latch set is of old-fashioned tumbler type, remove it from door as above. Unscrew cover plate and examine mechanism. If parts have slipped out of place, reassemble them properly; squirt in powdered graphite, and replace lock in door. If parts are broken, take set to a locksmith. Repair of this type of lock is easy, but parts are not generally available in hardware stores.

DOWNSPOUT

See leader.

DRAINS, PLUMBING

Lavatory drain clogged. Remove stopper and clean it. Fish down drain with a stiff wire hooked at the end. For serious stoppage, unscrew clean-out plug at base of U-trap and fish out obstruction with wire. If trap lacks a clean-out plug, unscrew large nuts at either end of trap and lift it out.

Sink drain clogged. Use chemical drain cleaner. If this doesn't work, pour boiling water mixed with a little household ammonia into drain. Let stand for a few minutes. Then fill sink with a little water, place suction cup of a plumber's friend over drain and pump up and down. If this still doesn't work, you'll have to remove trap and clean drain with a long, coiled-spring snake. It's probably easier to call a plumber.

Tub drain clogged. Remove stopper and clean out drain with a hooked wire. If this doesn't work, use boiling water, ammonia, and a plumber's friend as above.

Shower stall drain clogged. Remove cover on drain and clean like a tub drain.

Toilet drain clogged. Place plumber's friend over outlet and pump up and down. If this doesn't work, crank a coiled-spring auger down the drain.

Floor drain clogged. Take off strainer and clean drain with a stiff wire and spoon. Pour in several gallons of boiling water.

House drain clogged. Call a plumber. Special tools are required.

Leaks in joints of lavatory or sink drain. Unscrew large nut at joint where leaking occurs and pull it away from joint. Remove string which you will probably find wrapped around pipe. Wrap new cotton string around pipe four or five times to form a washer. Push nut over string and into place, and screw tight.

Leaks in joints of house drain. You can stop these temporarily by covering strands of hemp rope with asphalt roofing compound and forcing these into the joint. But you'd better call a plumber soon.

Drains frozen. Heat with a heat lamp or rags soaked in boiling water. Work from point where drain leaves house back toward fixtures.

DRAPERIES

Small holes, tears. Darn or patch. See clothing–fabrics.

Large tears. Anything you do for a large horizontal tear will be makeshift. If fabric is heavy, the least obvious repair will be made by bringing torn edges together carefully and covering with press-on mending tape. If fabric is sheer, machine stitching is best.

For large vertical tears, rip the material all the way to the bottom, turn edges under and sew on a machine. An even better job is done by putting a seam in all the way from the bottom to the top of the drapery.

See also clothing–fabrics; clothing–hems; clothing–seams.

DRAWER

See furniture–chest of drawers.

DRILL

See also electric drill.

Stiff, hard to turn. Remove rust with steel wool and liquid rust-remover. Then oil at all points that move.

Chuck stiff, doesn't hold bits tight. Unscrew to the left until the sleeve comes off. Clean jaws with liquid rust-remover and oil. Replace as you found them and screw back sleeve.

Bit dull, cutting edges bent. Place in a vise and sharpen with a small triangular metal file. Be careful not to flatten the bit on the outside.

DRIVEWAY, ASPHALT

Holes, cracks. Cut out loose material down to a solid base. Make sides of hole straight up and down. Wash with water and allow to dry. Then pack in patching asphalt, sold in small packages for repair work, and tamp hard.

Edges broken. Cut out loose material, wash with water, and allow to dry. Lay a board along the edge and stake in place. Pack patching asphalt between driveway and board. Remove board before asphalt dries. *Note:* Installation of steel edging strips will prevent recurrence of this problem.

Heaved by frost. Cut out heaved area, level the base. Then fill as above.

DRIVEWAY, CONCRETE

See floor, concrete.

DRIVEWAY CURB

Concrete curb broken. Break out loose concrete and brush surfaces clean. Coat two boards lightly with clean car grease and stake on either side of the curb so that the top edges are even with the curb top. Greased surfaces should face inward. Wet concrete between boards with water and let it stand for several hours. Then remove excess water and brush on a soupy grout of cement. Before this dries, trowel in a stiff mix of 1 part cement, 2 parts sand, and 2 parts pea gravel (or 1 part cement and 3 parts sand if hole is small). Compact thoroughly and strike off level with top of boards.

Brick curb broken. Crack out broken brick and surrounding mortar. Set in new brick. See brick.

DRYER, CLOTHES

Note. Call a serviceman if machine doesn't work properly, but before doing so check and correct points noted below.

Doesn't work. Check: Has fuse in machine blown (if there is one)? Has fuse at fuse box blown?

Shorts out. Check: Has a bobby pin or other metal object worked through a hole in the basket so that it rubs on parts behind it?

Pilot light on gas dryer out. Follow instructions in owner's manual.

DUREZ

See plastics—general.

EARTHENWARE

Broken. Wash edges and let dry thoroughly. Then coat both edges with epoxy glue and press together for 24 hours. The epoxy will withstand water and oven heat.

Pieces used for ash trays and ornamental purposes rough on bottom, scratch table tops. Cut a piece of felt to cover bottom and coat one side with Pliobond cement. Let dry. Then apply cement to earthenware and again to felt. Let dry until tacky and smooth felt down.

ELECTRIC APPLIANCES (other than those common types listed under specific headings)

See Basic Methods: How to Check Out Electrical Appliances.

ELECTRIC CORD

Note. Always disconnect cord before making repairs.

Outer insulation frayed, cut, or broken but wires intact. Wrap securely with black cellophane electrical tape. Cuts in rubber insulation can also be covered with plastic rubber.

Lamp cord, extension cord, or cord to motor broken. Cut cord in two. Strip off 2″ of insulation on the wires on either side of cut. Bend opposing wires around each other and then twist together. If you have a soldering iron, apply solder. Then wrap each of the two mended wires with cellophane electrical tape. Be sure no metal is exposed. Then overwrap both wires together with more tape.

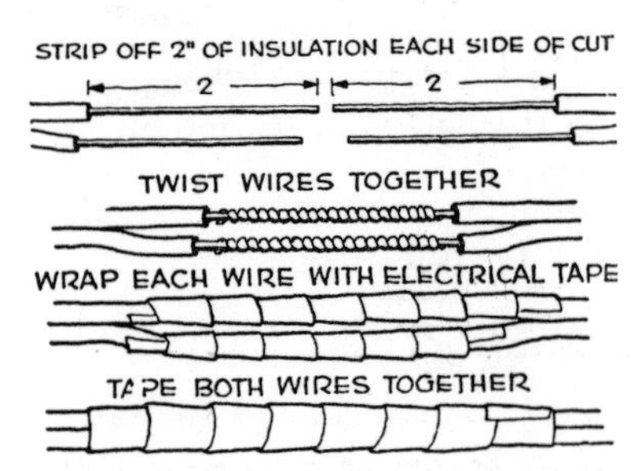

Heater cord (for irons, toasters, other heating appliances) broken.

In an emergency, mend as above. But replace cord with a new one as soon as possible.

Lamp cord broken at socket. Cut off below socket and pull socket apart. Loosen two screws that hold broken wires. Remove ¾″ of insulation from end of each of the wires in the cord and twist strands of small wires tightly together. Insert both wires through socket cap, tie Underwriters' knot and wrap each wire around one of the screws. Wrap from left to right so that wires are drawn in closer as you tighten screws. Reassemble socket.

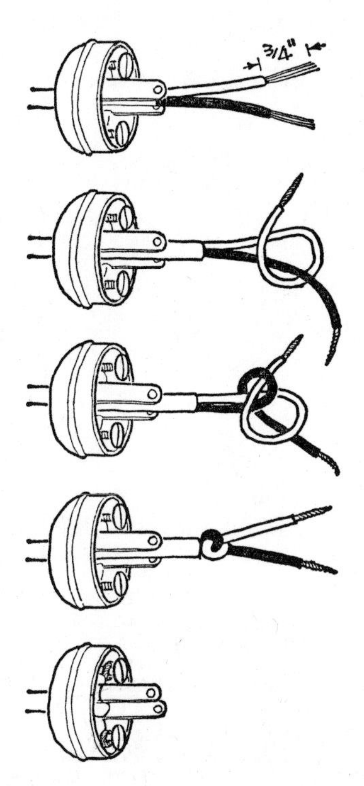

Cord broken at male plug. Cut off cord. If cord is used for lamps or extension cords, replace old plug with clamp-on type. Do not remove insulation from the wires. Just insert end of cord in plug and clamp in place according to manufacturer's directions.

If cord is too thick for clamp-on plugs, separate the two wires for 1½″ to 2″. Strip off ¾″ of insulation from end of each wire and twist strands. Push them through hole in back of plug and tie Underwriters' knot in the two wires above the exposed copper. Then loop one wire around one prong, wrap the copper strands around the adjacent screw, and tighten screw. Loop other wire around other prong and screw and tighten.

Cord broken at female plug. Use clamp-on plug on thin cord; screw-on plug on thick cord. Job is same as above.

ELECTRIC DRILL

Doesn't work. Check whether fuse has blown; outlet into which drill is plugged is defective; cord is broken.

Runs too slowly. Lubricate according to maker's directions.

Noisy. Lubricate according to maker's directions.

Sparks excessively. Carbon brushes may need replacement. See motor, electric.

ELECTRIC LIGHT

Socket of ceiling or wall fixture defective. Shut off current at fuse box. Take down fixture. Remove coverings on cord splices behind fixture and untwist wires (if they are soldered together, melt solder with a soldering iron or simply cut off soldered portion). Remove socket from fixture and replace with new one. Connect black wire on socket to black lead cable, white wire to white cable, by twisting ends of wires together. Cover the joined ends of the wires with insulated wire nuts, and screw nuts tight. Then wrap friction tape or cellophane electrical tape around base of nuts and wires. Reassemble fixture.

Pull-chain broken below light. Buy a new chain with a split clamp. Open one end of clamp, slip bottom bead of old chain into it and squeeze clamp together.

Pull-chain broken within light. Turn off current. Pull socket apart and note how the chain is threaded into it. Open or pry out the clamp holding the last bead of the chain, thread new chain into socket and place in clamp. Reassemble socket.

Light diffuser broken. If made of glass, apply Duco cement to both broken edges and press together. If made of plastic, use plastic-mending adhesive. In both cases, hold the broken pieces together with adhesive tape while glue dries.

ELECTRIC MOTOR

See motor, electric.

ELECTRIC OUTLET

Defective. Shut off current at fuse box. Unscrew outlet plate, then take out screws that hold outlet and remove it from box. Pull out gently to avoid breaking the wires. Loosen wires from outlet and install a new one. Always attach black wire to gold screw; white wire to silver screw. Push outlet into box carefully and make sure that bare wires and terminal screws do not touch sides of box.

ELECTRIC PLUG

See electric cord.

ELECTRIC SWITCH

Defective. Shut off current at fuse box. Unscrew cover plate, then take out screws and remove switch from box carefully. Unscrew wires from switch. Screw on new switch in exactly the way the old one was attached. In a three-way switch, black wire goes to the single screw; red and white wires to either of the other two side-by-side screws. When setting switch in box, make sure that screws and bare wires do not touch sides of box.

ENGINE, GASOLINE

Note. Let an expert make repairs on gasoline engines. But before calling on him, check and correct the points noted below for *small* engines such as those on lawn mowers.

Doesn't start. Check: Is valve on fuel tank open? Is stop-switch pushed away from spark plug? Is choke adjusted? Are you out of gas?

Runs unevenly. Check: Is gasoline stale, gummy? Is fuel filter clean? Is oil in crankcase at proper level and is it clean? Is oil filter clogged? Are cooling fins clogged with grass and dust? Is spark plug dirty or cracked?

EXHAUST FAN

See fan, ventilating.

EXPRESS WAGON, CHILDREN'S

Nut on steering yoke pulls out from bottom of wagon. Take off nut and pull out bolt. Slip a wide steel washer under head of bolt and insert bolt shank through hole in wagon bottom and yoke. Then screw on nut.

Handle loop bashed. If this can't be straightened, replace it with metal handle from a child's aluminum snow shovel. Bolt to handle post.

Axle broken. Cut a new axle out of round, brass-plated steel curtain rod. Drill holes in ends for cotter pins. Slip into frame. Put large, tight-fitting washers over the ends. Then put on wheels and more washers. Set cotter pins in holes.

Holes in steel wagon bottom. Scrape off paint around holes and clean metal with steel wool. Spread on plastic steel and smooth.

EXTENSION CORD

See electric cord.

EXTERIOR WALLS

See also entries following.

Open cracks between siding and window or door frame, chimney, etc. Scrape out loose caulking, if any. Fill with new caulking compound. This is easily applied with a caulking gun, but can also be packed in with a putty knife.

EXTERIOR WALL, ASBESTOS-CEMENT SHINGLE

Broken shingles. See roof, asbestos-cement shingle.

Copper and rust stains. Scrub with an abrasive household cleanser. If this is not completely effective, use special asbestos shingle cleaner. Mix 1 part of this to 5 parts of water; scrub on with a fiber brush, then rinse with clear water.

Fungus growth. See roof, asbestos-cement shingle.

EXTERIOR WALL—ASPHALT ROLL SIDING

Bulges. Carefully pry up bottom edge of the siding strip above the one affected and then slightly loosen the nails along the top edge of the bulging strip. If bulge does not disappear after a few days of warm weather, loosen the bottom edge of the strip and with a stick reach up under the strip and smear asphalt roofing cement under the bulge. Press down. If this does not eliminate bulge (don't count on it) the only thing left to do is carefully cut through the bulge along the "mortar" lines in the siding; spread asphalt roofing cement under the cut edges; overlap the edges, and wedge a board flat against them for several days.

EXTERIOR WALL, BRICK

Brick broken, loose. See brick.

Mortar joints cracked. See brick.

Efflorescence on brick. See brick.

Water leaks through wall. If walls become slightly damp on the inside during prolonged wet weather and the problem is not attributable to cracks, the entire wall needs to be waterproofed. Use either a transparent, colorless silicone waterproofing compound or cement paint. To apply former, clean walls, remove old oil paint and whitewash but not cement paint. Let walls dry. Then brush or spray on silicone. Use two coats on very porous surfaces.

To apply cement paint, remove old oil paint and clean wall thoroughly. With a scrubbing brush apply first coat of paint mixed according to manufacturer's directions. Work it well into pores. Let dry for several hours, then fog wall with clear water several times during next 24 hours. Apply a second coat of paint on damp surface. After it has set, keep damp for 48 hours.

Stains. See brick.

EXTERIOR WALL, CONCRETE

See concrete.

EXTERIOR WALL, STONE

Mortar joints cracked, crumbling. Chip out broken mortar. Blow out crumbs with vacuum cleaner. Then pack in 1 part cement and 3 parts sand mixed to the consistency of damp earth. Finish to match old joints.

Water leaks through walls which are not cracked. See exterior wall, brick.

Stains. See brick.

EXTERIOR WALL, STUCCO

Cracks. Cut open with a chisel so they are wider in back than on the surface. Blow out crumbs with vacuum cleaner and wet with water. Fill with mortar made of 1 part cement, 3 parts sand and 1/10th part hydrated lime. Keep damp for several days by misting with water.

Loose, broken, bulging. Remove all defective stucco. If wire lath is rusted, cut it out and nail in a new piece. Wet edges of surrounding stucco with water before applying each of three new coats of stucco.

All coats are made of 1 part cement, 3 parts sand, and 1/10th part hydrated lime. Trowel first coat on to lath and scratch the surface so that next coat will adhere. After stucco has set up, keep it damp for 48 hours; then let dry. Then sprinkle with water and trowel on second coat in the same way. After sprinkling and allowing to dry, apply third coat and trowel off to match old stucco.

Stains. See concrete.

EXTERIOR WALL, WOOD

Holes. Brush edges of hole with linseed oil. Fill with putty. If hole is large, cut a piece of wood to fit and nail in place. Conceal nail holes and cracks around edges with putty. Paint to match surrounding area.

Siding warped slightly. Nail down as well as possible and fill crack with caulking compound.

Badly warped, cracked or rotten siding. With saw, hammer, and chisel, cut out defective section and replace with new length of wood. Countersink nails and cover with putty. Repaint.

Stains. See wood.

EXTERIOR WALL, WOOD SHINGLE

Holes. Brush edges of hole with linseed oil. Fill with putty and groove lightly to match wood grain. If shingles are stained, mix matching stain into putty before applying.

Shingles cracked or warped. Loosen overlapping shingles slightly and reach up under them with a hacksaw blade and cut nails holding defective shingle. Replace with new shingle. To hold this in place, put several dabs of roofing cement on both sides near the thin end. Do not nail butts.

Stains. See wood.

EYEGLASSES

Plastic frame broken. Apply plastic-mending adhesive to break. Allow a little excess glue to remain on surface of frame; it will add strength but being transparent will not show. Press pieces together until glue sets.

FABRICS

See clothing–fabrics. Specific entries will be found for burlap, canvas, clothing–stretch fabric, felt, fiberglass, lace, lastex, leatherette, oilcloth, vinyl.

FAIENCE

Broken. Clean and coat both broken surfaces with a thin coat of Duco cement. Press together for several hours.

FAN, ATTIC

Doesn't run. Check whether switch is on. Check if fuse has blown. Then call a serviceman.

Runs slowly. Apply oil at oiling points. Examine drive belt and adjust tension. Check motor (see motor, electric). Then call a serviceman.

Vibrates noisily. Make sure fan is securely mounted. Examine and if necessary replace vibration dampeners under it. If noise continues, call serviceman.

Fan blades loose. Make sure fan is positioned properly then tighten. You may need an Allen wrench of the proper size to do this.

FAN, ELECTRIC

Doesn't run. Disconnect and examine cord and plug. If broken, repair (see electric cord). If the switch doesn't seem to work properly (the push type often fails to catch when it is old) and if it is possible to open fan housing easily, replace the switch. Should these measures fail, take fan to a service shop.

Runs slowly. Disconnect, and turn fan blades by hand. If they feel stiff, apply a couple of drops of light oil either at oiling point (if there is one) or on shaft at the point where it enters motor housing. Turn blades to loosen them. Then, if shaft was oiled, remove oil with a rag.

Doesn't oscillate. Clean grease, oil, and dirt from oscillating mechanism under fan and apply a couple of drops of SAE No. 10 oil to moving parts.

Fan blades bent. Try straightening by hand. If this is impossible, take blades off shaft, lay bent blade on a flat surface and hammer out bend with a block of wood.

FAN, KITCHEN VENTILATING

Noisy, slow. Remove grille. Clean out dust and grease carefully. Lubricate motor at oiling points with a couple of drops of light oil.

Doesn't work. Check if fuse has blown. If not, call an electrician.

FAUCET

Compression faucet drips. Shut off water to faucet. Unscrew large packing nut and screw out stem assembly. Unscrew old washer with screwdriver or, if head of screw is damaged, with pliers. If screw breaks off in stem, place stem in a vise and carefully drill out screw with a small metal drill. Replace old washer—and old screw if damaged—with new. Reassemble faucet.

If faucet continues to drip, the valve seat below the washer may be rough and uneven. Call in a plumber.

Compression faucet leaks around faucet stem. Turn off water, unscrew packing nut and stem assembly. Wrap graphite wicking around the stem and force it into the packing nut. Then reassemble faucet. If graphite wicking is not available, cotton string will do for a short while.

Aquaseal faucet drips. If tightening large cap nut under faucet handle does not stop drip, remove nut, lift out valve stem, take out rubber diaphragm below stem and replace with a new one.

Moen push-pull faucet drips. Take off handle escutcheon, handle and stop tube. Remove retainer clip and pull cartridge out of valve body. Replace with new cartridge and reassemble.

American-Standard single-lever faucet drips. Take off escutcheon and large cap nuts on sides of faucet assembly. Pick out wire screens and wash in water. Lift out stainless steel valves and clean valve faces and seats with a pencil eraser. Then reassemble.

American-Standard push-pull faucet drips. This is mended like a single-lever faucet. To get at faucet assembly, look for printed instructions concealed in back of faucet escutcheon.

Faucet aerator clogged. If it can't be unscrewed by hand, wrap with adhesive tape and use pliers. Clean strainers under running water. Be sure to replace them in the same sequence that you found them.

FEATHER

Ornamental feather bent, broken. Poke a stiff wire of appropriate diameter up through the quill and well past the break. If you can work some Duco cement up to the break, so much the better.

Edge of ornamental feather torn from quill. Usually there is a sliver of the quill still attached to the feathers. Glue this to the body of the quill with Duco cement.

FELT

Holes, slashes. Cut a patch about ¾″ larger in all dimensions than the hole. Feather edges with a razor blade. Apply a thin layer of Devcon Patch glue and smooth down.

Felt loose from wood. Clean off old glue. Apply a thin layer of Elmer's Glue-All to felt and smooth down.

Felt loose from glass, ceramics, metal, plastics, etc. Clean off old glue. Apply a thin layer of Pliobond cement to both surfaces. Let dry until tacky and press together.

FENCE, STEEL

Posts wobble. See fence, wood.

Rusted. Wire-brush metal thoroughly to remove loose rust, scale, and dirt. Only loose rust need be removed. Apply Rust-Oleum 769 Damp-Proof Red Primer. When dry, apply finish paint (see Basic Methods: How to Paint).

FENCE, WOOD

Posts wobble. If posts are sound, coat with preservative. Then dig holes 16″ deep and 12″ in diameter around them. Pour in concrete made of 1 part cement, 1 part sand, and 1½ parts coarse aggregate. Tamp well.

Posts rotten at base. Replace with wood that has been pressure-treated at a mill with wood preservative. If such wood is not readily available, soak bottom of post in pentachlorophenol or zinc or copper naphthanate for 24 hours. An alternative to using wood posts is to make concrete posts reinforced with steel. Insert bolts to hold rails while concrete is damp. For mortar mix, see above.

Posts rotting at top. If replacement is not called for, dig out soft wood and fill with plastic wood. Saturate with pentachlorophenol. For extra protection, cut aluminum flashing to fit over top and nail around the sides.

Rails or pickets rotting. If rot has not progressed too far, dig out soft wood and fill holes with plastic wood. Scrape off paint and saturate wood with pentachlorophenol.

Wide top rail holds water and splits as a result. Edges of rail are curved upwards. With a plane or drawknife, cut down edges so that water will run off. Fill splits with plastic wood or putty.

FIBERGLASS—FABRIC

Holes in fiberglass fabrics. Darn with fiberglass yarn or sew on a patch of matching fabric with cotton thread. See clothing–fabrics. Patches can also be glued to the fabric, but you must use methyl methacrylate "invisible" glue.

Grease stains on fiberglass fabrics. Place a blotter or absorbent rag under stain and drip carbon tetrachloride on stain. Don't rub. This method works pretty well on solid-colored fabrics but will probably fade prints (and unfortunately there is no other way to clean the latter).

Rust stains on fiberglass fabrics. These are impossible to remove. Make sure that drapery hooks and hardware you use are rustproof.

Other stains on fiberglass fabrics. Sponge on lukewarm, soapy water. Do not rub.

Paint on fiberglass fabrics. Pick paint off with your fingernails when it dries.

FIBERGLASS, REINFORCED

Shallow scratches in reinforced fiberglass. Sand clean and brush on polyester resin available from boat dealers.

Deep scratches, gouges in reinforced fiberglass. Sand. Mix ⅛″ cuttings of fiberglass mat or cloth with polyester resin to form a putty. Trowel into scratch. Sand smooth when dry.

Breaks in opaque reinforced fiberglass. Open small breaks with a file. Then with a disc sander, feather back the edges around the hole for about 3″. Out of fiberglass cloth or mat cut a patch to cover sanded area. Lay it on a sheet of cellophane, spread polyester resin uniformly over it, cover with another sheet of cellophane and with your hands or a wood paddle work the resin thoroughly into the fabric. Then brush polyester resin on area to be patched. Remove top sheet of cellophane from patch, lay patch over hole and smooth down. When the resin has set, remove cellophane. Sand the patch and apply additional patches of fiberglass in the same way until desired thickness is achieved. Then sand and brush on one or two more coats of resin to obliterate the weave of the cloth. See illustration for boat, molded fiberglass.

If break is large and compound, cut out the damaged area with a metal-cutting saw and feather back the edges of the hole. Mold a thin sheet of aluminum, or a piece of shirt-cardboard covered with cellophane, over the hole on one side and hold in place with pressure-sensitive tape. Then patch hole with fiberglass cloth or mat as above.

Polyester resin cures best at a temperature of about 70°. Below 55° it will not cure satisfactorily. However, you can use the resin at this or lower temperature if an infra-red bulb is directed on the patch from a distance of no less than 14″.

If the repair must match a colored surface, add a color pigment of the right hue to the resin. An exact match is difficult to achieve, however.

Breaks in translucent reinforced fiberglass. If this type of material is not used for decorative purposes, repair it like opaque reinforced fiberglass. However, if it is used in decoration, clean the broken edges, dry thoroughly and glue together with polyester resin. But note that this joint is very weak and will last only if the fiberglass is not subjected to strain; therefore it may be advisable to reinforce it by bolting small pieces of reinforced fiberglass at intervals across the back of the break.

FIGURINE

Wood figurine broken. If the break is large, apply Elmer's Glue-All to one edge and press together. But if the break is too small to offer an adequate gluing surface (for example, if an upraised hand breaks off at the wrist), a strong repair is difficult to make with glue alone. In this case, push a straight pin about ¼″ into one broken edge. Cut off all but ¼″ of the exposed pin. With a tiny drill or awl make a corresponding hole in the other broken edge. It can be larger than the pin in order to permit perfect alignment of the broken pieces. Apply a thin coat of Duco cement to both broken edges and let dry. Then apply a second coat to the edge with the hole and fill hole, too. Bring pieces together, align and hold in place until glue sets.

Instead of a pin, a round toothpick can be used if the broken edges are large enough to permit drilling for the toothpick. Use Elmer's Glue-All to stick pieces together.

Ceramic figurine broken. If the break is large, coat both edges with Duco cement and press together. If break is small and figurine is hollow, shape a short length of balsa wood to fill the hollow. (Lacking balsa wood, use a small roll of paper). Insert it half way in one broken piece. Then coat broken edges with Duco cement. Slip other end of the "splint" into other broken piece and press the pieces together until glue sets.

Wax figurine broken. If broken surface is large, hold the two pieces close together and melt both surfaces at the same time with a match. Immediately press together. If break is small, stick a needle halfway into one broken piece. Align edges as best you can. Then stick bottom end of needle into other broken piece. If figurine is not handled too much, this repair will be adequate, but there is a good chance that the top piece will swivel on the needle. If this happens, replace needle with a flat-sided toothpick or a small flat strip of metal.

FILE CABINET

See cabinet, file.

FILE, CARPENTER'S

Teeth clogged, file smooth. Brush with a wire brush. If soft metal such as solder has clogged teeth, scrape clean with a knife.

Tang loose in wood handle. Remove tang and squeeze into handle hole a little plastic steel. Replace tang.

FIREPLACE, MASONRY

Smokes. Have fireplace and chimney cleaned and examined by a professional (cleaning by burning chemicals in the fire is nowhere nearly so effective as mechanical cleaning). Remove or prune back any large tree that overhangs chimney. If smoking continues, hold a board across the fireplace opening and gradually lower it until smoking stops. Have a metal shield or hood installed in chimney opening at this point.

Draft poor. Check whether fire is properly placed at back of firebox and whether room ventilation is adequate (in a tight room, if you open a window when you start fire, good draft should be created and should continue after window is closed). If these measures don't help, call in a professional. Height of chimney may have to be adjusted or you may have to have chimney capped.

Wind blows down chimney. Consult expert about need for capping chimney.

Rain comes down chimney. Have it capped.

Damper defective. If it simply works stiffly, opens only partially, scrape off encrusted soot and apply oil. Some dampers can be removed to facilitate work. If damper is broken, have a mason replace it.

Mortar joints in firebox and in hearth cracked. Chip out bad mortar. Blow out crumbs. Wet edges of bricks or stones. Pack in fire clay available from a building supply dealer or mortar made of 1 part cement, 1 part lime, and 6 parts sand.

Hearth settling. Call in mason at once.

Large cracks between hearth and floor. These heel-catchers develop when the mortar along the edges of the hearth crumbles. Clean cracks out thoroughly and blow out crumbs with a vacuum cleaner. Wet edges with water. Pack in concrete mixture of 1 part cement and 3 parts sand.

Smoke stains on fireplace breast. Wash with detergent and/or household cleanser. To remove stubborn stains, see concrete.

FIREPLACE, PREFAB METAL

Dents. Hold a block of wood against concave side and hammer out with a rubber mallet. Use light blows, especially if exterior of metal is porcelain-enameled.

Joints open in fireplace or flue pipe. Brush off soot and wash with detergent. Dry and clean surface with steel wool. Then spread on plastic steel.

FIREPLACE SCREEN

Hole in mesh. Weave in steel wire and paint black or gold.

Flexible screen slides stiffly. Clean out channel with a toothbrush and kerosene. Squirt in powdered graphite.

Traverse-type flexible screens don't meet at center of fireplace. See curtain rod.

FIREPLACE TOOLS

Tip of poker loose. Remove tip by unscrewing, clean screw hole and threads on handle. Coat threads liberally with plastic steel and screw tip back in place.

Hole in bellows. Cut a patch out of any impermeable, flexible matching material, such as light leather or plastic, and glue over hole with Pliobond cement.

FISHING ROD

Line guide off or loose. Position guide on rod and wrap cellophane tape around one leg to hold it. Use silk or nylon thread to bind legs permanently in place. Start winding about 1/16″ ahead of the legs and continue winding up to point where they bend to form the loop. Turns of thread should touch. To anchor ends of thread without knotting, see drawing. When both of the guide legs have been bound down, coat thread thoroughly with varnish.

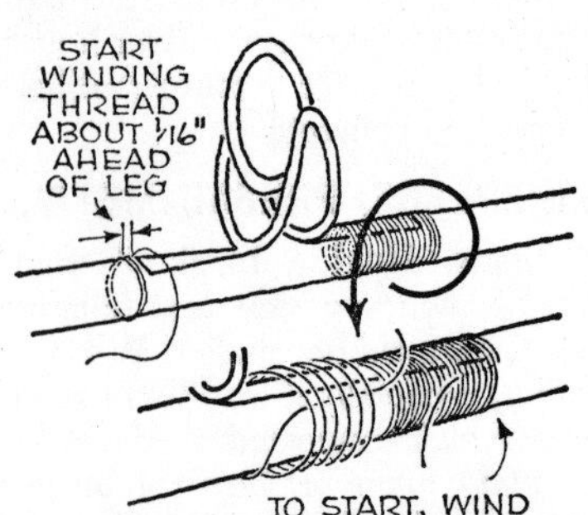

Bamboo rod broken. See bamboo. But note that it is best to have an expert repair an expensive fly rod.

Set (bend) in bamboo rod. Bend straight by hand. Be careful. But remember that once a rod develops a set, it can never be permanently straightened.

FLASHING, ALUMINUM

Small holes, tears. Steel-wool surface and smear on plastic aluminum.

Large holes, tears. Cut a patch out of aluminum sheet. Steel-wool area around hole and underside of patch. Spread plastic aluminum on flashing and embed patch in this.

Chimney flashing buckled or loose. Force together seams that have come apart, crimp edges, and seal with plastic aluminum. If metal has pulled loose from mortar joints or mortar is crumbling around metal, clean out the joints. Force aluminum back in place. Fill joints with caulking compound or asphalt roofing compound.

FLASHING, ASPHALTIC FELT

Small holes. Coat with asphalt roofing compound.

Tears, large holes. Cut a patch of asphalt roll roofing 6″ wider and longer than the tear. Apply roofing compound to both sides. Slip under tear and then apply more compound to edges of tear.

FLASHING, COPPER

Holes, tears. Solder on a patch. See copper. For safety, use a soldering iron rather than a blowtorch.

Chimney flashing buckled or loose. Force together seams that have come apart, and solder. If metal has pulled loose from the mortar joints or if mortar has crumbled away around the metal, rake out the joints, wet with water and pack in mortar of 1 part cement and 2 parts sand.

FLASHING, GALVANIZED IRON

Small holes, tears. Clean thoroughly with steel wool. Cover with plastic steel. Prime with rust-inhibiting paint and apply finish paint.

Large holes, tears. Cut a patch out of galvanized steel. Steel-wool one side of patch and metal around hole. Spread on plastic steel and weight down patch. Prime and paint.

Chimney flashing buckled or loose. See flashing, copper.

FLASHLIGHT

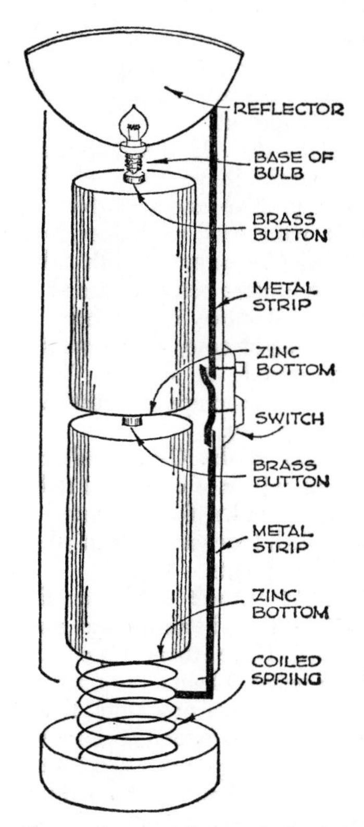

Note. For a flashlight to work, electric current must flow from the positive terminal (the small brass button) of the battery to the filament and back to the negative terminal (the zinc bottom) of the battery. In a tubular flashlight the current flows from the brass button of the top battery to the bottom of the bulb, through the filament, then out through the screw base of the bulb to the reflector, then to a metal strip attached to the bottom of the turn-on switch, then to the coiled spring in the base of the flashlight and finally to the zinc base of the bottom battery. For the circuit to be complete, the batteries must be arranged so that the brass button of the bottom battery touches the zinc base of the one next nearest the light; the brass button of the top battery must touch the base of the lamp; the metal strip on the bottom of the switch must touch the reflector; and the spring in the base of the flashlight must touch the zinc base of the bottom battery.

In an electric lantern the circuit is completed in the same way, but in this case the positive and negative terminals of the large square battery are close together on top of the battery. They make contact with the bulb and switch by an arrangement of metal strips which are readily located when the lantern case is opened.

Light dim. If the batteries are not weak (have them checked), clean positive and negative terminals with fine sandpaper, emery cloth or by scraping with a knife. Clean contact point at base of lamp socket. Remove spring from base of flashlight case, clean thoroughly and stretch it slightly. With a screwdriver scrape out rust in case below spring.

Light blinks. Clean and stretch spring in base of case. Seat reflector securely and make sure metal strip on switch touches it. Clean all other contact points.

Light doesn't work at all. Be certain that batteries are not reversed. Have them tested. Have bulb tested. Clean all contact points with sandpaper or a knife. If switch is difficult to operate, clean under the metal strip inside the case with sandpaper. Bend metal strip so it touches reflector.

FLOOR, ASPHALT TILE

Tile broken. Crack tile with a hammer, dig out pieces and scrape adhesive from subfloor. Spread in new asphalt tile adhesive. After it becomes tacky, set in tile. If subfloor is uneven, tile should be heated in an oven until it is pliable and then quickly set in place.

Holes. Replace tile as above.

Tile loose. This usually occurs when tiles are laid over a concrete floor that contains too much moisture. There's nothing to do but relay tiles with new adhesive after concrete has been allowed to dry completely.

Cracks between tiles. See floor, vinyl.

Stains. See floor, linoleum.

FLOOR, BRICK

See brick.

FLOOR, CERAMIC TILE

Cracks between tiles. Clean out old mortar. Blow out crumbs. Soak tile edges with water. Then smear a prepared tile grout into them and remove excess with a damp rag.

Other problems. See tile, ceramic.

FLOOR, CONCRETE

Cracks. Chip crack open with a cold chisel. Blow out crumbs with vacuum cleaner. Wet edges with water. Fill with mortar made of 1 part cement and 2 parts sand.

Concrete badly broken. Break out bad area with a heavy hammer; clean out dust. Wet edges with water. Fill with 1 part cement, 1 part sand, and 1½ parts coarse aggregate consisting of pebbles no more than ⅜" diameter. Compact mortar thoroughly to eliminate voids but don't work it so hard that water comes to the surface. Let it set until just before it is too hard to trowel. Then smooth off slightly above surrounding surface. Keep patch covered with damp burlap for several days.

Concrete pitted, uneven. Clean floor thoroughly. Spread on latex cement and trowel smooth. If cement needs to be more than ⅛" thick, apply it in two or more coats after preceding coat has dried.

Concrete dusting. Clean floor thoroughly. Then mix 1 part zinc fluosilicate with 4 parts magnesium fluosilicate. Mix ½ lb. of this mixture in 1 gal. water and mop evenly over floor. While this dries, mix 2 lb. of the fluosilicate in 1 gal. water. Mop on floor. When this has dried, mop floor with clear water to remove encrusted salts.

Stains. See concrete.

FLOOR, CORK

Holes, burns. See cork.

Tile damaged. See floor, vinyl. Stick tile down with linoleum cement.

Cracks between tiles. See floor, vinyl.

Stains. See cork.

FLOOR, LINOLEUM

Small holes. Grate a waste scrap of linoleum and mix with clear lacquer to form a thick paste. Spread in hole immediately. Sand smooth when dry.

Large holes. If in tiles, replace tiles. If in sheet linoleum, lay a scrap piece of matching linoleum over the hole, hold tight and with a very sharp knife cut through both layers at once. Then dig out old linoleum, scrape out adhesive and apply new linoleum paste. Set in patch and weight down.

Cuts, tears. Lift edges and spread linoleum paste underneath. Use a spatula or thin knife, or squirt paste from a clean oil can. Weight down.

Bulges. Make small cut through bulge, spread linoleum paste underneath and weight down.

Cracks between tiles. See floor, vinyl.

Tile damaged. See floor, vinyl. Use linoleum paste to glue new tile down. Note that if linoleum is laid over concrete laid on grade or below grade, the salts in the concrete will soon destroy it. Tear it all up and use flooring designed for on-grade and below-grade installation, such as asphalt tile and some vinyls.

Stains, rubber heel marks. Never use chemical cleaners. Scrub with a damp cloth and mild cleansing powder. Use fine steel wool if necessary.

Nail polish, tar, lacquer, varnish, other deposits on flooring. Scrape off with a dull knife and rub with fine steel wool.

FLOOR, RUBBER

Small holes. You can fill these with plastic rubber, but it will be difficult to make the patch smooth.

Tile damaged. See floor, vinyl. Use rubber tile adhesive.

Cracks between tiles. See floor, vinyl.

Stains. See floor, linoleum.

FLOOR, STONE

See stone.

FLOOR, VINYL

Small holes. Shred a scrap of the vinyl flooring into tiny shavings and mix with a small amount of methyl ethyl ketone or acetone until a putty is formed. Then add a small amount of lacquer or clear fingernail polish. Surround hole with cellulose tape to keep mixture from spreading. Apply putty with a spatula or knife to the level of the tape. After it has set for a few minutes, remove tape. Added thickness created by tape will allow for shrinkage of the mixture as it dries.

Large holes. Hold a piece of vinyl flooring tightly over the hole and cut through both layers at once with a sharp knife. Dig out old flooring and adhesive. Spread in new vinyl flooring cement. Set in patch and weight down.

Cuts, tears. Lay a 1″ strip of smooth, heavy-duty aluminum foil over the cut and fasten one end with friction tape. Smooth the foil down with your finger. Heat a hand iron to highest temperature. Then pull the point of the iron over the foil toward you several times. Do not bear down or hold iron in one spot. Edges of cuts should now be sealed together. Wipe foil with a damp rag and remove it. Clean vinyl with water and an abrasive household cleanser to remove dull streak left by foil.

Burns. Scrape with a dull knife until only a small residue remains. Then rub with a damp cloth and abrasive cleanser.

Tile damaged. Cut tile across the middle, insert chisel under cut and pry up two pieces. (Do not pry up a tile from the sides lest you damage adjacent tiles.) Scrape out old adhesive and spread in new vinyl floor cement. Set new tile and weight down.

Cracks between tiles. These result from laying the tiles on a single-thickness wood subfloor. The inevitable expansion and contraction of the wood causes cracks to open between the tiles (as well as between sheets of resilient flooring). There is no way to fix these short of relaying the floor on a double-thick wood subfloor.

Stains. See floor, linoleum.

FLOOR, VINYL-ASBESTOS TILE

See floor, asphalt tile. Unlike asphalt tile, however, vinyl-asbestos is flexible enough to be laid over an uneven surface without heating.

FLOOR, WOOD

Deep scratches, gouges. Fill with plastic wood. This must be stained to the color of the floor before you apply it. Better make several test batches first. After plastic hardens, sand smooth.

Burns. Scrape out charred wood with a sharp knife or razor blade. Work with the grain. Sand smooth. If hole is not deep, apply new stain and finish. If hole turns out to be too deep for this, fill it with plastic wood as above.

Splits. If board is loose, drill through it at an angle in several places along the break. Drive in 3″ or 4″ cement-coated finishing nails and countersink the heads. Fill the split and nail holes with plastic wood stained to color of floor. To replace a badly damaged section, see porch, wood.

Boards loose or raised. Drill small holes at an angle through the board near the edges. Drive in cement-coated finishing nails, countersink the heads and fill holes with plastic wood.

Parquet flooring loose or warped. If it is laid over a wood subfloor, nail down like strip flooring (see splits, above). If it is laid on concrete, better leave well enough alone. The only thing you can do, and it is not easy, is to insert a very thin chisel or putty knife into the cracks around the wood block and cut through the tongues connecting it with the adjacent blocks. Then lift out, clean out old mastic, and glue down with asphalt tile cement.

Wood plugs in pegged floor miss-

ing. Buy a hardwood dowel the size of the plug holes. Saw into lengths roughly equal to depth of hole. Coat with Weldwood plastic resin glue and set in hole. When glue has dried, trim plug flush with floor with a sharp chisel and sandpaper. Then stain.

Floor squeaks. If first floor squeaks, drive thin wood wedges between the joints and the subfloor. If there is a ceiling below the squeaky floor, drill small holes at an angle through the boards. Nail down boards with long cement-coated finishing nails or spiral nails. Countersink the heads and fill holes with plastic wood.

Graphite squirted into cracks between squeaky boards often silences them. But the graphite is very messy and the treatment is not permanent.

Floor sags. Raise on one or more steel jack posts or short screw jacks set on top of 4″ by 4″ timbers. Floors which sag badly and cannot be leveled by jacking can be covered with a mastic fill, provided they will support the extra weight. But you should get a flooring contractor to do this job.

Floor vibrates. Raise floor on jack posts and install additional bridging between the joists. If joists are too small, have a carpenter install additional ones.

Stains. See wood.

Water spots on shellacked floor. See varnished surface.

FLUORESCENT LAMP

Tube blinks repeatedly before staying lit. In older types of lamps, it is common for the lamp to blink once or twice; but if blinking continues longer than this, check whether tube is seated in sockets. If blinking still continues, replace the starter (the little metal cylinder near one end of the fixture). To do this, remove tube, press down the starter and turn to one side until it comes loose. New starter must be of the same size.

Tube lights at ends but not in middle. Replace the starter.

FORMICA

See plastics, laminated.

FORTICEL

See plastics—general.

FOUNDATION WALL

Leaking cracks. Scratch small cracks open with a nail or cold chisel, sprinkle with water and brush in two coats of a soupy grout made of equal parts of cement and fine sand. If cracks are large, chip them out at least ½″ deep. Blow out crumbs with a vacuum cleaner. Wet edges with water. Fill with a stiff mixture of 1 part cement and 2 parts sand.

If water comes through crack more or less continuously, ordinary cement mortar will not hold. Use quick-setting plugging cement. Chip out crack deeply and make it wider at the back than on the surface. Mix with water just enough plugging cement to fill the hole, and mold it in your hands until it begins to feel warm and starts to stiffen. Immediately cram it into hole and hold in place for several minutes.

Wall weeps over large areas. If wall is damp in prolonged wet weather, remove paint and clean thoroughly. Rinse with water. Before wall dries, mix cement paint with water according to manufacturer's directions and apply it to a small test area with a scrubbing brush. Use a circular motion. If test area becomes damp during the next rain, repeat application of paint. If this still doesn't do the trick, call in a masonry contractor. However, if first or second application of paint stops the leaking, go ahead and paint the entire wall. To cure paint properly, let it set up for an hour after you apply it. Then mist it with water several times during the next 24 hours.

Wall leaks badly over large areas. You need a masonry contractor. The wall must be waterproofed on the outside with asphaltic compound and cement plaster. You may also have to put in drainage tiles around the footings.

FOUNTAIN PEN

Pen leaks. The barrel of the pen can be unscrewed or pulled from the finger-hold, and the rubber ink tube replaced. However, since the new ink tube must come from a pen dealer, it is just as well to have him make the repair.

Point broken. Same thing applies.

FREEZER, FOOD

Note. Call a serviceman if machine doesn't work properly, but before doing so check and correct points noted below.

Doesn't work. Check: Is it plugged in? Has fuse blown?

Runs too cold or too hot. Check: Is thermostat set at zero as it should be? Does box need defrosting?

Labors. Clean out dust, cobwebs, etc., from operating mechanism with a vacuum cleaner hose.

Sweats. If sweating occurs only around the top rim, check if gasket is sealing tightly. Wash with soap and water. If sweating continues, call a serviceman. You also need a serviceman if box sweats in one or two spots on the surface but not over the entire surface.

FRYING PAN, ELECTRIC

See coffee maker, electric.

FUR

Seams in furs ripped. Loosen and turn back lining. With a very sharp needle sew heavy cotton twill tape to both leather edges. Use a back stitch. Fold tapes under and stitch together.

If the skins are very dry, the tapes must be sewn as far back from the edges as possible.

Coat cuffs worn. Loosen sleeve lining, pull worn fur up into sleeve and sew down. Then resew lining.

Other problems. Take the fur to a furrier.

FURNACE

See also coal stoker, gas burner, or oil burner.

Doesn't heat house properly. If furnace is coal fired, clean out soot every month with a long-handled wire brush. Whatever the fuel, have heating contractor check draft and clean soot out of entire system.

Heats house unevenly. Check whether all heating outlets are operating properly (see radiator). If thermostat is exposed to cold drafts or heat (a radiator, register, fireplace, etc.), call in heating contractor. Thermostat probably needs to be moved.

Grates jammed with clinkers. Don't shake grates vigorously. Break clinkers with poker passed up through grate from ash pit.

Air leaks around furnace doors. If doors are seldom opened, cover cracks with asbestos cement.

Small cracks in cast-iron shell. Scrape open and pack in iron cement.

Delivers dirt to rooms through warm-air ducts. Clean furnace filters if of cleanable type; renew throwaway type.

FURNACE FLUE

Small holes. Clean metal with steel wool and fill holes at once with plastic steel.

Large holes. Replace flue section immediately.

Joints between pipe sections loose. Straighten pipes and support them on wires from joists. Remove dirt and rust with steel wool. Then cover joints with asbestos cement.

Joint between flue pipe and chimney open. Plug with asbestos cement.

FURNITURE—BED

Slats fall out. Check whether small rails on which the slats rest are secure. If they're not, screw them to the side rails with several more screws. The problem may also be attributable to the fact that the slats are too short. Cut new ones that are only ¼″ shorter than the space between the rails.

Boxspring sags. One or more of the bed irons (the heavy angle irons on which the spring rests) may be loose. If it cannot be tightened because screw holes are worn, remove it and install it where wood is sound.

Bedpost finial (ornamental top) broken off. Sometimes finials are integral parts of bedposts; sometimes they are separate pieces that are doweled into the posts. If the former type is broken, turn the repair job over to a professional. If the latter type is broken, saw off the dowel flush with the base of the finial. Carefully drill a hole in the finial for a new dowel. Glue dowel in finial with Weldwood plastic resin glue. Don't glue bottom end of dowel in bedpost.

Other problems. See furniture—wood chair. Also see mattress.

Stains. See wood.

FURNITURE—CANED SEAT OR BACK

Small holes. Buy matching cane and soak in warm water until pliable. Trim off old broken ends under the seat or behind the back. Weave in new canes and conceal ends under the old. When cane is dry, glue ends in place with Elmer's Glue-All, cover with wax paper and clamp between boards.

FURNITURE—CANVAS SEAT OR BACK

Holes, tears. See canvas.

Canvas done for. Rip it off. Pull tacks out of frame if there are any. Using old canvas as a pattern, cut new canvas to size. Sew edges if necessary for strength or to prevent raveling.

If canvas is tacked to wood, double the material at the tacked ends. Use 5⁄16″ copper tacks and space them about 1½″ apart.

Stains. See clothing–fabrics.

FURNITURE—CARD TABLE

Legs wobble. Tighten all screws.

If screw holes are worn, fill them with plastic wood before setting screws. If top of wood leg is attached to a wood axle and the joint is loose, remove leg entirely. Separate leg slightly from axle and fill joint with glue. Then screw tight.

Top on wood table torn. This can be patched with adhesive-backed mending tape. But it will look better if it's replaced. Rip off fabric and carefully dig out the fabric in the slots around the edges of the opening. Clean glue from slots. Nail wood base of top down tight. Cut new fabric top just large enough to cover the opening and fit into slots. Cover wood top with thin cotton batting or felt. This should come just to the slots. Lay the fabric and notch the four corners slightly. Run a little Elmer's Glue-All into the slots. Then carefully push edges of fabric into slots.

Top on metal table torn. The fabric top is wrapped around a wood base. Loosen cleats holding the base, lift out and tear off fabric. Use old fabric as a pattern, but add an inch to all sides of the new fabric. Wrap this over the wood base and down around and under the edges. Set top back in table and anchor one side with the cleats. Then pulling on the extra fabric under the table, tighten the fabric top on the other sides and anchor with cleats. Cut off excess material.

FURNITURE—CASTERS

Loose. If caster fits into a metal socket in the furniture leg, remove it from socket and wrap the shank with friction tape. If shank of caster is set directly in wood, hold in place with epoxy glue. If caster is secured to furniture with screws, fill screw holes with plastic wood and reset screws.

Frozen, won't swivel. Check whether sticking is caused by thread or string wrapped around the caster. Clean thoroughly. Apply a drop of oil and work caster back and forth. Remove excess oil.

FURNITURE—CHEST OF DRAWERS

Drawer sticks in summer. Rub edges with paraffin. If this doesn't help, burn a light bulb inside the drawer to shrink the wood. (Don't let bulb rest on wood; keep drawer open slightly for ventilation.) Then coat all surfaces with shellac or varnish to prevent wood from soaking up moisture from the summer air.

Drawer sticks in winter. Try rubbing edges with paraffin. If this does no good, plane down the bottom edges of the sides a fraction of an inch and sand smooth.

Drawer joints loose. Pull sides apart and scrape off old glue. Apply Weldwood plastic resin glue and refit sides. Tighten with a tourniquet as shown in drawing.

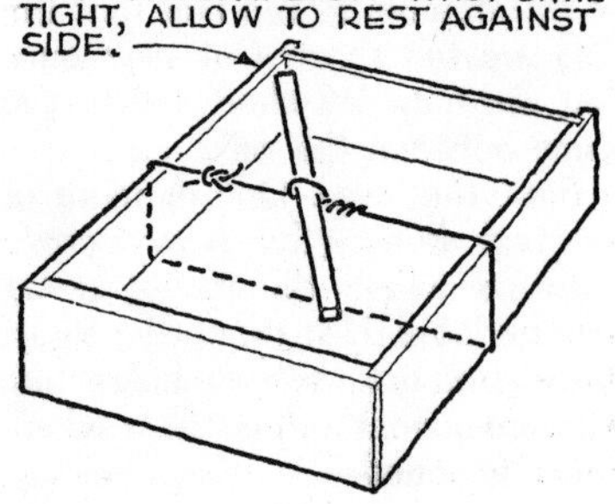

Bottom of drawer loose. Remove bottom and scrape glue from edges. Also clean glue out of rabbets in the sides and front of the drawer. Spread Weldwood plastic resin glue in rabbets and set in bottom. Nail a small brad through the bottom edge of the back of the drawer into the drawer bottom. If bottom panel is loose in the rabbets, force glue-coated toothpicks into the cracks.

Bottom of drawer broken. Cut a piece of ⅛″ hardboard to the size of the drawer and lay it over the old bottom. For a better job, replace the bottom entirely with hardboard or plywood of the proper thickness. Glue this in place as above.

Wood damaged. See wood. Also see veneer.

Side panels split. Remove the drawers. Working on the inside, pry one side of panel loose from frame with a knife. Join with other side. Then glue a very thin strip of wood, as from a bushel basket, lengthwise to the back of the split.

Stains. See wood.

FURNITURE—DESK

Wood top damaged. See furniture—table.

Veneered top damaged. See veneer.

Felt top torn. Remove felt and scrape and sand wood base clean. Cut new felt top to fit. Apply Elmer's Glue-All to wood and smooth felt into this. Trim edges as necessary with a razor blade.

Leather top torn. If tear is not obvious when leather is pressed down, simply spread Elmer's Glue-All under torn edges and weight down. If damage is severe, replace top as you would a felt top.

Lucite top cracked. See plastics—general.

Linoleum top damaged. See linoleum.

Burn in leather top. Carefully scrape out charred particles. If the scar is not too deep, you can pretty well conceal it with leather polish. If burn goes through leather, however, lay a scrap of matching leather over the hole; hold tight, and cut through both layers at once with a razor blade. Make a round or oval hole if possible. Apply Pliobond cement to back of patch and to base. Let dry until tacky and then stick down patch. Polish well and often.

Roll top on desk split at seams. Even though only one or two seams may be split, this is a sign that the backing material is old and likely to split again. Therefore, it is advisable to remove the roll top from the desk (this is done by taking off the back of the desk) and to replace the backing material in its entirety. To do this, lay the top upside down on a flat surface and peel off the fabric. Scrape off old glue. Then cut a piece of lightweight canvas to fit. Cover backs of wood strips with Elmer's Glue-All. Hold strips edge to edge and smooth out canvas on them.

To make a somewhat less permanent but satisfactory repair, do not remove roll top from desk. Cut out any old backing that is loose along the split. Cut a 2″ or 3″ strip of lightweight canvas the width of the top. Cover this with glue. Push roll top up far enough to get your arm under it. Hold wood strips together and smooth canvas under them.

Stains. See wood or entry for appropriate material.

FURNITURE—FOLDING CHAIR

Slat seat in wood chair broken. It's difficult for anyone except an expert to set in a new slat. But you can make a sound seat simply by cutting a piece of ⅛" hardboard to the size of the seat opening and gluing it to the slats with Weldwood plastic resin glue.

Holes in upholstered seat of folding wood bridge chair. Replace with new covering. See furniture—upholstered chair (seat of side chair torn).

Holes, tears in upholstered seat of metal chair. Unscrew the seat from the frame (if the chair is assembled in this way). Remove old fabric and use it as a pattern for the new cover. Cut, fold around seat, and tack in place. Then reset seat in frame.

In an older type of chair, the seat is slipped into a frame made of U-shaped metal. The part that forms the back of the seat frame is held to the rest of the frame by strong steel clips. Pry one of the clips loose with the claw of a hammer. Remove seat, take off cover, and cut a new cover out of vinyl fabric or leatherette. Tack to the base of the seat. Then slide seat into frame and hammer on the back channel.

Rubber tips on metal legs broken. Replace round, cup-shaped tips (like those on crutches and many ironing boards) with new tips available from most hardware stores. The rubber "tips" used on chairs with more or less flat, rectangular legs are another matter. These consist of a straight piece of hard rubber stuck to the bottom of a more or less T-shaped metal piece. To replace them, knock rubber and metal T off the bottom of the leg with a hammer. Then insert an entirely new tip, available from the chair supplier, in the hole in the end of the leg.

Chair wobbly, squeaky. Tighten up all bolts and screws, and oil the joints lightly. That's about as much as you can do.

FURNITURE—KNOBS AND PULLS

Wood knob loose. Cut two small washers from a sheet of medium-grade emery cloth. Paste back to back. Insert between the knob and the drawer.

If knob is loose because the screw hole in the back of it has enlarged, fill hole with plastic wood and reset screw at once.

Threads on bolt of metal knob gone; nut pulls off. Try a smaller nut. If this doesn't work, rub plastic steel into threads, tighten old nut, and coat joint between nut and bolt with more plastic.

FURNITURE, METAL

See aluminum, cast iron, steel as the case may be.

FURNITURE—ROCKING CHAIR

Rocker split. Spread Weldwood plastic resin glue on split surfaces and clamp wood together with C-clamps. If additional reinforcement is needed, drill ¼" holes up through the rocker after glue has hardened. Coat ¼" dowels with glue and tap into holes. Cut dowels off flush with surface when glue sets.

Other problems. See furniture–wood chair.

Stains. See wood.

FURNITURE—ROPE SEAT OR BACK

Sags. Find starting point of the rope. Working from there, pull each succeeding loop of rope taut. Put a new knot in the end and cut off the excess.

Broken. Don't remove rope. Make a rough measurement of the amount of new rope required and purchase this at hardware store. Then, when you're ready to install this in the chair, study how old rope is laced into frame and make a rough diagram on paper. Then cut out old rope and lace in new. Pull it up as tightly as possible to accommodate somewhat for eventual sagging.

FURNITURE—RUSH SEAT

Rushes broken, frayed. Buy chairmaker's rush to match. Cut old broken rushes off cleanly—preferably under the chair. Cut new rush strips long enough to fill in the breaks and add about 4″. Flatten the ends of the old and new rushes. Glue new strips to old with Elmer's Glue-All.

FURNITURE—SOFA

See furniture–upholstered chair.

FURNITURE—TABLE

Legs wobbly. Try to break joints and reglue, or try to force new glue into joints. If this is impossible, cut a triangle out of a piece of 1″ thick wood. Notch 90° corner to fit around the leg. Place block tight

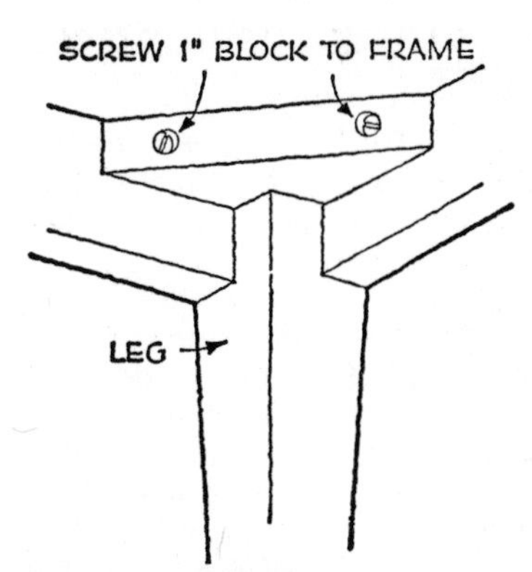

against inside surfaces of leg and screw it to the frame.

Wood damaged. See wood. Also see veneer.

Top or leaf warped. Remove top from frame and lay it concave side down on several layers of damp rags. Over the top hang one or two heat lamps. Keep lamps lighted and rags wet until wood straightens. If warp returns, repeat process. Once you're sure wood is stable, varnish the unfinished underside.

If warp is irregular, so that top is actually twisted, follow above procedure and weight down the highest parts with heavy weights.

Note. This repair is likely to damage the finish on the wood, but you have no choice.

Joined boards in top separated. Remove top from base. Scrape the old glue from edges of boards. Apply Weldwood plastic resin glue and press boards together. To assure that joints are tight, nail a straight board to the floor or to a sheet of plywood. Cover floor with wax paper. Push one end of table top against the board and, when joints are tight, nail a board along the opposite end of table.

Top split. Same as above.

Stains. See wood.

FURNITURE—UPHOLSTERED CHAIR

Seat of side chair torn, shabby. Turn chair upside down and remove the four screws that hold seat in place. Remove old cover and use it as a pattern for new cover. (If using a strongly patterned print, be sure that feature of design is centered.) Wrap new cover tightly around seat and secure four sides with tacks. Miter corners. Then tack all the way around the seat with 5⁄16″ tacks spaced about 1½″ apart.

Seat of overstuffed chair sagging. Turn chair upside down, remove dust cover and webbing. Tie bottom coils of springs together and to the frame. Be sure springs are evenly spaced in straight lines. Replace old webbing with new. The strips should be spaced so that each spring rests squarely on a crossing of the strips. Double the ends of the webbing to increase holding strength and fasten to bottom of chair frame with ¾″ tacks. Webbing should be interwoven and pulled flat and tight across bottom of frame. To pull it tight, use a webbing stretcher, or fold end of webbing around a board, brace board against chair frame and bend it down. Tack webbing strip once to hold. Then cut it off about 2″ beyond the chair frame, double back the end and put in three or four more tacks. To assure against movement of springs, sew them to webbing with coarse thread or light string. Replace dust cover.

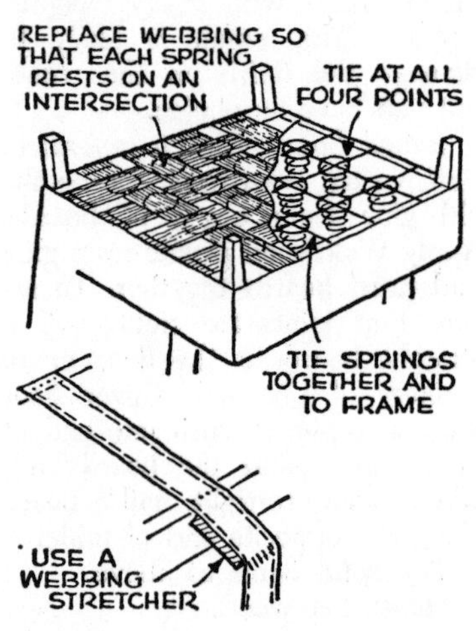

Seat of overstuffed chair lumpy, holey. Remove upholstery fabric and muslin underneath. Note well how they were attached to chair frame. Smooth out padding. If necessary to add new padding, use cotton and lay it in thin sheets with tapered edges. Use old upholstery fabric as a pattern and cut new seat cover to size. Tack and sew in place like the original upholstery.

Wood damaged. See furniture wood.

Stains. See wood or clothing—fabrics.

FURNITURE, WICKER, RATTAN, REED, OR BAMBOO

Bindings loose, broken. If full length of binding remains and is not too brittle, apply Elmer's waterproof glue to joint, rewrap binding over it and nail end in place with small brad. If binding needs to be replaced, soak new strip in water until pliable. Dry with a rag. Then apply waterproof glue to joint, wrap binding around it and secure with a brad.

Wicker, rattan, reed, or bamboo strips broken, split. If possible (the angle of the break and size of the material may cause trouble), coat the broken edges with Elmer's Glue-All or Duco cement and press together. To hold the ends while glue is drying and to strengthen the joint, it may be necessary also to wrap thread tightly around the break or to insert a pin (sharpened at both ends) or a wood dowel into the opposing ends.

If the broken strip is part of a rather dense weave (as is often the case with wicker), an easier solution may be simply to coat it with glue and clamp it to the other strips in the weave. The break can be further reinforced by tiny wires wound through the weave and around the broken strip.

FURNITURE, WOOD

Minor scratches. Rub with paste floor wax, the meat of a nut, or a mixture of equal parts boiled linseed oil, turpentine, and water. Hide with shoe polish if necessary.

Severe scratches. Rub with a wax stick of the proper color.

Burns. With a sharp knife carefully scratch out all charred wood. Work with the grain. Clean with benzine. Smooth with fine steel wool or sandpaper. Apply oil stain to match surrounding finish.

If scar is deep, instead of applying stain, fill it with stick shellac matching the finish. Heat a small spatula over an alcohol flame or on an electric burner, press it against shellac stick and let the melting shellac drip into hole. Smooth with heated spatula. Sand with fine sandpaper when dry and rub down with rottenstone and a rag dipped in sewing machine oil.

Dents. Cover with a damp cloth. Place a bottle cap upside down directly over dent and rest a warm flatiron on top. If dent doesn't rise after several applications of heat, remove finish with steel wool and try again.

Stains. See wood; also lacquered surface, shellacked surface, or varnished surface as case may be.

FURNITURE—WOOD CHAIR

Joints loose. Sand off old glue on the tenon and in the mortise. Apply Weldwood plastic resin glue and reset the joint. Keep joint under pressure for 24 hours. This is most easily done by looping a strong cord around legs, arms, or back of chair and tightening like a tourniquet. Pad the cord where it bears on the wood.

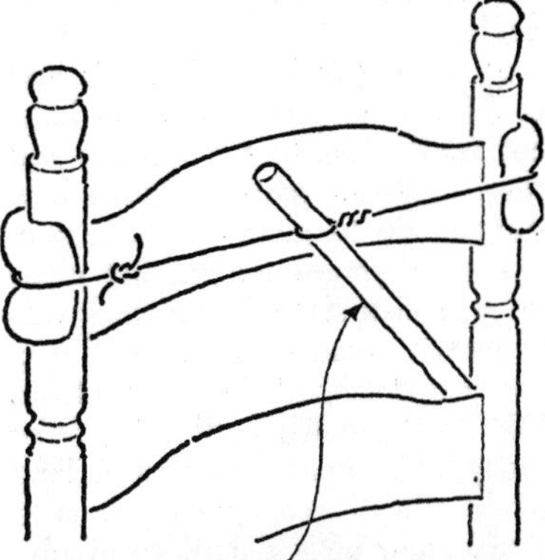

TIE HEAVY CORD LOOSELY AROUND BACK OF CHAIR. PASS STICK OR OTHER RIGID OBJECT UNDER, THEN OVER CORD TO FORM LOOP. TWIST UNTIL TIGHT. REST STICK AGAINST UPRIGHT OR WHERE CONVENIENT.

If joint keeps coming loose no matter how much glue is applied, try one of the following tricks: (1) After joint is glued and set, tap glue-coated toothpicks into mortise around the tenon. Cut them off flush with joint when glue dries. (2) Apply glue to tenon, wrap with thread, apply more glue and force into mortise. (3) This is frowned on by cabinet-makers, but it works. After joint is glued and set, drive a small screw into the tenon from the outside of the mortise. Countersink head and cover with plastic wood stained to match chair.

Broken rung, slat, leg. If the break runs with the grain, apply Weldwood plastic resin glue to the split and clamp together for 24 hours. If clamps are difficult to adjust because of contours of wood, bind wood with wax paper and string.

If break is across the grain, the piece must be doweled together. Let an expert do this. Lining up the holes in the two pieces is difficult.

If a rung is beyond repair and is difficult to pull out of its hole, cut it off close to the mortise and then drill out mortise. Have new rung made to match the old one.

Legs different length. Set chair on a level surface. Put a thick dab of plastic wood on a piece of wax paper and embed short leg into it. File to shape when dry. If you're lucky, this repair will last a long while. But a better procedure is to stand chair on a flat piece of plywood. Lay saw flat on the plywood and saw off end of longest leg. Repeat process as necessary, sawing off only the thickness of the saw blade each time.

Legs wobble. Try to break joints and reglue; or force glue into cracks of joints. If this doesn't work, either turn chair over to an expert or brace legs with angle irons.

If chair wobbles even though all joints seem tight, you can brace it with a metal stretcher. Insert metal hooks in four legs and connect them to turnbuckle. Tighten turnbuckle until wobbling stops. This is not an attractive repair.

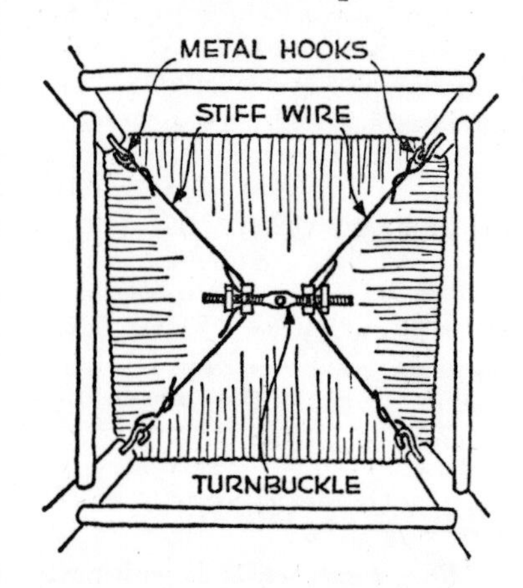

Wood seat splits. Apply glue to crack. Lay boards across top and bottom of seat and hold together, but not tightly, with C-clamps. Then loop strong cord around the seat and tighten like a tourniquet. If clamping boards are not too tight, tourniquet will draw broken seat pieces together; the clamping boards will keep it from buckling.

For additional reinforcement of a split seat, screw iron mending plates across the bottom. If seat is cracked in several places, cut a piece of ¼" plywood slightly smaller than the seat and screw it to bottom instead of mending plates.

Wood damaged. See wood.

Stains. See wood.

GALOSHES

Holes, tears in rubber or rubberized areas. See tire (tube punctured).

Holes, tears in canvas. See canvas.

Holes, tears in plastic. Use plastic-mending adhesive kit. Cut plastic patch that comes with kit to proper size, coat with plastic adhesive and smooth over tear. Patch can also be made out of any transparent or translucent flexible plastic.

GALVANIZED IRON

Small holes. Remove rust and dirt with steel wool. Cover hole with plastic steel.

Large holes. Steel-wool surface thoroughly. Cut a patch out of galvanized iron sheet. Spread plastic steel around hole and weight patch down in it.

GARBAGE CAN

Hole in metal. Scrub with soap and water and clean with steel wool. Cover hole with plastic steel.

Metal bottom rusting. Scrub clean and sand as smooth as possible. Paint with asphalt roofing cement. Let dry thoroughly before using. This is a good precaution to take with any new metal garbage can.

Hole in rubber. Scrub with soap and water and roughen surface with sandpaper. Cover hole with plastic rubber. If hole is large, set a patch of rubber in the plastic rubber.

GARDEN DUSTER

Nozzle clogged. Clean with a fine wire. If necessary, take off nozzle and wash it. Dry thoroughly.

Flit-gun type doesn't pump air. Remove cap at end of air cylinder, pull out plunger, and coat edges of leather with car grease. If end cap is not easily removable, pull plunger out as far as possible and apply heavy oil through holes in end of cylinder on leather. If duster still doesn't throw dust properly, replace the leather entirely.

Crank on crank-type duster works hard. Apply a few drops of oil to handle. On some dusters, there is a grease cap under the handle. Remove this, clean out old grease and apply new.

This kind of duster also works hard when the gears become clogged with dust. Remove end housings and clean dust compartment and gears thoroughly. Do not apply oil to moving parts except as noted above.

GARDEN HOSE

Rubber hose broken. Cut in two and join pieces with a metal hose-mender.

Rubber on hose cracked. Rejuvenate hose by painting it with liquid neoprene rubber or plastic rubber.

Vinyl hose broken. Cut in two and join pieces with a plastic hose-mender (different from a rubber hose-mender). Tubes of mender are slipped into opposite pieces of hose and held in place by metal rings on the outside of the hose.

Hose leaks at coupling. If a new washer doesn't help, replace entire coupling.

GARDEN SHEARS

Blades do not come together properly. Tighten nut holding two blades together. If this does not correct problem, check whether one blade (or handle) is bent;

then disassemble shears, place defective blade in vise and bend slightly. Do not exert too much pressure, especially on cheap shears.

Dull. If cutting edges are scissors-like, clamp shears in a vise and run a fine-toothed metal file up and down them several times. Be careful not to change the angle of the cutting edges.

If cutting edges are knife-like, take shears apart and sharpen on a carborundum stone.

GARDEN SPRAYER

Sprayer does not hold pressure. Check gasket under top of air cylinder. If worn or distorted, replace it. If this is not the cause of trouble, examine tank for pinholes, especially in or near the bottom. Solder these if tank is copper. Seal with plastic steel otherwise.

Pump action does not produce air. Make sure that rubber diaphragm at bottom of air cylinder is not stuck to metal and that air holes are clear. For a temporary repair, pry cylinder from handle and coat leather on bottom of plunger handle with heavy grease. For a permanent repair, install new leather.

On sprayers of the Flit-gun type, pump action can be improved somewhat by pulling the plunger all the way back and squirting heavy oil through the hole near the end of the cylinder on the leather.

Spray nozzle clogs continually. Trouble may be caused by nothing more than undissolved chemicals and bits of garden debris. But it may also be caused by corrosion products in bottom of tank. In this case, partially fill with kerosene and let it soak for several days. Empty and scrape sides and bottom as well as you can with a long stiff brush or stick of wood. Soak with kerosene again. Then empty and rinse with soap and water.

Hose cracked. Smear plastic rubber on the holes. If hose is badly cracked at end near tank, cut it off and clamp the new end over the pipe stub on the tank.

GARDEN SPRINKLER

Clogged. Clean spray holes with a fine wire. If trouble persists, soak sprinkler in kerosene for several days and then clean with wire.

GARDEN TOOLS

See also axe, garden shears, garden duster, garden sprinkler, garden sprayer, lawn mower, rake (leaf), watering can.

Handle broken. File off heads of rivets, if any, and drive them out. Dig or drill wood out of ferrule. If this proves difficult, put tool head in a fire and burn handle out. Insert new handle in ferrule and rivet in place with steel rivets.

Tool head bent. Place in vise and bend slowly. Hammering does little good.

Hoe, spade, trowel, mattock, dull. Clamp tool head in a vise and sharpen with a medium-coarse metal file. Hold the file at both ends and stroke it toward the cutting edge of the tool. Do not file on the back stroke. And do not feather the cutting edge too much —it should resemble a chisel edge, flat on the back and beveled in the front.

Sickle, scythe, grass whip dull. Stroke an oval scythe-stone along the beveled edge of the blade. The stroke should not be completely parallel with the blade edge but at a slight angle toward it (in other words, at the start of the stroke the top edge of the stone is touching the blade; at the completion of the stroke, the stone is touching the blade near its bottom edge). Stroke from the point of the blade toward the handle.

Shears dull. See garden shears.

Tools rusted. Rub with coarse steel wool, then smear on liquid rust-remover and rub with a rag. Henceforth, clean and dry tools thoroughly after you use them, and store them in a dry place.

GARMENT BAG

Tears. Cover tear on the inside with adhesive-backed mending tape.

Zipper broken. See zipper.

GAS BURNER FOR HEATING SYSTEM

Doesn't come on. Check whether thermostat is set below room temperature. Check whether pilot light is out. If pilot is out, first shut off the A valve, which is the main gas valve to the burner, and the B pilot valve. Wait five minutes. Then turn on B valve and ignite with a match. (In some burners there is a magnetic valve directly in front of the burner, and B valve is attached to or built into a solenoid valve. A red button represents the B valve. Depress this and then put match to pilot tip. Keep the red button depressed for 1 minute to energize the magnetic valve.) Finally, turn on the A valve. If burner still doesn't go on, call a serviceman.

Note. Instructions for lighting pilot lights are mounted on the burner. Don't let these get obliterated with dirt and grease.

Pilot lights, but burner doesn't work. Check whether electric fuse controlling burner circuit has blown.

Smells. Shut off main gas control valve at once and call a serviceman. Don't under any circumstances go hunting for the leak with a lighted match. Don't even turn on the electric light in the furnace room.

GASOLINE ENGINE

See engine, gasoline.

GATE

Sagging. See door, garage.

Wood posts rotting. See fence.

Support post loose from masonry to which it is attached. The post is probably held to the masonry with screws set in lead anchors. If anchors do not hold when driven back into the masonry, replace them. See Basic Methods: How to Support Things, etc.

GLASS

Broken. Apply thin layer of Duco cement to both broken edges and press together immediately. Hold until glue sets.

Edges rough, cutting. Polish with silicon carbide cloth available from hardware store. Keep edges wet while working.

Separated from other materials to which it is joined. See household decorative accessories.

For how to cut glass, see Basic Methods.

GLASS BLOCK

Mortar joints cracked, broken. Scrape clean. Blow out crumbs with a vacuum cleaner. Pack in mortar of 1 part cement, 1 part lime, and 4 parts sand. Smooth to match surrounding joints.

GLIDER

See swing, porch.

GRASS CLOTH

See burlap.

GUTTER, METAL

Small holes. Clean metal with steel wool and cover holes with plastic steel or plastic aluminum.

Large holes, tears. Clean out dust and debris. Spread a liberal coat of asphalt roofing compound on metal over and around hole. In this lay a strip of freezer-grade aluminum foil. Smooth down and cover with more roofing compound.

Gutter sags. Adjust hangers or install new ones. If gutter is bent, take it down and straighten it on the ground.

Straps on hangers broken. Most gutter hangers consist of a loop of metal strapped around the gutter. From the top of this strap another strap runs to the roof. The straps are riveted together, but frequently the rivet breaks. When this happens, join the two straps with a small nut and bolt.

Ice builds up in gutter, backs up water, which leaks through the roof. This can be prevented by looping electric soil-heating cable in a zigzag along the edge of the roof and over the gutter. When the cable is warm, it cuts channels through the ice and permits water to run off. But the only permanent cure is to install an eaves flashing strip under the roofing over the roof deck. Get a roofing contractor to do this.

Corroded. If gutter is aluminum, clean with a heavy-duty aluminum cleaner and steel wool. Then prime with zinc chromate and apply house paint. If gutter is galvanized, clean off rust with a wire brush and prime with Rust-Oleum 769 Damp-Proof Red Primer. Then paint with house paint.

GUTTER, WOOD

Splits. Clean out dust and debris. Coat the trough with asphalt roofing compound. Smooth freezer-grade aluminum foil into this. Then cover with more roofing compound.

If splits are bad, try to nail wood together. If this is impossible, tack a large sheet of heavy aluminum flashing to bottom of gutter. Then use asphalt roofing compound and aluminum foil in the trough. However, it may be smarter to have gutter replaced entirely.

Ice builds up in gutter, backs up water, which leaks through roof. See gutter, metal.

GYM, CHILDREN'S OUTDOOR

Rocks when children are playing on it. Attach legs to T-shaped steel anchors which are buried in the ground (gym-set dealers have these). Or dig holes about 12″ wide and 15″ deep under the legs. Pour in concrete made of 1 part cement, 1 part sand, and 1½ parts coarse aggregate. The concrete should come to within about 2″ of the ground level. Slip large nails or steel rods through the holes in the ends of the gym legs. Then sink the legs and nails into the concrete several inches and firm concrete around them.

Swing chains broken. Buy replacements from dealers.

Supports rusted. Remove rust with a scraper and wire brush. Apply Rust-Oleum 769 Damp-Proof Red Primer, then finish coat of paint.

GYPSUM BOARD

See interior wall, gypsum board.

HAIR DRYER, ELECTRIC

Doesn't work. Check whether fuse on house circuit has blown. Disconnect dryer and examine cord and plug for breaks and make necessary repairs (see electric cord). If dryer still doesn't work, take it to a service shop.

Tear in hat. Lap edges of tear and glue together with plastic-mending adhesive. Or apply a patch cut out of matching material with plastic-mending adhesive. Let glue dry several hours before using.

Hole in hose. Use plastic-mending adhesive kit. Coat patch in kit with the adhesive and smooth over hole.

Hose loose from end connectors. Coat end of hose with plastic-mending adhesive and screw into connector. Let dry overnight.

HAMMER

Head loose. Hold hammer, head up, on a firm base. Drive small metal wedges, available from hardware store, into top of handle. You can also use hardwood wedges, but in this case it is necessary first to make a small split in the top of handle.

Handle broken. Saw off handle just below head. Then drive rest of handle out through bottom of head. Shape new handle to fit with a rasp, drive into head, and secure with a metal wedge.

HANDBAG

Frame sprung. Bend straight by hand. If this proves difficult, wrap the sprung edge with paper and squeeze it straight in a vise.

Twist-type catch hard to open or close. Wrap the two prongs, or knobs, with adhesive tape and carefully bend them slightly apart. If this proves difficult, overlapping edges can be filed down with a metal file; but of course this ruins the finish at that point.

Twist-type catch doesn't stay closed. Wrap the prongs with adhesive tape and bend toward each other. Or melt a blob of solder on one of the prongs and then file it smooth.

Spring-type catch doesn't catch. Check whether frame is bent, and if so, correct this. Otherwise, with a small metal file, open the catch as far as possible and deepen the groove which fits over the small prong on the other half of the frame.

Handle off. Sew back on. Or use appropriate glue or metal rivet.

Lining at top of handbag loose. The lining should be wedged into the channel in the frame. With a screwdriver, pry up edge of channel just enough to stick the lining back underneath. Squeeze frame back together with pliers (wrap the jaws with adhesive tape).

Handbag material damaged. See appropriate material entry.

HARDBOARD

Paint finish marred. See painted surface.

Scratches. Rub a hammer head over the scratch. Press down hard. Then rub with a wax stick of the proper color.

Stains. See wood.

Pieces of hardboard separated. Bolt or rivet together, or coat surfaces with Weldwood plastic resin glue and clamp pieces together overnight.

Hardboard separated from another material. If the other material holds nails and screws, hardboard can be rejoined to it with either of these. Otherwise use bolts or rivets or appropriate glue (see household decorative accessories and use same glues as specified for wood).

HEATER, ELECTRIC

Doesn't heat. Proceed as follows until you find problem: 1. Check whether fuse on house circuit has blown. 2. Check whether outlet is defective. Just plug in a light. 3. Disconnect and check whether heater cord is broken and if so, replace it. 4. Disassemble heater (each one is put together differently but the manner in which they come apart is usually obvious). Tighten wires at terminals. 5. If heater still doesn't work, element has burned out. Some of these unscrew like a light bulb and are easily replaced. If heater is equipped with another type, take it to a service shop for repair.

HEATING PAD, ELECTRIC

Doesn't heat. You can repair a broken cord or cord plug (see electric cord), but don't fool with the pad otherwise. Buy a new one.

HINGES

Stiff. If pin is removable, tap it out with a nail and scrape off paint. Scrape paint from hinge leaves, too. Coat pin with light oil and replace. If pin is not removable, scrape off paint around it and the joints and squeeze powdered graphite into the joints.

Leaves bent. Place on a hard surface and hammer straight.

Shift position. Screw down tight. If screws don't hold, take them out and fill holes with plastic wood. Then reset screws. Note that some hinges have elongated screw holes to permit the position of a cabinet door to be changed. With these, if door is accidentally knocked out of place, simply position door properly and tighten hinges.

Screws tear through hole in hinge. This happens sometimes in cigar-box hinges, piano hinges and others made of light metal. If the leaves do not come together when the hinge is shut, you can make a washer out of thin aluminum sheet or a tin can, place over screw hole and drive in a round-headed screw. Then file top of screw flat. If the hinge leaves do come together when shut, drive screw almost all the way through the enlarged hole in the hinge, then coat edges of hole with epoxy glue and turn screw tight.

HOCKEY STICK

Broken. Coat the broken edges with epoxy glue and clamp together for 24 hours. Sand finish off the stick in the area of the break and coat the wood with polyester resin used in fiberglass boat construction. Then wrap fiberglass tape diagonally over the break. Butt the edges of the tape and smooth it into the resin. Let dry. Then sand and brush on two more coats of resin.

HOTPLATE, ELECTRIC

Doesn't heat. Examine element to see if it is broken. If so, disconnect appliance, take out element and install a replacement in same way. Check also whether cord is broken, whether fuse on house circuit has blown, whether outlet used for hotplate is defective (just plug in a light). If these measures don't produce results, take hotplate to service shop.

HOT WATER BOTTLE

Holes, tears. See tire (tube punctured).

HOT WATER HEATER

See water heater.

HOUSEHOLD DECORATIVE ACCESSORIES such as book ends, ash trays, sconces, candle-holders, ornaments, etc.

See also figurine, vase.

Material of which object is made broken. See appropriate material entry.

Different materials separated. In almost all cases the materials can be rejoined with the appropriate glue as shown in chart below. (For how to glue, see Basic Methods.) The addition of screws or rivets may also be advisable.

	Ceramics (earthenware, china, etc.)	Cork	Felt	Glass	Leather	Metal	Plastics	Rubber	Stone
Ceramics (earthenware, china, etc.)									
Cork	Pc								
Felt	Pc	Pc							
Glass	D or E	Pc	Pc						
Leather	Pc	Pc	Pc	Pc					
Metal	D or E	Pc	Pc	D or E	Pc				
Plastics	Pm	Pc	Pc	D	Pc	Pm			
Rubber	Pc	Pc	Pc	Pc	Pc	Pc	Pc		
Stone	E	Pc	Pc	E	Pc	E	D	Pc	
Wood	D or E	Pc	G	D	Pc	D or E	E or Pm	Pc	E

Key to chart:
D–Duco cement
E–Epoxy glue
G–Elmer's Glue-All
Pc–Pliobond cement
Pm–Plastic-mending adhesive

INTERIOR WALL, CERAMIC TILE

Crack between tiles and bathtub. See bathtub.

Crack between tiles and wood or metal. Clean out old filler, if any. Since there is a difference in the rate of expansion and contraction between the materials, fill crack with tub-caulking compound (which has considerable flexibility).

Other problems. See tile, ceramic.

INTERIOR WALL, COMPOSITION BOARD (Celotex and the like)

Tears, cracks. If board is textured, there is no way of fixing it so it will look right. Replace. If board is smooth and sufficiently rigid, spread cement used in gypsum-board construction over hole and embed in it a strip of gypsum-board tape. Smooth and cover with a thin layer of cement. Let dry. Then sand smooth and spread on more cement in a wider strip. Let dry and sand again. A third application of cement may be necessary if ridge made by cement is too apparent.

Joints between boards expand and contract. This happens with changes in weather. There is no cure. Cover joints with wood molding strips.

Holes. Replace panels.

INTERIOR WALL, CONCRETE

See concrete.

INTERIOR WALL, GYPSUM BOARD

Nail holes, gouges. Fill with spackle and sand smooth.

Small holes. Cut a piece of cardboard slightly larger than the hole. Insert a string through the center of the cardboard and knot at the back. Push cardboard through hole, center, and hold on to string. Fill hole part way with patching plaster. When plaster has set, cut off string and fill hole rest of the way with more plaster, spackle, or gypsum-board cement.

Large holes. Cut gypsum board back on the sides until at least ¾″ of the front surface of the studs is exposed. Cut board straight across the top and bottom of the hole. Cut a 2′ by 4′ into two pieces the width of the opening. Nail them into place along the top and bottom edges of the opening so that the old wall surface and new patch will bear on them. Cut a new piece of gypsum board to fit exactly in the hole. Nail to studs and, if crosspieces of 2′ by 4′ are sturdy enough, to them. Fill cracks with gypsum-board cement and embed in this strips of gypsum-board tape. Cover with a thin layer of cement. When dry, sand smooth and apply another thin layer of cement in a wider strip. Sand when dry.

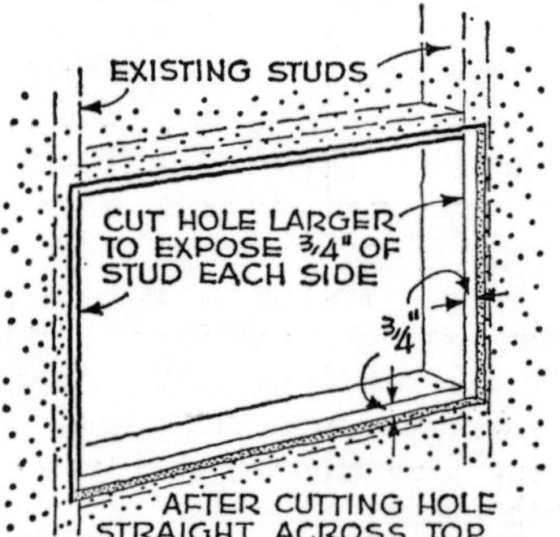

Boards bulging at the edges. Renail with ring-grooved nails spaced every 6″. Fill nail holes and cracks along edges of board with gypsum-board cement. Let cement spread over surface of board. Sand smooth when dry and apply additional cement if necessary to make wall perfectly smooth.

Nails, screws don't hold in wall. See Basic Methods: How to Support Things, etc.

INTERIOR WALL, METAL TILE

See interior wall, plastic tile.

INTERIOR WALL, PLASTER

Hair cracks, small holes. Scrape open slightly with a beer can opener and fill with spackle. Sand smooth when dry.

Large cracks, large holes. Scrape open to ¼″ width. If possible, make the opening wider at the back than on the surface. Dampen crack with water. Fill immediately with patching plaster. If the job is not too extensive, the plaster can be mixed with water only. The mixture hardens quickly. To slow hardening, if you are doing a big job, mix plaster with ⅔ water and ⅓ vinegar.

If the lath is missing behind a hole (as where a light was installed), cut a piece of cardboard a bit larger than the hole. Insert a string through the center and knot in back. Push cardboard through hole. Center it. Hold on to string. Fill hole part way with patching plaster and when it is dry, cut string. Then fill hole rest of the way with plaster.

Very large holes if surrounding surface is irregular. Chip out loose plaster and sprinkle exposed surfaces with water. Fill with wood-fiber plaster. If hole is deep, fill hole part way and scratch plaster in criss-cross fashion with your trowel. Let set. Then fill rest of the way. When surface is completely dry, sand lightly to smooth over exposed fibers.

Very large holes in a smooth wall. Call in a plasterer.

Holes and cracks in walls above bathtub. Repair as above but for plaster use Keene's cement and dry hydrated lime mixed in the proportion of 4 lb. to 1 lb.

Bulges. Break out bulging plaster and repair as above.

Note. If any walls to be repaired have a sand finish, mix 1 part clean sand with 1 part plaster.

Plaster soft, dusty, crumbly, stained. Check for water leak. Replace plaster if badly eroded. If it isn't, brush off loose powder and wash spot with a solution of zinc oxide. Follow with two coats of aluminum paint. Imperfections in surface can be smoothed out then with spackle.

Picture hook nails chip plaster, don't hold. Fill hole as above. Stick a scrap of masking tape over spackle when it is dry. Drive nail through this.

Screws don't hold in plaster. Fill hole with steel wool and drive in screw. Or insert a Rawl plug and drive screw into this. If screw still doesn't hold, replace screw with a spring-wing toggle bolt (see Basic Methods: How to Support Things, etc.).

INTERIOR WALL, PLASTIC TILE

Tiles broken. See below.

Tiles loose. With a thin putty

knife, carefully pry off tile (don't use too much pressure or tile will break). Scrape out as much of the adhesive as possible. Make sure wall is sound and dry underneath. Butter back of tile with plastic-tile cement and press tile firmly in place. Smooth out joints.

If wall behind tile is unsound, it must be repaired before tile is reset.

Cracks between tiles. Scrape out old cement and fill joints with new plastic-tile adhesive. Smooth off with a small knife, nail head or blunt pencil point. Remove excess from surface with plastic-tile adhesive cleaner. Let joints dry 24 hours before exposing to moisture.

INTERIOR WALL, PLYWOOD PANELED

See interior wall, wood paneled.

INTERIOR WALL, WOOD PANELED

Joints open. If joints open and close as weather changes, you can tack batten strips over them. The strips should be attached only on one side of the joints. If the joints are permanently open, you can apply batten strips or have a carpenter fill the joints with narrow wood strips set flush with the surface. Note, however, that any such treatment may end up in a wall that is worse looking than the one you have now.

Gouges, dents, etc. See wood.

Finish marred. See lacquered surface, painted surface, shellacked surface, or varnished surface as case may be.

IRON

See cast iron, galvanized iron, or wrought iron.

IRON, ELECTRIC

Doesn't heat. Check whether fuse on house circuit has blown. Check whether outlet into which iron cord is plugged is defective (just plug in a light). Disconnect iron and examine it for a break or loose connection at terminals. Tighten connections. Replace cord if broken. If these measures don't work, take iron to service shop.

Soleplate scratched. Smooth with very fine emery cloth. Then melt beeswax on soleplate and rub it off with a clean, dry cloth.

IVORY

Broken. Coat broken edges with Duco cement or epoxy glue and press together for six hours.

Separated from another material. See household decorative accessories. Use glue recommended for ceramics.

Stained yellow. Rub with alcohol and expose to sunlight. But note that ivory yellows naturally with age and you may not be able to change its appearance very much.

JAPANESE LANTERN

Paper torn. Spread a sheet of wax paper inside lantern under tear; then stuff lantern with newspaper until torn surface is smooth. Bring torn edges together and spread a little white paste on them. Then tear a strip from thin white tissue paper, rub it into paste and smooth down over the length of the tear. When paste is dry, carefully tear off excess tissue paper, tearing it toward the rip.

Paper torn from frame. Reglue with Elmer's Glue-All.

JEWELRY, COSTUME

Stone loose. Try bending little prongs or claws that hold stone secure. If these are worn or broken off and if jewelry is not valuable, glue stone in place with Duco cement.

JUNGLE GYM

See gym, children's outdoor.

KITCHEN CABINET

See cabinet, kitchen.

KITE

Tears in paper. Out of tissue paper cut a patch ½″ larger than the tear in all directions. Paste down with Elmer's Glue-All.

Wood-framing pieces broken. If break parallels the grain of the wood, coat the broken edges with Elmer's Glue-All and clamp together. If break is across the grain, use epoxy glue and reinforce with a short strip of very thin wood, such as a veneer, glued to one side of the broken piece. Match sticks laid edge to edge, parallel with the grain, may be used instead of the veneer.

For a neater joint, cut a shallow recess in the framing member wood, on one side, and lay the reinforcement in this.

KNIFE, POCKET

Handle sides (bone, plastic, etc.) loose. Spread epoxy glue between body of knife and handle and clamp.

Blade broken. If knife is worth saving, reshape blade on a grinding wheel.

Dull. Lay blade almost flat on a carborundum stone and sharpen with a circular motion.

KNIFE, TABLE

See cutlery, table.

LACE

Holes. Cut a patch of matching lace, place under hole and whip it down. Then carefully snip out old material.

LADDER

Also see stepladder.

Note. Don't let a hasty, patchwork job kill you. A new ladder is cheaper than a broken neck.

Rung of wood ladder broken. If the rung passes all the way through the side rails (so you can see the ends), saw it off close to the inside of the rails. Then drill out wood remaining in rails with a brace and bit and cut out the nails which held the ends of the rung with a triangular metal file. Secure a piece of hickory the same size as the holes. Apply Elmer's waterproof glue in the holes and insert the rung by driving it carefully through from one side of the ladder to the other. Anchor the ends of the rung with finishing nails.

If the broken rung is set into mortises in the rails (the ends are not visible), cut it off about 3″ from each rail. Then with a hammer and chisel split the remaining pieces and pull them out (but don't bend them back and forth so violently that the rails are split). Cut nails that held rung with a file. With a brace and bit, bore one of the holes all the way through the rail. Apply glue in holes. Then insert a new hickory rung by driving it through the open rail hole across the ladder and into the mortise in the other rail. Secure ends with finishing nails.

Rail cracked. This can be braced with a long 2′ by 4′ bolted to the rail, but that will make the ladder even more awkward to handle; and anyway, why take chances? Get a new ladder.

Rung in metal ladder broken. If the rung is bolted to the rails, as is the case in cheap ladders, you can easily install a new one. But if the ladder is welded, let a metal-worker make the repair.

LAMP

Note. Always disconnect lamp before making repairs.

Cord broken. If socket is mounted on top of a straight stem, unscrew socket from stem, pull it apart, loosen screws holding wires and pull cord out through bottom. Run new cord up through base and stem and attach to socket (see electric cord—lamp cord broken at socket).

If socket is mounted on an arm attached to the stem, unscrew wires from socket as above. Then unscrew nut in base of lamp and pull out cord. The various pieces of which the lamp is made will now either fall apart or you can unscrew them. This will make it possible for you to thread new cord into arm on which socket is mounted. After cord is in, reassemble pieces and tighten them together. Then install socket.

Socket broken. Simply unscrew it from lamp and install new one. See lamp socket. Also see electric cord (lamp cord broken at socket).

Table lamp loose at joints. Remove felt (if any) from base. Tighten nut on the spindle that holds parts of lamp together.

If metal base that holds socket wobbles on top of a glass or ceramic pedestal, loosen nut in base of lamp until socket base can be pulled free of pedestal. The socket base, in many instances, is a cup that fits over the top of the pedestal. Clean this out, fill with wet plaster of Paris, and place over pedestal immediately.

Light diffuser broken. If made of glass, coat broken edges with Duco cement and press together. If made of plastic, use plastic-mending adhesive. To hold pieces together while glue is drying, put strips of adhesive tape across the break.

LAMP CORD

See electric cord.

LAMPSHADE

Shade loose from wire frame. Remove binding at top or bottom as case may be and replace with adhesive-backed mending tape. Stick tape to outside of shade first and smooth it carefully. Then wrap over frame wire and stick down.

LAMP SOCKET

Lamp won't light. Disconnect. Pull halves of socket apart. Tighten screws around wires and make sure cord is not broken at any place. If lamp still doesn't light, remove bulb again and, with a screwdriver, bend metal contact in bottom of socket upward. If lamp still doesn't light, difficulty is in the switch. Replace socket with a new one. See electric cord (lamp cord broken at socket).

LACQUERED SURFACE

Minor scratches. Dip a tiny artist's brush in lacquer thinner and lightly run it along the scratch. Thinner will soften lacquer, obliterate scar.

Larger scratches. Fill by rubbing with a colored wax stick made for use on furniture. Or touch up with matching lacquer.

Water spots. Rub with cigaret ashes and a cloth dipped in salad oil or sewing machine oil. If this doesn't work, rub with rottenstone and cloth dipped in salad oil. Clean off residue with benzine.

Heat marks. Rub with rottenstone and oil as above.

Alcohol spots. Rub with rottenstone and oil as above.

Paint spots. Scrape off the paint with the point of a sharp knife. If surface is damaged slightly in the process, rub down with rottenstone and oil.

Nail polish. Handle like paint spots.

Candle wax on lacquer. Remove as much as possible with your fingers, then scrape off residue with a dull table knife and wipe entire surface quickly and lightly with benzine.

Crayon or lipstick. Rub with Jubilee cleaner-wax.

LASTEX

Tears. Baste twill tape under tear, then stitch edges of tear and edges of tape with sewing-machine zigzagger.

LAUNDRY TUB

Porcelain chipped. See bathroom fixtures.

Stains. See bathroom fixtures.

Drain clogged. See drains.

Faucet problems. See faucet.

Basket-type strainer-stopper leaks. Buy a new one.

LAWN MOWER, HAND

Rattles, stiff. Tighten all bolts. Lubricate at oiling points regularly.

Blades stick. Lower the front edge of the underknife by loosening bottom screws at the side of the knife and tightening top screws. Turn reel by hand to make sure contact is even along the entire blade. Some mower underknives are adjusted by thumb screws.

Doesn't cut. Reverse above procedure: raise the underknife.

Dull. You can touch up edges of blades with a fine metal file, but it's better to take mower to a shop where blades can be sharpened properly.

Wheels spin, reel doesn't. If you loosen the bolts that hold the wheels and remove the wheels, you will find inside a cogged gear. Pull this off its shaft and you will then find a short piece of steel inserted through the shaft. This is beveled on the ends and positioned so that when you push the mower forward it catches in slots inside the gear and turns the reel, but when you pull the mower backward, the gear does not catch. When this metal piece becomes worn (as it does in time), it no longer catches properly in the gear when you move forward. Then it needs to be replaced. Take it to a lawn-mower dealer and buy a new piece, or have a metal-working shop make one.

Wood roller falls off. Stuff the holes in the end tightly with steel wool and reset the screws that hold it on the mower.

LAWN MOWER, POWER

Note. Follow instruction-manual directions for care and adjustment of mower. But let an expert make repairs. Before calling on him, check and correct points noted below:

Doesn't start. On gasoline mower, check: Is valve on fuel tank open? Is stop-switch pushed away from spark plug? Is choke adjusted? Are you out of gas? On electric mower, check: Is there a break in the cord? Has fuse on house circuit blown?

Runs unevenly. On gasoline mower, check: Is gasoline stale, gummy? Is fuel filter clean? Is oil in crankcase at proper level and is it clean? Is oil filter clogged? Are cooling fins clogged with grass and dust? Is spark plug clean? Is it cracked? For an electric mower, see motor, electric.

Blades rotate unevenly. Adjust tension on drive belt according to manufacturer's directions.

Rotary mower blade nicked, dull. Remove it from housing, set in a vise and file with a fine-toothed metal file. Stroke file towards the cutting edge; do not cut on return stroke.

Reel blades dull. Leave sharpening to a professional.

LEAD

Small holes. Clean metal thoroughly with steel wool and cover hole with plastic steel.

Large holes. Clean area around hole until metal shines. Cut a patch out of sheet lead and clean one side. Sprinkle shavings of tallow on both surfaces and melt it with a warm iron (this serves as the flux). Then tin both surfaces with a special tin-lead-bismuth solder. Hold patch over hole and heat it with a not-too-hot iron until the solder melts. Do not let iron rest long in one place, because lead has a low melting point.

LEADER (DOWNSPOUT)

Seam split. Leader seams split when the leader is clogged with twigs and leaves and the water trapped above the clog freezes. Remove clog before making repair. Then bend metal back in shape, heat with a torch and apply solder.

Joints broken. Clean metal with steel wool. Slide lower length of leader up over upper length. Heat with a torch and apply solder.

LEATHER

Tears, slashes. If leather has a solid backing, apply Elmer's Glue-All under torn edges, butt edges carefully and press down. Several applications of polish will help to conceal the scar. If leather is not backed, apply adhesive-backed mending tape to one side of tear. Or cut a patch out of leather, coat with Pliobond cement, and coat torn area with cement. Let dry until tacky and then press together. Very soft leather can also be patched with needle and thread (see clothing–fabrics).

Holes. Cut a patch out of matching leather and feather the edges with a razor blade. Lay over hole and draw a pencil line around it. Coat back of patch with Pliobond cement. Apply cement around the hole within the pencil line. Let glue dry until tacky. Then smooth down patch.

Stitches in leather articles ripped out. If leather itself is sound, resew with thread of appropriate strength and color. Very soft leather, like that in gloves, can be sewed on a machine. Thick leather must be sewed by hand with a very sharp needle. Don't try to resew leather that is old, worn, and weak. Use glue.

Layers of leather delaminated. Coat facing surfaces with Pliobond cement. When this becomes tacky, press together. If stitches along edges are ripped, resew them.

Leather separated from wood, glass, ceramics, metal, rubber, paper, plastics. Clean surfaces. Apply light coat of Pliobond cement to both surfaces. Let dry until tacky and then clamp together.

Leather stiff, brittle. Wet a rag, rub it in saddle soap, and rub on leather. Work soap in well. Rinse with a damp sponge and then polish with a dry cloth.

Grease stains. As soon as possible brush rubber cement over the stain and peel off when dry. Repeat operation several times, if necessary. Don't count on success, however.

General discoloration. Rub a damp cloth in saddle soap and then rub evenly over leather. Work soap in well. Then rinse with a damp sponge and dry.

LEATHERETTE

Holes, tears. Cut a patch out of matching material. Apply a thin coat of Devcon Patch glue to the back and smooth over the hole. Let dry several hours.

LIGHT SOCKET

See lamp socket.

LIGHTNING ROD

You can reset a loose rod, solder a broken cable, or solder a loose joint between the cable and the ground. But whatever you do must be considered only a temporary measure. Call in a professional installer at once.

LINOLEUM

See floor, linoleum.

LUCITE

See plastics–general.

MAILBOX, OFFICIAL U.S.

Loose or broken from post. Remove board screwed under bottom of box. If necessary, replace with a new board of same size. Check whether post wood is sound. Center board on post and nail down securely with 4″ nails. Then set box over board and drive screws through sides of box into board.

Post wobbles. See fence.

MAJOLICA

See faïence.

MARBLE

Small scratches. Rub with very fine (10-0) sandpaper. Then wet surface with water, sprinkle on a pinch of tin oxide available from drugstore, dampen a cloth and rub briskly until shine appears.

Large scratches, pits, general roughness. The flaws can be removed only by rubbing evenly with abrasive materials of successively finer grit sizes. The job is messy and very difficult. Better call in a marble dealer or finisher.

Broken. Wash edges if dirty and let dry. Apply epoxy glue to one edge and press together for 24 hours.

Loose from wall, floor, etc. Lift out and scrape loose cement from back of marble and the base. Apply several large dabs of Miracle Adhesive to back of marble and press firmly into place.

Separated from another material. See household decorative accessories under stone.

Oil stains on marble. Soak a white blotter or thick white cloth with Vermont 50–50 Liquid Cleaner (made by Vermont Marble Co., Proctor, Vt.), lay on stain and cover with a piece of glass for 24 hours. If stain persists, mix the liquid cleaner with whiting to form a thick paste. Trowel on stain and keep paste covered with a damp cloth and piece of glass for 24 hours; then allow to dry for 24 hours.

Organic stains. Pour hair bleach or hydrogen peroxide mixed with a few drops of household ammonia on stain. Let stand until stain disappears. If stain persists, mix bleach with whiting to a thick paste; spread on stain, and cover with a damp cloth for 24 hours.

Rust stains. Sprinkle Vermont Crystal Cleaner (made by Vermont Marble Co., Proctor, Vt.) on stain. Let stand for a very short time. Follow manufacturer's directions. For persistent stains, mix cleaner with whiting and water to form a thick paste; trowel on stain, and cover with a piece of glass for 24 hours.

Note. Never try to clean marble with lemon juice or other acid. They etch the surface.

MATTRESS

Buttons off. With a needle long enough to go all the way through the mattress, thread a strong cord (upholsterer's twine preferably, or the equivalent of fishing line) from the bottom of the mattress to the top. Run cord through button and then thread it back through to other side of mattress. Loop through the bottom button. Have some one compress the mattress as much as possible at that point. Draw ends of string tight and knot them securely.

If you don't have a long needle, you can try doubling a small, stiff wire in two lengths greater than the thickness of the mattress. Make the bend as sharp and pointed as possible. Push the wire through from the top of the mattress to the bottom. Thread cord through the bend and pull the cord back to the top of the mattress. After looping cord through button, insert bent wire from bottom of mattress, secure end of cord and draw it back to the underside.

Holes in fabric. Patch with press-on mending tape.

MATTRESS, AIR

Holes in rubberized mattress. To find hole, inflate mattress and immerse in water. Bubbles will rise from hole. Then let all air out of mattress and dry fabric completely. Use patching kit provided by mattress maker or cut a patch out of rubber or rubberized fabric. Apply rubber cement to patch and mattress and let dry. Apply a second coat to patch and smooth over hole.

Holes in plastic mattress. Find hole and release air as above. Use patching kit provided by manufacturer or use plastic-mending adhesive kit. Spread adhesive around hole and immediately smooth on plastic patch in kit. Let dry overnight before inflating mattress.

MEDICINE CABINET

See cabinet, medicine.

MELAMINE

See plastics—general.

MELMAC

See plastics—general.

MICARTA

See plastics—laminated.

MIRROR

Broken. See glass.

Silver gone or discolored. Have mirror replated.

Loose from wall to which it has been cemented. Cement alone will not hold a mirror permanently. Screw plastic or metal mirror clips to wall where bottom of mirror should be. Apply Miracle Adhesive to back of mirror (don't try to scrape off old). Set mirror in clips and press to wall. Then install additional clips along top and sides of mirror.

Sliding medicine cabinet doors stiff. See cabinet, medicine.

MIXER, ELECTRIC

Doesn't work. Check whether fuse on house circuit has blown, whether outlet into which mixer is plugged is defective (just plug in a light). Then disconnect mixer and examine cord for a break. Repair or replace if necessary (see electric cord). If mixer still doesn't work, take it to a service shop.

Bowl doesn't turn. Lift turntable and scrub off gummy residues underneath. Put a drop of sewing machine oil on spindle.

Beater shafts bent. Clamp in a vise and carefully bend straight. But note that it is difficult to do a perfect job.

Beater blades bent, broken. Bends can be removed with pliers. If joint where blades cross at the bottom is broken, it can be resoldered. See stainless steel.

MODELS OF SHIPS, AIRPLANES, ETC.

See toys.

MONK'S CLOTH

See burlap.

MOP

Screw-in mop handle loose. When wood is dry, unscrew handle from head of mop, spread plastic wood in the threads and replace handle. If handle is still not tight enough, drive a small brad through mop head into screw threads of handle.

MOTHER-OF-PEARL

Broken. Clean edges, coat with thin layers of Duco cement and press together for several hours. *Note:* Don't let a baby have a glued mother-of-pearl teething ring.

MOTOR, ELECTRIC

Note. Oil motors only in accordance with manufacturer's instructions. If you don't have these but if motor has obvious oiling points, put in a few drops of SAE No. 10 oil every two or three months. If motor has no oiling points, leave it alone.

Doesn't run. Check whether fuse has blown on house circuit. Plug a light into outlet into which motor is plugged to see if outlet is defective. Disconnect motor and examine cord and plug for breaks. Make necessary repairs (see electric cord). If these measures don't produce results, call in an expert.

Hums but doesn't start. Disconnect and examine mechanism driven by motor to make sure it turns freely. Apply oil at oiling points in mechanism if it is stiff. Check whether belt driven by motor (if any) is too tight (see belt, machine). If trouble continues, call a serviceman.

Turns too slowly. Disconnect and check mechanism driven by motor as above. Make sure that motor is securely bolted or screwed into motor housing.

Overheats. Turn off at once and get a serviceman.

Sparks excessively, runs unevenly. If you have oiled an AC-DC motor frequently, it may be that commutator and brush ends are covered with oil. Shut off current. Remove housing and clean commutator with a toothbrush dipped in carbon tetrachloride. Do not use gasoline or benzine. Unscrew metal or plastic caps on brush holders and slide out little springs and brushes. Clean these, as well as holders, with carbon tetrachloride. Then replace in exactly the same position that you found them.

If carbon tips (called brushes) on ends of springs are badly worn and if motor continues to spark a great deal after cleaning as above, stretch springs slightly to increase tension of brushes on the commutator. But buy replacement brushes as soon as possible.

MOLDING

Pulled away from wall or ceiling, floor or baseboard. Drive 3″ or 4″ finishing nails (depending on thickness of molding) diagonally through molding into the corner. If crack remains along either edge of ceiling molding or at top edge of base molding, fill with spackle and sand smooth. If base molding cannot be nailed down tight to floor, check whether there are bobby pins, grit, or dirt underneath.

MOVIE PROJECTOR

Follow manufacturer's directions for oiling and adjusting; but when machine breaks down, let the dealer fix it.

MOVIE SCREEN

Torn. Bring edges of tear close together. Coat a patch of lightweight canvas with Devcon Patch glue and smooth it over back of tear. When glue dries, touch up line of tear with paint.

MUSICAL INSTRUMENTS

Note. If a good instrument is damaged, let an expert repair it. Anything you do may alter the tone. On inexpensive instruments proceed as follows.

Dents in metal parts. Where possible to do so, place a wood block on the concave side of the dent and tap the reverse side lightly with a block of wood or, preferably, a rubber mallet. In cases where it is impossible to do this, solder a short length of stout copper wire to the center of the dent. Grasp the end of the wire with pliers and pull out the dent. Then melt off the solder on the instrument.

Wood parts cracked. Coat edges of crack with Elmer's Glue-All and press them firmly together for five hours.

Plastic parts cracked. Coat edges with plastic-mending adhesive and press together firmly overnight.

Hole in accordion bellows. Cut small patch out of matching material or vinyl sheet. Coat back of patch and area around hole with rubber cement. Let dry, then apply a second coat of cement to patch and immediately press into place.

NAPKIN

See clothing–fabrics or clothing –hems.

NETS—BADMINTON, BASKETBALL, FISHING, ETC.

Holes. Repair with cotton twine. In a square-meshed net, first tie new lengths of twine to the broken cords (or knots) along the top of the hole. Call these Strings 1, 2, 3, 4, etc. Then tie a length of twine to the topmost broken string at the left side of the hole. Call this String A. Now draw String A to the right to meet String 1; form desired mesh opening, and tie strings together with a square knot. Then draw String A to String 2 and knot, and so on across the hole. Repeat process with horizontal strings B, C, D, etc. until hole is filled.

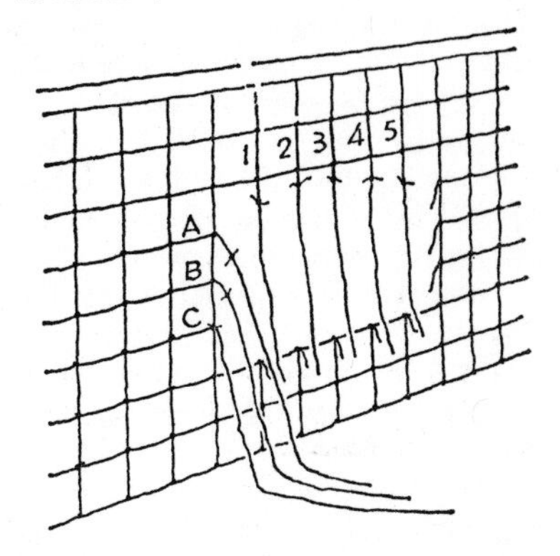

The procedure is the same in a net with a diamond-shaped mesh except that all strings run diagonally downward.

Professionals use a special net knot instead of a square knot, but this is more difficult for the amateur to make.

OAR

See canoe paddle.

OIL BURNER

Doesn't start. Check whether thermostat is set below room temperature. Is fuel tank empty? Check for blown fuse. Press reset button on control box (burners may start but shut off in a few seconds). Call a serviceman.

Operates, but house doesn't get warm. Open fire door. If flame seems small, call a serviceman.

Smells of oil. Call a serviceman.

Note. Don't take chances. At

first suspicion of trouble, tell the serviceman to come on the double.

OILCLOTH

Holes. Trim out hole neatly. Place a scrap of matching oilcloth, shiny side up, underneath and draw an outline of the hole on it. Take out patch and scrape off the shiny surface around the outline. Then spread thin layer of Elmer's Glue-All on the scraped area and press the patch on the oilcloth under the hole.

Rips. Bring edges together. Glue a scrap of fabric underneath with Elmer's Glue-All.

ONYX

Broken. Clean edges of break and coat with Duco cement or epoxy glue. Press together until glue dries.

PAIL

See bucket.

PAINTED SURFACE

For how to remove and apply paint, see Basic Methods: How to Paint.

Paint chipped, flaking, peeling, alligatored, etc. Remove paint down to the base. Make sure surface is dry. Apply new paint. Use same type for all coats.

Paint deeply scratched. Sand to remove any loose paint. Fill scratch with spackle and sand smooth when dry. Apply new paint.

Exterior paint blistered. Remove it down to the wood. Be sure surface is absolutely dry before applying new paint. Don't paint at all if blistering is a common occurrence, because you may have a condensation problem within the walls, and until this is rectified, blistering will continue.

Paint on metal chipped, scratched. Wash with detergent or ammonia solution. Sand defect with very fine sandpaper. Be sure to remove any rust. Fog on spray enamel recommended for use on metal in several thin coats.

Paint peeling off galvanized iron. Scrape off loose paint and sand well. Wash metal with detergent solution and then rinse with clear water. Brush on zinc-dust paint.

Paint surface stained by knots that bleed. Paint over stained areas with a phenolic and vinyl primer, aluminum paint or shellac. Then apply finish paint.

Copper or rust stains. Sand thoroughly, wash with turpentine, then repaint surface.

Mildew stains. Wash with a strong detergent solution and rinse. To prevent recurrence of mildew on a painted surface, mix a prepared mildew retardant (available from paint stores) with your paint the next time you apply it.

Fingernail polish on painted surface. Nail-polish remover will take it off but may also mar the paint finish. Try scraping the polish off with the point of a sharp knife.

PAINT SPRAYER

Gun doesn't deliver paint, sputters, or leaks. Clean gun thoroughly according to manufacturer's directions. If paint has dried on fluid tip, soak tip in paint thinner. Clean air nozzle. Tighten packing nut.

Compressor makes hammering noise. Check and tighten loose

pulley on motor or compressor shaft. Tighten set screw holding eccentric to shaft.

Pressure is low. If air-intake filter on compressor is covered with paint, replace it. Tighten hose nuts and belt if it is slipping. Replace worn diaphragm.

Compressor pumps oil. Check whether oil level is too high. Examine for worn piston rings according to maker's directions.

PAINTING, OIL

Canvas loose. Turn picture frame on its face and tap in wedges in back.

Joints of picture frame open, loose. See picture frame.

PANELYTE

See plastics–laminated.

PAPER

Torn. Cut a paper patch to cover. Coat patch and area around tear with rubber cement and smooth surfaces together. See also book (page torn).

Separated from another material. Glue down with rubber cement.

PARTICLE BOARD

Finish marred. See lacquered surface, painted surface, shellacked surface, or varnished surface as case may be.

Gouges, dents. Fill with plastic wood and sand smooth when dry. Note that if particle board is stained, matching stain should be mixed into the plastic wood before it is applied.

Burns, scratches. See furniture, wood.

Stains. See wood.

Pieces of particle board separated. Nail or screw together, or coat both surfaces with Weldwood plastic resin glue and clamp pieces together overnight.

Particle board separated from another material. Refasten with screws or bolts or use appropriate glue (see household decorative accessories and use same glues as specified for wood).

Edges rough. See plywood.

PARTITION

See interior wall.

PATENT LEATHER

Cracked. You can't mend this. Just conceal the crack as best you can by dyeing the fabric underneath. In future, to prevent cracking, rub leather with vaseline and don't expose to heat.

PENCIL, MECHANICAL

Lead doesn't hold or doesn't draw back in. The tiny metal tube which holds the lead is clogged. To get at it, wrap the tip of the pencil case with adhesive tape and unscrew it with pliers. The lead-holding tube can then be brought into view by turning the top of the pencil to the right. Stick a pin point through the slit in the side of the tube and force out the obstruction.

PENCIL SHARPENER

Jammed with a broken pencil or crayon. Remove sawdust holder. Unscrew slotted bolt in one of the grinding wheels and pull wheel to one side but don't try to remove it entirely. You should then be able to reach and pry out the stoppage with a knife or small screwdriver. If you can't, loosen the other grinding wheel.

PERCOLATOR, ELECTRIC

See coffee maker, electric.

PEWTER

Note. If the pewter to be mended is a prized piece, let a professional fix it.

Small holes. Clean the metal inside the pewter object with steel wool, then cover hole with plastic steel.

Joints between pewter surfaces cracked. Use plastic steel as above if the repair cannot be seen. Otherwise, remove tarnish from the surfaces and clean metal carefully with fine emery cloth. With a warm soldering iron melt shavings of tallow on the surface (this serves as a flux). Use a special tin-lead-bismuth solder. Hold the soldering iron against the pewter; hold the solder against both the iron and the pewter, and melt solder into the joint. Do not hold soldering iron long in one spot because pewter has a low melting point.

Dents. First try to press it out with your fingers. If this doesn't work, hold a block of wood over concave side of dent and tap the reverse side sharply but not too heavily with another block of wood.

Pewter separated from other materials, such as felt. See household decorative accessories under metal.

Tarnished. Clean with silver polish.

PHONOGRAPH

See record player.

PHONOGRAPH RECORD JACKET

Seams torn. Bind with adhesive-backed cloth tape.

PHOTOGRAPH

Torn. Coat both edges with a thin coat of rubber cement, and before this dries, press the edges together. Smooth carefully so as not to damage the emulsion. Then cover a sheet of paper or cardboard and the entire back of the picture with rubber cement. Let dry, and apply a second over-all coat to the picture. Smooth it down on the paper.

PIANO

Keys stick. Raise heat and try to lower humidity in room for several days. Work the keys up and down and sideways. If stickiness doesn't disappear, call in a piano tuner.

Keys stained yellow. Age causes this and it cannot be corrected. Ordinary dirt stains can be removed with mild soap and water.

Top off key. Carefully scrape off old glue. Spread a thin layer of Duco cement on back of key top and press down on the base for five minutes. Be sure to wipe off any glue that squeezes out at the sides.

Wood damaged. See wood.

PICTURE FRAME

Joints open, loose. Open joint wide enough to insert a thin knife or spatula. Spread in Elmer's Glue-

All. Press together and tap in brad in edge of frame. To make sure corners are square, nail two strips of wood to a piece of plywood at right angles (use a carpenter's square). Set frame against these. Then nail two more strips of wood along the other sides.

Glass broken. See glass.

Carving on gilt frame broken. Clean broken surface with a damp rag. Mix spackle with just enough water to make a thick "dough" and apply a large blob to the break. Mold roughly to shape with your fingers while still damp. Then let dry and carve to correct shape with a sharp knife. Finish with sandpaper. Paint with gold paint.

PILLOW

Holes. On bed pillows apply a patch with Devcon Patch glue. Holes in sofa pillows and the like are best mended by darning. See clothing–fabrics.

PING-PONG PADDLE

Rubber face loose. Scrape off glue and apply rubber cement to back of rubber and to wood. Let dry. Apply a second coat to one surface and smooth rubber down.

Cork face loose. Scrape off glue and reglue with Elmer's Glue-All.

Sandpaper face loose, damaged. If face is simply loose, scrape off old glue and reglue with Elmer's Glue-All. If paper is damaged, peel it off completely (wetting the surface will help). Stick down new sandpaper with rubber cement.

PING-PONG TABLE

Table wobbly. If filling loose screw holes with plastic wood and generally tightening screws and metal braces does not help, cut a 3″ board into 2′ lengths. You will need one board for each table leg. Cut a 90° V-notch into end of each board. At the other end, hinge boards to short cross blocks of wood. Position the blocks on the bottom of the table top so that they are 18″ from the legs and bisect the corner angles of the table. Glue or screw the blocks to the bottom of the table top at this point. Press notch of each brace against the leg it is designed to support. Drive a screw through one edge of brace into the table leg.

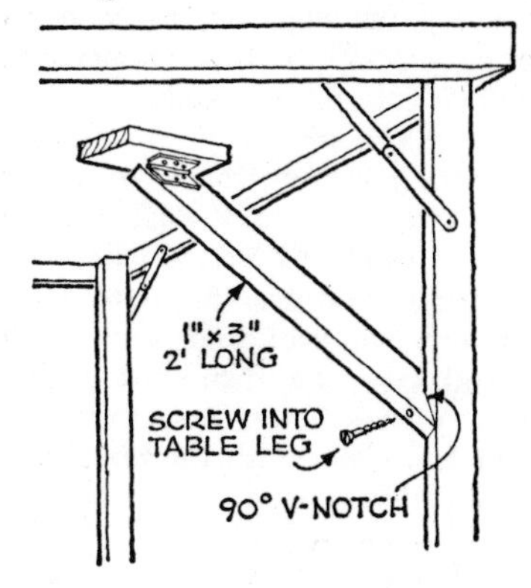

Veneer on table top split, delaminated. See veneer.

Dents in top. Sand paint from dent. Fill with plastic wood. Sand smooth when dry and repaint.

Net torn. Sew torn edges together with strong cotton thread.

PIPE, HEATING

Insulation broken or missing at joints. Remove defective insulation. Wet remaining insulation with water. Mix asbestos cement with water into a stiff paste and apply to pipe when it is cold.

Leaks. See pipe, water–copper, or pipe, water–steel.

PIPE VALVE

Shut-off valve doesn't shut off water. Turn off water and drain line. On stop valves (most commonly used type in homes), loosen cap nut. Then remove nut next below it. Screw out handle. Replace washer with one of proper size. On gate valves, unscrew large nut below cap nut. Pull out spindle; then pull out gate with pliers. Replace entire body of valve.

Shut-off valve leaks around handle. Tighten cap nut just enough to stop leak. If leaking persists, remove nut and wrap new graphite wicking around stem.

Shut-off valve frozen open by corrosion products. Don't try to force valve closed. Scrape off visible corrosion products. Saturate joint between cap nut and stem with Liquid Wrench penetrating oil. Then unscrew cap nut, take out stem and clean both thoroughly.

PIPE, WATER

Also see entries following.

Leaks. See pipe, water–copper; or pipe, water–steel.

Clogged. Clogging may be caused by corrosion products or mineral deposits. There is no cure. Have pipe replaced with pipe of another material. Install a water softener if clogging is caused by hard water.

Sweats. Wrap with fiberglass tape and over-wrap with kraft paper tape.

Pipes thump or hammer. If this happens when a faucet is turned on, make sure cap nut on faucet is tight and faucet washer is in good condition (see faucet). If hammering is more or less continual, shut off main water valve, open all faucets in house and drain system at lowest drain point. This will let in air which should cushion against hammer. However, if hammering persists or returns, call in plumber.

Frozen. Open all faucets on the line. Direct an electric heat lamp on the pipe, starting at the faucet end and working backward to the supply end. Or wrap rags soaked in boiling water around pipe. But do not use a torch of any kind.

PIPE, WATER—BRASS

Leaks in pipe. For temporary and permanent repairs, see pipe, water—copper. If mending plate is installed, buy same size as for steel pipes (see pipe, water–steel).

Leaks at fittings. See pipe, water—steel.

Leaks at unions. See pipe, water—copper.

PIPE, WATER—COPPER

Leaks in pipe. Temporary repair. Apply a mending plate. To determine which size plate is needed, tie a knot in a piece of string and loop string once around the pipe until it touches the knot. Remove string from pipe and measure from the "touching" point to the knot.

If string measures	*copper pipe size is*
1⁹⁄₁₆″	⅜″
2″	½″
2⅜″	⅝″
2¾″	¾″
3⁷⁄₁₆″	1″
4⁵⁄₁₆″	1¼″

Place the rubber gasket that comes with the mending plate over the hole in the pipe. Fold the plate around the pipe over the gasket and lock in place with bolts.

Permanent repair. Drain pipe. Clean hole and area around it with steel wool. Apply acid flux. Heat pipe with torch or soldering iron and apply solder.

Note. If copper tube springs many leaks, water should be treated to remove or reduce corrosive elements.

Leaks at soldered joints. Drain pipe. Clean joint with steel wool. Heat joint with torch until solder melts. Apply a little new solder.

Leaks at joints made with flared or compression fittings. Tighten the nut on the fitting with a wrench. If this doesn't stop leak, drain the pipe, loosen nut completely, pull joint apart and make sure it is clean and properly aligned, then retighten nut. If leak continues, call plumber.

Leaks at unions. Leaks occasionally develop if the male and female sides of the union are not properly aligned or clean. Drain pipe. Loosen large central nut and pull joint apart. Check alignment and clean faces of joint. Retighten nut. If leak continues, call plumber.

PIPE, WATER—STEEL

Leaks in pipe. There is not a satisfactory permanent repair. For a temporary repair, see pipe, water —copper. To determine size of mending plate needed, use string measuring technique.

If string measures	*steel pipe size is*
2³⁄₁₆″	⅜″
2⅝″	½″
3¼″	¾″
4⅛″	1″
5¼″	1¼″
6″	1½″

Leaks at fittings. Don't try to tighten fitting or pipe; you may only aggravate the problem. For a temporary repair, drain the pipe and dry fitting with a torch. Clean off rust, dirt and pipe dope. Smear on plastic steel and let set for several hours before turning on water again.

Leaks at unions. See pipe, water —copper.

PLACE MAT

See clothing–fabrics; clothing–hems; straw, or cork as the case may be.

PLANE, CARPENTER'S

Bottom rough, rusted. Remove rust by rubbing with liquid rust-remover. Then, after removing or pulling back cutting blade, polish bottom with fine steel wool. To smooth out scratches, rub with emery cloth.

Blade dull, nicked. Here's a tricky job. You can use a grinding wheel, but it is safer to work on a large (about 2″ wide) carborundum stone. The blade must be held firmly at an angle of about 25°. You can buy a special blade holder or simply cut a block of wood to the proper angle. Hold blade against this and at right angles to the long side of the stone. Then move blade up and down the stone. Sharpen first on the rough side of the stone; finish on the smooth side. When job is done, turn blade over so that beveled edge is up; lay it flat on the smooth side of the stone, and move it sidewise several times.

PLANT TUB

Rotting at bottom. If rot has not progressed too far, unpot the plant. Clean and wash tub thoroughly and let dry. Dig out soft wood and fill holes with plastic wood. Apply two liberal coats of zinc or copper naphthanate wood preservative to the wood inside and out. Line bottom and well up the sides with freezer-grade aluminum foil or heavy polyethylene film and poke drainage holes through it to correspond with holes in tub bottom. Pour in 2″ or 3″ of coarse gravel before repotting plants. Keep tub raised off floor about 1″ to provide air circulation underneath.

PLANTER

Wood planter rotting at bottom. See plant tub. But a better remedy —possible with rectangular planters but difficult with round tubs—is to make a liner of copper flashing metal. Solder all seams. If planter has drainage holes, fit copper tube or a ring of copper flashing through holes and solder to bottom of liner.

Concrete planter broken. See concrete (thin sections of ornamental concrete broken).

Hollow tile planter broken. See tile, hollow.

PLASKON

See plastics—general.

PLASTER

Plaster ornament broken. Coat broken surfaces with Duco cement and let dry. Apply a second coat of cement to one surface and press together firmly.

Ornamental plaster surface chipped. Saturate with water. Mix plaster of Paris with water to form a stiff paste. Apply to chipped surface and mold roughly with your fingers. When dry, the plaster can be shaped accurately with a knife, file, and sandpaper.

Plaster ornament separated from another material such as felt. Apply Duco or Pliobond cement to the separated surfaces and press together. See also household decorative accessories. Hard plaster can be glued much like ceramics.

Plaster wall and ceiling problems. See interior wall, plaster.

PLASTICS—EMBEDDED WITH DECORATIVE MATERIALS

See plastics—general.

PLASTICS—FABRICS

Note. Plastic fabrics, such as rayon, nylon, Dacron, Orlon, Acrilan, etc., are mended like fabrics made out of cotton, silk, wool, etc. See clothing—fabrics.

Problems with vinyl fabrics. See vinyl.

PLASTICS—FILMS

See cellophane or polyethylene, as case may be.

PLASTICS—FLEXIBLE

See vinyl or polyethylene. Otherwise, if plastic is of unknown brand or type, see plastics–general.

PLASTICS—FOAMS

See styrofoam or urethane foam.

PLASTICS—GENERAL

Note. Plastics included under this heading are those used in kitchenware, appliances, radio cabinets, toys, decorative accessories, etc. If you cannot identify the type of plastics used in something that needs to be mended, follow directions below. If these repair methods do not work, chances are that you are dealing with polyethylene, which see.

Broken, cracked. Wash edges and dry thoroughly. Apply plastic-mending adhesive to one edge and press broken pieces together overnight. If the broken section is thin, it is then advisable to reinforce the joint by gluing a thin plastic patch over it. Use the same adhesive.

Scratched. Better leave well enough alone. However, if you want to take a chance, dip a rag in sewing-machine or salad oil and then in powdered pumice. Rub on the scratch until it is obliterated. Then wipe surface clean and repeat the process with rottenstone. When the area dulled by the pumice begins to shine, wipe clean again. And then rub with powdered rouge (available at the hardware store) and water. This should restore the original shine pretty well.

Note. If you value the plastic article, test this scratch-removal method on the underside of the article or on a piece of similar plastic.

Deformed. Heat and very hot water soften and deform such thermoplastic plastics as acrylics, nylon, polyethylene, styrene, and vinyl. All you can try to do–and it probably won't be successful–is to reheat the deformed object and try to mold it back into shape.

Stains. Wash in soap and water. Do not use abrasives. If stains remain, leave them alone.

Separated from another material such as wood. See household decorative accessories. Plastics can also be drilled and screwed to wood or bolted or riveted to metal.

PLASTICS—LAMINATED (FORMICA AND THE LIKE)

Plastic surface loose from wood base. Scrape out old adhesive as much as possible. Make sure surfaces are dry. With a spatula spread waterproof counter-top adhesive (but not contact cement) in crack according to manufacturer's directions. Then clamp or weight plastic in place. If plastic is under tension at a nearby point–for example, if a faucet escutcheon is bearing on it –release tension before clamping plastic.

Holes, deep burns. First secure a scrap of matching material. Draw a rectangular outline around the defect. Then with a very sharp chisel, cut out along the outline. Do not hammer chisel too hard. Hold chisel so that beveled side of blade faces the damage. Heat damaged piece with a torch to loosen adhesive, then pry piece loose. Clean the base smooth. Out of the scrap material, cut a piece to fit hole. Use a fine-toothed saw and cut piece slightly larger than necessary, then trim to size with a file. Spread waterproof counter-top adhesive (not contact cement) on base. Set in patch and roll down. To fill cracks around patch, heat a small spatula or knife in an alcohol flame, hold it against stick shellac of proper color and drip shellac into cracks. Scratch off excess with a sharp knife.

Note. This is a very tricky repair; think twice before attempting it. Just filling the hole or burned spot with stick shellac might be better.

Stains. Wash with soap and water or mild household cleanser. Try nothing else.

PLAYPEN, BABY'S

Plastic on top rails cracked. Don't try to fix it. Peel it off and either leave wood unfinished or apply non-toxic paint.

Slat broken. If broken with the grain, coat the edges with Weldwood plastic resin glue and clamp together with C-clamps for 24 hours. If break is across the grain, saw off slat flush with bottom rail and pull it out of mortise in top rail. Cut new slat the same length and shape top to fit in mortise. Apply epoxy glue in mortise and set in slat. To hold slat on bottom rail, daub epoxy glue on end and press in place on rail. When glue is dry, drive a long thin screw up through the rail into end of slat or join the slat to the rail with a steel corner brace.

Bottom weak. Check hinges, angle irons or wood strips on which bottom rests. Reglue wood strips which reinforce the bottom.

PLEXIGLAS

See plastics—general.

PLIERS

Jaws do not meet squarely. Tighten nut that holds halves of pliers together. Then lock nut tight by holding a steel punch on the line where the nut goes through the bolt and rap with a hammer.

Teeth dull, rounded. Clamp pliers in vise and deepen grooves between teeth with a small triangular file.

PLYWOOD

Note. When buying plywood, always specify "exterior grade" if it is to be used outdoors.

Finish marred. See lacquered surface, painted surface, shellacked surface, or varnished surface as case may be.

Veneer loose, broken, bulging. See veneer.

Burns, dents, scratches. See furniture, wood.

Holes, gouges, rot, stains. See wood.

Warped. See furniture—table (top or leaf warped). Note that exterior grade plywood is less subject to warping than interior grades.

Pieces of plywood separated. Nail or screw together, or coat both surfaces with Weldwood plastic resin glue or Elmer's waterproof glue and clamp pieces together overnight.

Plywood separated from another material. Refasten with screws or bolts. Or use appropriate glue (see household decorative accessories and use same glues as specified for wood).

Edges rough, splintered. Wrap sandpaper around a block of wood and sand edges as smooth as possible. Holes and roughness that remain can be filled with plywood edge filler or plastic wood which is spread on with a putty knife and sanded when dry.

If plywood is stained, coat the edge (after sanding) with Weldwood plastic resin glue or Elmer's waterproof glue. Press a plywood edging strip (a very thin, narrow strip of pine, mahogany, birch, etc.) in place. When glue dries, trim off the edges of the strip flush with the plywood surface with a very sharp knife. The edging strip can then be stained to match the plywood.

POCKETBOOK

See handbag.

POLYETHYLENE

Holes, tears in polyethylene film. Experiment first on some scrap material to get the hang of making this repair. Overlap the edges of the film or cut a patch out of polyethylene and lay it over the hole. Place a sheet of white paper on top. Heat a flatiron to about the middle temperature setting and hold it on the paper for several seconds. The polyethylene edges should heat-seal together. If they don't, increase iron temperature slightly. But beware using too high temperature, because it will disintegrate the plastic.

Breaks in thick polyethylene. A perfect repair is impossible. But broken parts can sometimes be joined by touching the edges quickly to an electric range burner set at middle temperature and then immediately pressing them together.

POOL, CONCRETE

Cracks, open joints. Scrape open slightly and scrub clean with detergent and water. Rinse and let dry. With a caulking gun, squeeze in synthetic rubber sealant made by Thiokol.

Fine cracks, rough areas. Scrub surface with detergent, rinse, and let dry. Brush on concrete adhesive made of epoxy resin and polysulfide liquid polymer.

Stains. If concrete is painted, scrub stains with household bleach or strong detergent. Try same treatment on painted concrete. If this doesn't work, see concrete.

Algae. Pour ten times normal daily amount of chlorine into pool and scrub walls and floor with a steel brush. If algae persist, call in pool contractor.

Scale deposits. Remove with sandpaper. If necessary use a power sander with medium-grit paper. Be careful not to damage the wall. If scale becomes a serious, continuing problem, consult pool contractor.

POOL, FIBERGLASS

See fiberglass. If seams are split, call in a pool contractor.

Stains, algae, scale deposits. See pool, concrete.

POOL, PLASTIC

Holes, tears. Repair with mending kit sold by pool manufacturer. Or cut a patch out of sheet vinyl and glue over hole with plastic-mending adhesive. Pool surface must, of course, be absolutely clean and dry for patch to hold.

Stains, algae. See pool, concrete.

POOL, RUBBER

Holes, tears. Apply rubber patch. See tire (tube punctured).

Stains, algae. See pool, concrete.

POOL, STEEL

Rust spots. Scrub with steel wool. Then apply Rust-Oleum 769 Damp-Proof Red Primer. When dry, apply pool paint.

Badly pitted. Fill holes, after cleaning thoroughly, with plastic steel. Smooth down. When dry, prime as above.

PORCELAIN

Broken. See china.

Chipped. Clean chipped area and let dry. Then apply epoxy resin sold for porcelain repairs.

Rust or copper stains on surface. Wash with household ammonia and water, or a solution of 3 tbsp. Javelle water to 1 qt. water. If this doesn't work, scrub with a non-abrasive cleanser such as Zud.

PORCH, MASONRY

Floor cracked, uneven. See brick, concrete, or stone as the case may be.

Columns rotting. See column.

Wood railings rotting. See fence.

Iron railings wobbly. Chip out weak mortar around base of posts (or bolts holding posts). Blow out crumbs with vacuum cleaner. If opening is fairly small, force in plastic steel. If opening is large, dampen edges of masonry. Cram in mortar made of 1 part cement and 3 parts sand. In either case, brace the railing in vertical position until filler material hardens.

Collects water in low spot. Floor can be leveled by troweling on latex cement or by chipping out concrete in low spot to a depth of 1" and filling with mortar of 1 part Portland cement and 3 parts sand. See Basic Methods: How to Mix and Handle Concrete. However, patch will not match surrounding surface unless you paint it; and paint does not hold up very well on concrete paving.

PORCH, WOOD

Floor board weak, rotten. If entire board is gone, replace it. To remove, split it lengthwise in several places and pry it out from the center toward the edges. Be careful not to damage tongue and groove of adjacent boards. To set in new board in a tongue-and-groove floor, chisel off the bottom part of the grooved edge. Tongue of new board can then be slipped into groove of adjoining board, and grooved edge will fit over tongue of the other adjoining board.

If only a small part of a floor board is defective, locate position of nearest joists and draw pencil

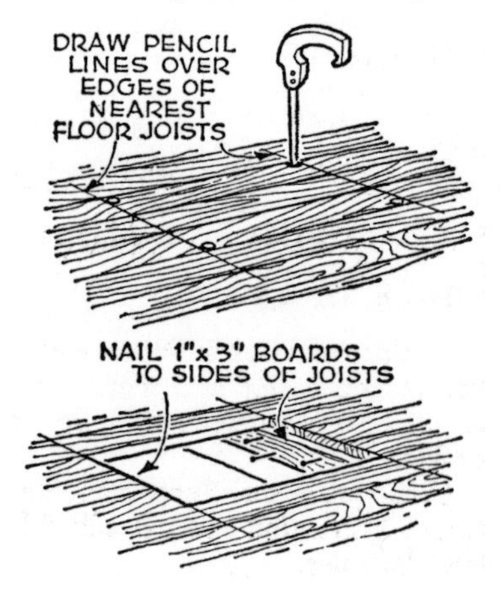

lines across the top of the floor to mark these. Then drill 1" holes in the corners between the pencil lines and the edges of the bad board. With a keyhole saw cut across the two pencil lines from hole to hole. The saw cuts should be almost flush with the inner edges of the joists. Split defective board and pry it out. Nail 1" by 3" boards to the sides of the joists under the hole. Cut new board to fit the opening. Remove bottom part of the grooved edge. Then set in and nail.

Columns rotting. See column.

Railings rotting. See fence.

Railings wobbly. Secure to columns or floor with angle irons.

Porch sagging. Rent a steel jack post (or maybe two) and jack up sagging joists. Then place 4" by 4" timbers treated with wood preservative under joists and remove jacks.

POST

See column.

POTS AND PANS

See cooking utensils.

POTTERY

See earthenware. Use epoxy glue if pottery is used for cooking; Duco cement if it is a purely ornamental piece.

POWER TOOLS

Don't work. Check whether fuse has blown, outlet into which tool is plugged is defective, cord is broken.

Other problems. Keep manufacturer's instruction manual and follow the rules.

PRESSURE COOKER

Gasket worn, cooker leaks. You can usually pull off the gasket (you may need pliers, because when it is old it sticks to metal) and replace with a new one available from the pressure-cooker dealer. But it's easier and costs no more to take the cooker to the dealer and let him do the whole job.

QUARRY TILE

See tile, ceramic.

RADIATOR, HOT WATER

Radiator doesn't heat properly. Hold a pan under vent valve; open valve with valve key to let out accumulated air; close valve when water begins to run out. If difficulty continues to arise, replace manually operated valve with an automatic one.

Note. If radiator is painted with metallic paint, heat output is reduced. Repaint with interior paint. (The metallic paint need not be removed first.)

Leaks at inlet valve stem. Tighten nut at top of valve. If leak doesn't stop, loosen nut completely and wrap graphite wicking around stem a couple of times. Bring nut down over this and tighten.

RADIATOR, STEAM

Radiator doesn't heat properly. Unscrew valve from radiator, carefully clean venting port with a tiny wire. Blow hard through stem of valve. Shake out accumulated water. (Valves can also be cleaned by soaking in gasoline for a few minutes.) Then replace. If radiator continues not to heat, lay a carpenter's level on it to determine whether it is pitched properly. If it isn't, insert wood shims under legs. In a one-pipe heating system, radiator should pitch down to the supply line. In a two-pipe system, it should pitch toward the return line. If radiator still doesn't heat, replace valve with a new one.

Note. Heat output is reduced if radiators are painted with metallic paint. Over-paint with ordinary interior paint or special radiator paint.

Banging in radiator and pipes. Insert ½″ blocks of wood under the legs of the radiator to correct the pitch of the pipe leading to it. If this doesn't work and it is possible to do so, insert thicker blocks of wood under legs. If this still doesn't work, call a plumber.

Water leaks from around stem of inlet valve. See radiator, hot water.

RADIO

Won't play. If battery operated, you probably need new batteries. Otherwise, take tubes to radio shop and have them tested. Replace any that are gone. If radio is still silent, let the shop take over.

Tuning knobs loose. Remove knob. Coat hole in knob and end of spindle to which it is attached with rubber cement and press together. This, unfortunately, is not a very good repair and the knob will loosen up again. But if you use glue that will really hold, it may be difficult to take the radio apart if it ever needs repairs.

Plastic case cracked. Clean edges of crack and coat with plastic-mending adhesive. Bind case together for 24 hours.

RAINCOAT

Tear in vinyl. Cut strip of vinyl to cover tear or use patch in plastic-mending adhesive kit. Apply plastic-mending adhesive to patch and smooth in place over tear.

Tear in polyethylene. See polyethylene.

Tear in rubber. Cut a patch out of rubber. Roughen undersurface of patch and area around hole with sandpaper. Apply thin coat of rubber cement to both surfaces and let dry. Then apply a second coat to the patch and smooth down.

Tear in cloth. Out of similar material cut a small round patch and glue under tear with Devcon Patch glue.

Placket ripped in cloth coat. For a small rip, see clothing–plackets. If rip is large, rip out stitches in the entire back seam, pull edges together so that rip is concealed and sew a new seam on a sewing machine. There is generally enough fullness to raincoats to make such a repair possible without materially changing the appearance of the coats.

RAKE, LEAF

Bamboo tines loose—too far apart or too close together. The tines are held between two bamboo strips bolted to the bottom end of the handle and by laced wire about 6″ further down. Remove lower wire and position the tines properly. Wrap wire tightly around one end of the bamboo cross brace. Then lace it tightly between the tines and around the brace to the other end of the brace. Tighten at this point and lace back through the tines to the starting point.

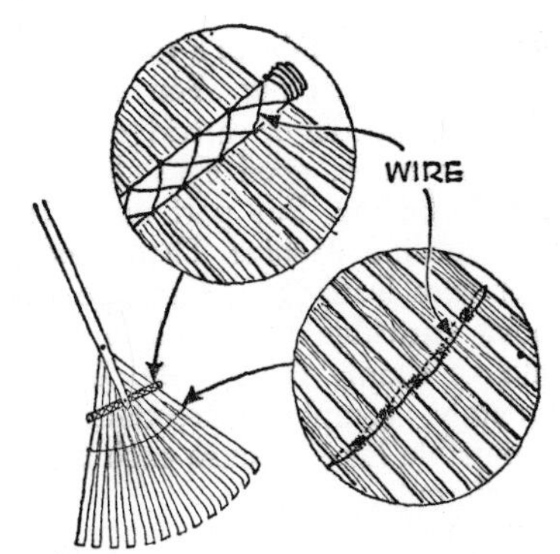

Now take a long length of wire and bend it in half around the tine at one side of the rake 4″ to 6″ below the cross brace. Loop it around the tine and twist together three or four times. Then loop it around the next tine and twist together; and so on to the opposite side of the rake. The wire should form an arc more or less paralleling the arc formed by the ends of the tines.

Bamboo tine missing. If it is not broken, set it back in place in the rake and lace to the bamboo cross brace with wire. Also wire it to the other tines where they come together at the handle. If the missing tine is broken, either leave the rake alone or, if you wish, reposition the other tines to reduce the gap left by the tine.

Head of bamboo rake wobbles on handle. Tighten the nuts on the U-bolt holding the tines to the handle. If the U-bolt still wobbles, wrap the handle at this point with friction tape and tighten the bolt over this.

Bamboo handle split. See bamboo.

Tines in steel rake broken. There's nothing you can do to this kind of leaf rake except keep the head tightly bolted to the handle. Use the rake until a number of tines are broken and then throw it away.

RANGE, ELECTRIC

Note. Call a serviceman if range doesn't work properly, but before doing so check and correct points noted below.

Doesn't heat, lights off. Check: Has fuse in bottom compartment (or wherever it is located on your particular make) blown? Have fuses blown at fuse box?

Single surface unit doesn't heat. Make sure switch is off. Raise unit, remove reflector and check whether wires are connected to terminals or whether one or more of them is broken. Reconnect wires. If unit still doesn't heat, it is probably burned out.

Oven units don't work. Check whether element is pushed firmly into outlet. If unit doesn't heat, remove it and clean terminals and try in outlet again. If it still doesn't work, unit is probably burned out.

Oven food too light or too dark on top or bottom. The problem is probably with the utensil you are using and where you place it in oven. Check range instruction book.

Oven walls and bottom encrusted with spillages. Turn oven on for a few minutes, then turn off. Pour straight household ammonia into a pan and set in oven overnight. Wash walls and bottom clean in the morning with water. Dry thoroughly. Wipe or spray on silicone preparation made to prevent food sticking.

Surface unit reflectors encrusted with spillages. Soak for several hours in a strong solution of household ammonia. Then polish with steel wool and rinse clean.

RANGE, GAS

Pilot light out. From the pilot follow the little gas inlet tube back to the manifold, where you will find an adjusting screw. Hold a lighted match at the pilot and turn the screw on the manifold counterclockwise until the gas ignites. Then turn the screw clockwise till the flame is three-quarters of the height of the flash tube leading to the burner.

Top burners light but oven doesn't. This happens on only a few modern ranges. Check whether electric fuse on house circuit into which range is connected has blown. If it hasn't, call a serviceman.

Lights don't light. Check whether range is plugged into electric outlet. Check whether fuse on house circuit has blown.

Burners encrusted with spillages. Lift out burner and soak in solution of household ammonia. If necessary, boil in a weak solution of washing soda. Then dry thoroughly.

Oven food too light or too dark. See range, electric.

Oven walls encrusted with spillages. See range, electric.

Other problems. Call a serviceman.

RATTAN

See furniture, wicker, rattan, reed, or bamboo.

RECORD PLAYER

Doesn't work. Check whether fuse on house circuit has blown. Disconnect player and examine cord and plug for breaks. Repair as necessary (see electric cord). If player still doesn't work or doesn't work properly, take to a radio shop.

Needle worn out. You can replace the needle or cartridge if you have patience, good eyesight, and nimble fingers. Buy part made for your specific machine. Then disconnect wire leads from cartridge, remove cartridge and replace it in toto or simply the needle. Unfortunately, complete directions are impossible here because each make is different.

REFRIGERATOR

Note. Call a serviceman if machine doesn't work properly, but before doing so check and correct points noted below.

Doesn't work. Check: Has temperature control dial been turned off? Is refrigerator plugged in? Has fuse blown? On a gas refrigerator, is pilot light out? Relight according to directions on tag attached to refrigerator.

Heats up. Provide more air circulation at sides and especially at top if refrigerator exhausts heat from the back. If you have a modern front-exhaust box, call a serviceman.

Seems to labor. Clean out dust, cobwebs from operating mechanism with a vacuum cleaner hose. Clean filter on gas refrigerator.

Plastic parts broken. Clean with soap and water and rinse. When dry, coat broken edges with plastic-mending adhesive. Clamp together for 24 hours. If break needs to be reinforced, cover it with plastic patching material that comes with plastic-mending adhesive kit.

Ice cube release broken. Buy a new tray.

Door doesn't seal. Wash gasket with soap and water. If this doesn't help, call a serviceman to check a magnetic-door gasket. In refrigerators with conventional latches, loosen the strike plate and move it into the box a fraction of an inch so that it pulls latch and door tight shut.

Door swings open or shut too fast. Pull off bottom front panel. Tilt refrigerator backward and raise or lower leveling screws under front corners. Check leveling screws at back corners, too. *Note:* Some leveling screws can be turned by a screwdriver without lifting appliance.

REGISTER, WARM AIR

Stains walls with soot. Remove grille and clean inside of duct with vacuum cleaner hose. Clean or replace furnace filters monthly.

RETAINING WALL

Cracked. This is caused by the pressure of the water and soil behind the wall. The crack may now permit adequate drainage, so if wall does not seem in danger of collapse, do not fill crack (you can grow vines over wall to conceal it). If you do fill crack, drainage tile must be installed behind wall so that water is carried away around the ends of the wall or through it.

The whole situation is complicated and possibly dangerous. Call in a mason who understands such things.

RIVETS

Broken or loose. Cut or file off head. Poke out shank. Insert new rivet. If this is too long, cut off shank about ⅛″ above surface. Place head on a vise or other heavy metal surface. Pinch pieces of metal being riveted together. Hammer down end of rivet shank until it overlaps hole.

ROOF

Also see entries following.

Leaks. Finding a leak is often the hardest part of fixing one. The best method, if you can get up under the roof, is to look for pinpricks of light and then to stick long wires up through the holes. If you can't see any holes, try to trace the course of the water back to its source. If both of these methods are unsuccessful or if you cannot get under the roof, the only thing you can do is examine the top of the roof inch by inch. For repair of leaks, see following entries.

Ridge sags. Rent one or two steel jack posts, set them under the ridge pole and jack them up evenly. When ridge is straight, join the rafters on opposite sides of the ridge pole with a series of collar beams cut out of 2″ by 6″ lumber. The beams should be approximately 4′ below the ridge pole and securely spiked to the rafters.

ROOF, ASBESTOS-CEMENT SHINGLE

Broken shingles. If the shingles are lapped only at the bottom, shatter the cracked shingle with a hammer and remove the pieces. Slip a hacksaw blade up under overlapping shingles and cut off nails that held broken shingle. Insert a new shingle. To hold it in place, drill a hole through the joint between the overlying shingles and through the top of the new shingle. Drive one roofing nail through this until it is flush with the face of the new shingle. Then slip a 3″-wide strip of copper or aluminum flashing between the shingles over the nail and bend it slightly so it will hold in place.

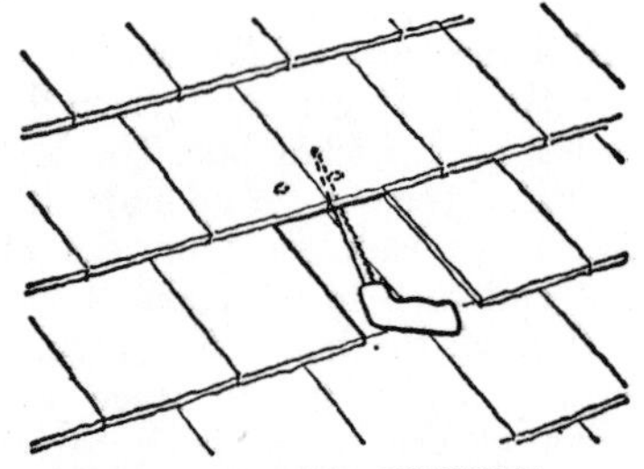

REMOVE BROKEN SHINGLE, CUT OFF NAILS WITH HACKSAW

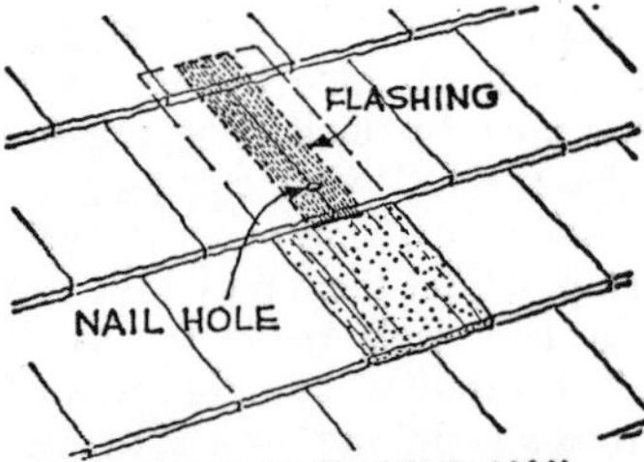

BORE HOLE AND DRIVE NAIL FLUSH WITH TOP OF NEW SHINGLE. SLIP FLASHING BETWEEN NEW AND OLD SHINGLES

If shingles are lapped at the sides as well as at the bottom, have broken shingle replaced by a roofing contractor.

Fungus growth on shingles. Scrub with an abrasive household cleanser. If this doesn't work, mix 1 part copper sulfate with 10 parts hot water in a non-metallic container. Brush on liberally. The stain will disappear and color of material return in a month or so.

ROOF, ASPHALT ROLL

Small holes. Dab on asphalt roofing cement.

Large holes. Open the seam between pieces of asphalt roll below the hole and slip up through it a new piece of roll roofing large enough to extend 6″ beyond all sides of the hole. When it is in place, spread asphalt roofing cement under and around the edges of the hole. Press down torn roofing and close opening in seam below the hole.

Leaks in seams. If leaks are not stopped by applying asphalt roofing cement to them, coat the seam thoroughly with cement and then embed in it a 6″ strip of 35-lb., smooth-surfaced, asphalt roll roofing. After the cement has set for two hours, paint the strip with asphalt roof coating (a non-fibrous asphalt cement).

ROOF, ASPHALT SHINGLE

Small holes, tears. Lift shingle carefully and put a dab of asphalt roofing cement under the hole. Press shingle down into cement.

Badly torn shingles. Cut out the damaged tab. Cut new shingle to proper width and long enough to fit up under cut-off shingle several inches. Smear asphalt roofing cement on bottom of patch and set in place. You do not need to nail a patch unless it is two or three tabs long.

Curled shingles. Anchor tabs with asphalt roofing cement.

Mineral surface gone but felt intact. This is not serious but is unsightly. If mineral surface is gone only in small spots, collect minerals that have washed off into the gutter or scrape them off a scrap of shingle. Dab asphalt roof coating on the bare spot and scatter granules thickly in this. If a large part of the surface is gone, paint the entire roof with asphalt roofing paint which comes in various colors.

ROOF, BUILT-UP TAR AND GRAVEL

Leaks. Scrape back gravel and spread asphalt roofing cement liberally over the hole. Replace gravel.

ROOF, CLAY TILE

Leaks. Slip a piece of aluminum or copper flashing metal under the tiles over the hole and hold in place with asphalt roofing cement applied to underside. The metal must be long enough so that its entire top edge is covered by the overlapping tiles.

Broken tiles. Call in a contractor.

ROOF, METAL

Small holes. Clean metal thoroughly with steel wool. Cover hole with plastic steel.

Large holes. For a semi-permanent repair, clean metal thoroughly. Cut a patch out of similar metal. Coat bottom of patch with plastic steel and press into place.

Seams parted. Call in a roofing contractor.

Rusted. Scrape off as much rust as possible. Prime with Rust-Oleum 769 Damp-Proof Red Primer. Then paint (see Basic Methods: How to Paint).

ROOF, REINFORCED FIBERGLASS

Leaks at seams. Loosen nails. Clean out joint and spread in clear mastic sealer supplied by roof manufacturer.

Holes, cracks. See fiberglass, reinforced.

ROOF, SLATE

See roof, clay tile.

ROOF, WOOD SHINGLE

Holes, cracks. Slip a piece of aluminum or copper flashing metal up under the shingle over the hole and hold it in place with asphalt roofing cement. The metal must be long enough to extend well up under the overlapping shingles.

Shingles rotten, badly damaged. Loosen overlapping shingles. Split defective shingle and pull out pieces. Slip a hacksaw blade up under overlapping shingles and cut nails which held defective shingle. Insert a new shingle. Put one or two dabs of asphalt roofing cement under this to hold it.

Leaks in a closed valley. (A closed valley is one in which shingles come together instead of being

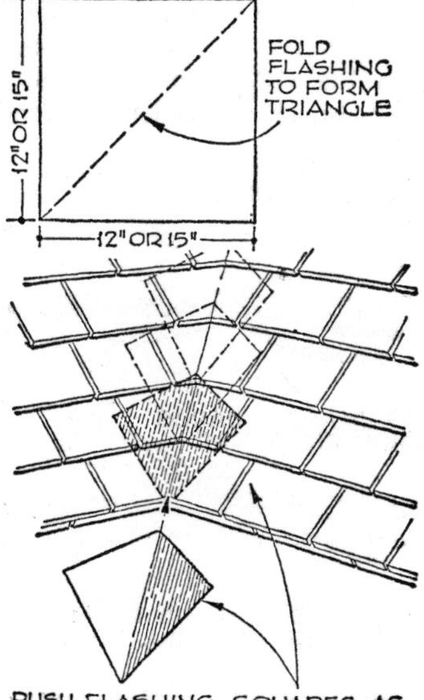

separated by an open strip of flashing material.) Cut 12"- or 15"-wide aluminum or copper flashing metal into squares and bend into equal triangles. Push the metal up under shingles as far as possible. If a series of metal patches are required, work from the bottom of the roof up.

ROPE

Broken. Cut the broken strands off cleanly, then separate the strands on each length of rope for several inches (the separation must be longer on thick ropes than on thin). Crotch the strands on the opposing pieces together just as you intertwine your fingers. Tie a string around the strands and the rope on your left. Then, starting with any strand on the right, tuck it over one strand and under one strand of the rope on the left. Do the same thing with the other two strands on the right. You may need a spike to open the strands in the rope in order to slip the loose strands through. Now remove the string and do the same thing with the strands on the left. When the splice is completed, do not cut the strands off next to the rope; let them protrude an inch or two to give extra strength.

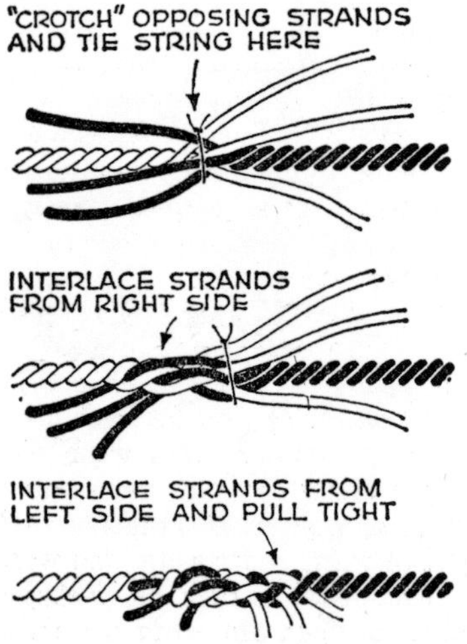

"CROTCH" OPPOSING STRANDS AND TIE STRING HERE

INTERLACE STRANDS FROM RIGHT SIDE

INTERLACE STRANDS FROM LEFT SIDE AND PULL TIGHT

Usually the strands need to be tucked only twice, as described. But for greater strength, you can make a third tuck.

End of rope raveling. Cut off cleanly and bind the end with friction tape.

RUBBER

Small holes. Clean surface thoroughly with gasoline or benzine. Roughen with sandpaper. Spread on plastic rubber.

Large holes, tears. Clean surface with gasoline or benzine and roughen with sandpaper. Cut patch out of an old tire tube or other rubber, clean and roughen surface. Coat both surfaces with rubber cement and let dry. Then apply a second coat to one surface and immediately smooth patch over hole.

A tire-tube patching kit will make a slightly stronger repair.

Rubber worn thin. Clean with gasoline or benzine and roughen with sandpaper. Apply plastic rubber or So-Lo rubber.

Rubber loose from another surface. Clean both surfaces, roughen with sandpaper and apply Pliobond cement. When this becomes tacky, press materials together and hold under pressure overnight.

RUBBER BALL

See ball, inflated rubber.

RUBBER TILE

See floor, rubber tile.

RUBBERIZED FABRIC

See rubber.

RUBBERS

Holes, tears. See tire.

RUG

Edges frayed. Whip the edge with carpet-binding thread or cover with gummed carpet-binding and press with a warm iron.

Worn in spots. Wear is caused by traffic and may be aggravated by condition of floor underneath. There is no way to mend worn spots satisfactorily, although you can conceal them to some extent by dyeing the rug backing to match the pile. If condition of floor contributes to the problem, take up rug and level the floor by sanding down high spots, filling wide cracks, and padding low spots with newspapers.

Holes. Stitch burlap to wrong side of rug. Then with a crochet hook, pull matching material through this to match the surrounding weave as closely as possible. To secure the yarn further, press gummed carpet-binding over the underside.

Rug indented by heavy furniture. Set steam iron in steaming position and hold over dents.

Rug limp. Have it sized by a rug cleaner. But if you don't care too much about it, mix 1 lb. of wallpaper size with about 4 qt. of water. Stir smooth. Lay rug upside down on a flat surface. Brush size on back and let dry. If rug is loosely woven, make size mixture thicker than above formula.

Corners curled. Curl back by hand. Steam with a steam iron.

Edges scalloped. Try steaming with a steam iron. Cut edge of rug cushion back 3″ from edge of rug. If these measures don't produce results, you will have to tack the edges down.

Fiber rug damaged. If fibers are only broken or frayed, glue them in place with Elmer's Glue-All. If damage is extensive and rug is made up in small squares, it is a simple matter to cut out the bad squares and sew in new ones. But if rug is of over-all weave, the only solution is to cut it into two or more smaller rugs. Finish the edges with gummed carpet-binding.

Burns in rugs. Carefully clip out the burned tufts and sponge with mild detergent.

Urine stains. Sponge immediately with water. Then sponge with Skip-Stain or equivalent preparation.

Grease stains. Cover with French chalk, allow to dry, and take up with vacuum cleaner. Repeat several times. Then sponge with carbon tetrachloride.

Tar on rug. Scrape up as much as possible. Then clean with carbon tetrachloride.

Non-greasy food stains, alcohol stains. Sponge with water.

Ink stains. Sponge with water, working from edges of stain toward the center. Only washable inks can be removed. Call a professional to remove others.

Shoe-dye stains. You're sunk. But call a professional rug-cleaner anyway—just on a dim chance.

Blood stains. Sponge fresh stains with cold water, then wash with warm suds. For old stains mix 1 tbsp. of household ammonia in ½ gal. of warm sudsy water and wash.

Nail polish on rugs. Pinch stained fibers in cloth dipped in nail-polish remover and wipe upward so as not to spread the stain.

Chewing gum and candle wax on rugs. Scrape off as much as possible and then treat with carbon tetrachloride.

RUG CUSHION

Edges frayed. Cover with gummed carpet-binding and press with a warm iron.

SALT CELLAR

Top and base corroded together. Soak the salt cellar in warm water until top can be removed. If this fails, soak it in rust-breaking penetrating oil for several days. When pieces come apart, remove as much of the corrosion as possible with a rag, then use very fine emery cloth. To prevent recurrence of trouble, store salt cellars only in a dry place. Remove, clean, and thoroughly dry top frequently.

SANDWICH GRILL, ELECTRIC

Doesn't heat. Check whether fuse on house circuit has blown. Plug a light into outlet used for grill to see whether outlet is defective. Try another cord on grill; the original may be defective. Lift out grids and check whether heating elements are broken. If one is, buy a replacement and install it in the same way. If all these measures fail, take grill to service shop.

SAW

Blade bent. Reshape with hands. If the blade has a sharp kink, place it on a flat surface, lift handle slightly, then hammer out kink with a wood mallet.

Rusted. Smear on liquid rust-remover and rub with a rag. When blade is as clean as you can get it this way, go over it with fine steel wool.

Dull. Sharpening is a tedious job and trickier than it may appear. Let an expert do it.

SAW, CHAIN

Won't start. Check whether it is turned on and gas tank is full. If there is no spark, replace plug.

Doesn't run well. Clean air filter. Change fuel filter. Replace spark plug. Drain tank and carburetor and clean. Readjust carburetor. Not all of these steps are required, of course; any one of them may do the trick.

Doesn't cut well. Apply oil. Tighten all screws, bolts, and nuts. Adjust tension on chain so that it slides easily around bar when moved by hand. Check whether bar holding chain is pinched and pry it open. Sharpen dull chain.

Note. Keep manufacturer's instructions and follow them faithfully.

SCISSORS

Don't cut—simply fold material being cut. Tighten screw joining the two halves of the scissors.

Dull. Cut a piece of medium sandpaper in two. Turn sandpaper over and cut again. But for a real sharpening job, stop the scissors-grinder next time he passes your house.

Point broken. File metal smooth. The scissors may not be perfect, but they are still usable.

SCREEN, WINDOW

Holes in metal screening. If

wires are simply pushed apart, as by a pencil point, straighten them with a small nail or ice pick. If wires are broken, buy screen patches at hardware store and hook into place over hole. You can make large screen patches out of a scrap of screening.

Holes in fiberglass screening. Push strands together if they are not broken. If strands are broken, you can fuse a fiberglass patch to the screening by applying heat. Practice on some scrap material until you get the hang of this. Have some one hold an iron frying pan or something similar to one side of the torn screening. Cut a patch to overlap hole and hold it against screening on other side. Then run the tip of a hot iron over it until it is stuck tight.

Holes in plastic screening. Cut a patch out of similar screening and sew it over the hole with nylon thread.

Metal screening corroded. Set on a flat surface and dust with a stiff bristle brush. Wash with soap and water, rinse and let dry. Paint both sides with two coats of spar varnish or prepared screen paint. To avoid clogging the mesh, apply finish with a piece of carpet.

Screening badly torn. Install new fiberglass screening (which is very durable, corrosion resistant, and easily stretched by hand). Pry off moldings on frame; remove tacks or splines holding old screening; rip off screening. Lay screen flat. Tack new screening securely across the top of the frame opening. Pull to the bottom and tack there. Then tack sides. Use ¼″ copper tacks and space them about 2″ apart. Cut off excess screening with a razor blade. Replace moldings.

If screening is held in place by splines instead of tacks, you can install new screening with these. Simply lay the screening over the grooves around the edges of frame and press it down into grooves with the splines.

Screen frame weak, wobbly. Brace four corners with iron angles. If you object to the appearance of these, drill ¼″ holes deep into the corner edges. Holes must go through both of the joined pieces of wood. Coat ¼″ wood dowels with Elmer's waterproof glue, drive them into holes and cut off flush with frame edges.

SCREWDRIVER

Tip broken, rounded. Hold screwdriver in a vise and file across the tip with a metal file. Hold file flat and file only on forward stroke. If repaired tip is too blunt, taper sides at the same gradual angle of original taper.

Shank loose in handle. Remove shank and squeeze a little plastic steel into handle hole. Then insert shank as far as possible. Allow plastic steel to set before using screwdriver.

SCREWS

Screw loose in screw hole. Remove from hole and cram hole with steel wool, solid wire solder, plastic wood, or a glued wood plug. Then reset screw.

Screw "frozen" in place. Heat screw head with a soldering iron. Then unscrew it.

Head damaged so that screwdriver won't hold. If necessary to salvage screw, reslot head with a hacksaw.

Shank broken off in wood. If wood is thick enough and new screw must be reset in same place, drive screw deep into wood with a nail set. If this is impossible, punch a small hole in the top of the screw with a steel punch. Then drill out screw with an electric drill.

SEASHELL

Broken. Apply Duco cement to both sides of break and press together until glue sets.

SEPTIC TANK

Clogged. Despite claims to the contrary, chemical septic-tank cleaners and yeast are of very little value. Have tank pumped out. To prevent future clogging, have tank checked every 12 to 18 months.

Roots clogging pipes in disposal field. These must be cut out with a special auger. Call septic-tank service.

SEWING MACHINE

If you don't have an instruction booklet, get one and follow directions for making adjustments and repairing damage. Otherwise, take the machine to the dealer.

SHAVER, ELECTRIC

Working badly. Clean head according to manufacturer's directions. If operation doesn't improve, return shaver to dealer or manufacturer for servicing.

SHEET

Tears, holes. See clothing–fabrics (holes).

Hemstitching broken. This can be mended but it's a painstaking job. Better separate hem edge from sheet entirely and rejoin with a strip of straight-edge lace. Or if appearance is not important, simply sew the hem edge over the sheet edge on your sewing machine or by whipping.

Contour sheet split at corners. Apply press-on mending tape over the tears. Then, if you dry sheets in a dryer, stitch down the edges of the tape and the torn edges of the sheet.

SHELLACKED SURFACE

Shallow scratches. Rub with alcohol.

Deep scratches. Apply several coats of new shellac with a fine brush. Then rub lightly with alcohol to smooth out surface.

Shellac gummy. Remove with denatured alcohol. In future, don't use shellac that is more than six months old.

Alcohol spots on shellac. Alcohol dissolves shellac, so mop it up quickly. Then rub with rottenstone and a cloth dipped in salad oil or sewing-machine oil. Remove residue with benzine.

Other stains. See varnished surface.

SHELVING

Sagging. If there is no support in the middle of the shelf, nail a strip of wood about 1″ thick to the wall under the shelf. This should be 16″ long or more so that you can nail through to two of the studs (which are spaced roughly 14″ apart). An alternative is to screw an iron angle to the wall (the screws must enter a stud).

If the shelf is warped as well as sagging, install a metal shelf support (like an iron angle but larger) under it. Or put a screw eye in the front edge of the shelf in the middle of the sag; install another screw eye in the ceiling overhead, and connect the two by a stout wire. *Note.* Do not support a warped shelf from a stable shelf in this way, because it will only result in warping of the upper shelf.

SHINGLE, WOOD

See roof, wood shingle and exterior wall, wood shingle.

SHINGLE, ASPHALT

See roof, asphalt shingle.

SHINGLE, ASBESTOS CEMENT

See roof, asbestos cement shingle.

SHOES

Leather scuffed. Trim off flaps of leather with scissors or a razor blade. Rub rest of scuffed area with the palm of your hand. Brush on liquid stain polish and buff. Then apply paste polish.

Leather water-stiffened. Rub a damp rag in saddle soap and rub vigorously on leather. Rinse with a rag dampened in clear water. Let dry (don't expose to heat). Then apply polish.

Patent leather cracked. You can't mend cracks but you can prevent additional cracking by rubbing vaseline vigorously into leather.

Moccasin seams split. Pick out broken threads. Resew with heavy cotton or linen thread coated with beeswax. Run thread through old holes.

Inner sole loose. Remove and scrape off old glue. Apply Pliobond cement to lining and to base. Let dry until tacky, then stick inner sole down.

Hole in leather lining. Trim out neatly with scissors. Cut a patch out of thin, soft leather like that used for inner soles. Feather the edges as much as possible with a razor blade. Then apply Pliobond cement to back of patch and around edges of hole. Let dry until tacky, then smooth patch in place.

Woman's shoe heel broken. Apply epoxy glue to both broken edges and press together for 24 hours.

Tap off heel. Reglue with epoxy glue.

Nail in heel. Hold heel on a solid metal surface. With a hammer and nail set, hammer down nail point on inside of shoe. If sole of shoe is so old and brittle that bent point of nail won't hold in it, however, grasp the point with pliers and pull nail out. Fill hole in inner sole with plastic rubber.

Hole in rubber sole. Clean rubber thoroughly with gasoline or benezine. Roughen surface if it is smooth. Fill hole with plastic rubber.

Hole in leather sole. If shoe does not warrant resoling by a shoemaker, apply a stick-on rubber sole. Clean old sole thoroughly and roughen with the rasp enclosed in the resoling kit (available at the Five and Ten). Apply thin coat of rubber cement to sole and let dry for 15 minutes. Apply a second coat and let it dry, too. Then remove paper backing from new rubber sole, apply cement to rubber, let dry for 20 minutes or more and press on leather sole.

Leather sole delaminated. Clean out dirt. Wedge opposing surfaces apart and coat both with Pliobond cement. Let dry until tacky, then remove wedge and press surfaces together.

Sole squeaks. Try rubbing neat's-foot oil deeply into the leather.

Polish on leather shoes blotched. Remove all polish with a cloth dampened with benzine. Then re-polish.

SHOES, TENNIS

Holes in canvas. Cut a small round patch of canvas, coat with Devcon Patch glue and stick on outside of shoe.

Rubber torn loose from canvas. Coat rubber and canvas with Pliobond cement and let dry. Then apply a second coat of cement to both surfaces and press together when cement is tacky.

Hole in sole or sole thin. Clean thoroughly with gasoline or benzine. Roughen surface with sandpaper. Fill with plastic rubber or So-Lo rubber. Let dry 24 hours. *Note.* Since plastic rubber is black, this repair looks good only on dark soles.

SHOWER CURTAIN

Tears in canvas. Glue a patch of matching canvas to the inside with Devcon Patch. See canvas.

Tears in rubber or rubberized material. Clean surface and let dry. Cut a patch from the bottom of the curtain. Coat curtain and patch with rubber cement. Let dry. Apply a second coat to patch and press in place.

Tears in oiled silk. Cover with cellophane tape.

Tears in plastic. Cut a patch out of matching plastic material and glue down with plastic-mending adhesive.

Mildew stains. Brush stains with strong detergent solution. Hang curtain out to dry.

SHOWER HEAD

Clogged. If shower head is modern, take off head, clean out sediment with a wire and rinse thoroughly. On old shower heads, poke a slim wire through the ports.

SHOWER STALL

Leak at top of receptor (bottom of stall). Clean crack thoroughly and let dry. Fill with tub-caulking compound.

Leak in base of receptor. Call a plumber.

Water leaks into wall behind faucet escutcheons. Wrap escutcheon with adhesive tape and unscrew with a pipe wrench. Cut out weak plaster around faucet. Let dry. Then fill hole with tub-caulking compound and replace escutcheon.

Metal stall rusted out. If hole is small, clean surface with steel wool and apply plastic steel. If hole is large, clean the surface and apply a thin layer of auto-body solder or plastic steel. Immediately embed in this a patch of wire screen cloth and cover it at once with more body solder. When solder dries, spread on still more to form a smooth surface. Let dry. Then file and sand smooth.

Ceramic tile cracked, broken, missing. See tile, ceramic.

Sliding doors stiff. Clean tracks with a toothbrush and detergent. Drop in a little light oil.

Drain clogged. See drains, plumbing.

SHUTTER

Sagging. Remove loose screws from hinges and fill holes with plastic wood. Then reset screws and draw all screws up tight.

Rotting along top edge. Dig out soft wood and saturate the entire top of the shutter with pentachlorophenol wood preservative. When this has dried, fill holes with plastic wood. To protect against further rotting, tack a strip of aluminum flashing over top of shutter.

Adjustable louver broken. Try to glue pieces together with Elmer's waterproof glue and tack a strip of aluminum to the back of the louver for extra reinforcement.

If louver is beyond repair, remove it and make a new one. After you have shaped the wood pivots on the ends, cut a U-shaped slot about 1″ long and the width of the pivot into the louver at the end of one of the pivots. With this pivot removed, you can now fit the louver into the frame. Then coat the sawed-out end of the removed pivot with Elmer's waterproof glue; insert the pivot end in the frame; slide the sawed-out end into the slot in the louver and bind it in place with adhesive tape until glue dries. Final step is to secure the louver, at the middle, to the adjusting arm with small staples

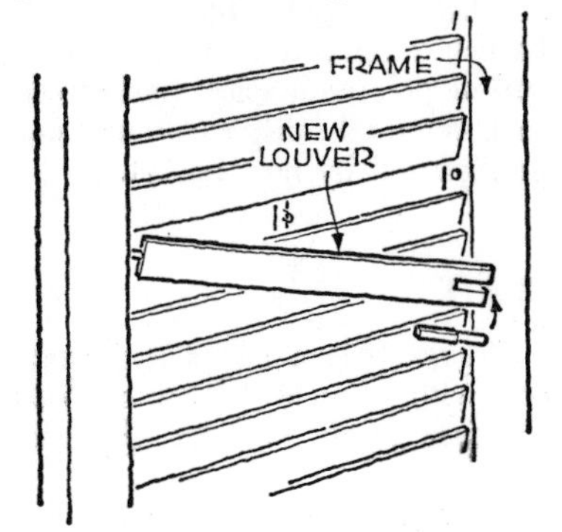

SILL, DOOR

See door, threshold.

SILL, HOUSE

Rotting. If rot has not progressed too far, chisel out the soft wood. Brush pentachlorophenol wood preservative into the holes and over the surrounding wood. Apply at least two coats. Then fill holes with plastic wood.

If rot has progressed so far that sill must be replaced, the entire rotten section should be sawed and chiseled out. Let a carpenter do this job if the cut-out piece is over 4′ long, but you can replace a shorter piece yourself. Don't worry about the wall collapsing. Just cut a new timber to size, saturate it with wood preservative, and shove it into place under the studs.

After repairing a sill, be sure to correct whatever condition caused it to rot.

SILVER

Note. Whether you want to repair silver or let an expert do it depends on how much you value the piece. You can do the job, but without a professional's tools and experience, you may not produce a good-looking result.

Small holes. Clean metal. Apply acid flux. Solder with solid-core solder.

Joints broken between metal pieces. Clean metal and flux with acid. Clamp joints together. Heat metal with tip of soldering iron and melt solid-core solder on surface.

Dents. Try to bend out with your fingers. Otherwise, let a jeweler work on them.

Silver separated from other materials, such as plastics, felt, etc. See household decorative accessories.

Silverplate off, base metal exposed. Have it replated by a jeweler. In the future, don't wash plated silver in a dishwasher. Never clean it with a dip cleaner.

Tarnished. Rub on silver polish (paste or liquid) with a soft cloth. Use a toothbrush to get into crevices. Rinse in hot soapsuds and dry.

SINK, KITCHEN

Porcelain chipped. See bathroom fixtures.

Stains. See bathroom fixtures.

Drain clogged. See drains.

Faucet problems. See faucet.

Basket-type strainer-stopper leaks. These are very unreliable gadgets, and when they no longer can be made to seat properly in the drain opening, it is best to buy new ones.

SKATES, ICE

Blade dull, rough. Buy a skate sharpener if you do a lot of skating. Otherwise have a sports shop do the sharpening.

Problems with shoes. See shoe.

SKATES, ROLLER

Action sluggish. Take off wheels and soak in kerosene to remove dust, dirt, gummy grease in bearings. Fill bearing sleeve with vaseline and replace wheels.

SKI

Split. Apply epoxy glue to one of the split edges and clamp pieces together for 24 hours. For reinforcement you can screw a sheet of aluminum flashing over the break, but this is not really necessary.

Splintered. Splintering usually occurs along the edges of a ski. Trim out the broken wood as cleanly as possible with a knife and small chisel. Form a stick of hardwood to fill roughly into the gap. Glue in place with epoxy glue (use plenty) and let dry for 24 hours. Then trim down with a knife and sandpaper.

Holes in wood. Fill with plastic wood and sand smooth when dry.

Steel edges loose. Fill screw hole in wood with plastic wood, let dry and then set in screw. If this does not hold, fill hole again with plastic wood. Then drill a new hole through the metal and slightly into the wood. Drive in screw.

Note. If plastic-covered skis are damaged, let an expert repair them.

SKI POLE

Basket worn out, broken. Baskets are held on poles by friction. If basket is difficult to remove, coat end of pole with soap. Basket will then come off fairly easily and can be replaced by new basket.

SLATE

Broken. Clean edges and cover one with Miracle Adhesive. Press together firmly and let glue dry for 24 hours.

Loose in floor. See stone.

SLED

Stiff. Sometimes the runners are actually stiffer than they should be for easy steering. But as a rule the stiffness is traceable to the binding of the various moving metal parts. First examine the way the sled is put together, and as you move the handle back and forth, notice the points at which there is some give, or slippage, between wood and metal. Clean rust from metal at these points. Slip sandpaper between metal and wood and sand wood lightly. Rub paraffin on wood surfaces that you can reach, and squirt powdered graphite on inaccessible surfaces. Oil rivets holding metal to metal

Seat broken. The planks are screwed or nailed to the wood cross braces but may be riveted to the rear strap of the metal steering yoke. File off the rivet on the broken plank, then unscrew the rest of the plank from the frame. Replace with a new hardwood plank. If large-headed rivet like the original one is difficult to obtain, replace it with a nut and bolt. Be sure to use lock washer under nut.

Center plank attached to steering handle cracked at end. Replace plank if you wish, but it can be reinforced adequately by screwing one or two short steel mending plates across the break.

SLEEPING BAG

Holes, tears. Cut a patch out of matching fabric, coat lightly with Devcon Patch and smooth over hole.

SLIDING BOARD

See gym, children's outdoor.

SLIPCOVER

Cording worn. Rip seam, remove cording and rip off covering. Cut matching or contrasting material on the bias into 1½″ strips. Fold these around cord and stitch. Then sew covered cord into slipcover seam.

Other problems. See clothing—fabrics.

SLIPPERS

Inner sole loose. Coat with Devcon Patch glue and smooth down.

Bow off. Staple in place with an office stapler. If it is impossible to get the stapler into the slipper, coat back of bow and top of slipper with Pliobond cement. When this is tacky, press bow in place for 15 minutes or more.

Pompon off. Apply Devcon Patch glue to the back and press down.

Patch of fur torn from furry slippers. Glue down with Devcon Patch glue.

Problems with leather slippers. See shoes.

SNAP FASTENER

Won't hold. With pliers, slightly flatten the prong on the male side of the fastener.

Won't close. Squeeze sides of the prong on the male side.

Note. In the long run you'll be better off to replace defective fasteners. Inexpensive kits of fasteners and the tools used to install the non-sew-on type are available.

SNEAKERS

See shoes, tennis.

SNOW SHOVEL

Handle strap loose from back of shovel. Bend strap and blade of shovel into line. Remove loose rivets by filing off the heads. Then set in new aluminum rivets.

Edge of blade bent, cut. File with a metal file.

SNOW THROWER

See lawn mower, power. The machines are essentially the same. But remember that snow throwers get wet when you use them and must therefore be dried off thoroughly to prevent corrosion and resultant malfunction or breakdown. Spraying frequently with a silicone spray of the type used to keep ovens from becoming dirty will help to shed water besides making movement through snow easier.

SOAP DISH

See bathroom accessories.

SOLDERING IRON

Tip pitted. Smooth tip with a fine metal file; then apply flux to surface and melt solder on it.

Tip worn out. Most tips can be unscrewed. Then all you do is screw in a replacement tip. However, if tip refuses to turn, do not try to force it. Let serviceman make repair.

Electric iron won't heat. Heater has burned out. If you have manufacturer's instruction sheet, disassemble iron according to directions and put in a replacement heater. Otherwise, give iron to an expert for repairs.

SPRING, COILED (as in door springs)

End broken off. With pliers firmly grasp the top coil at a distance from the end equal to a full turn of the coil. Hold spring below this point with another pair of pliers. Bend top coil sharply upward. Form new loop that will hook into the screw eye or whatever the spring was attached to.

Coils misshapen. All you can do is pinch them together with pliers.

Not springy enough. Lengthen slightly by stretching.

STAINLESS STEEL

Dents. If you can get at the back of the metal, hammer out dent—preferably with a hard-rubber mallet. Work from edges of dent toward the center.

Seams cracked, open. Clean well. Close seam and resolder. Use special flux and solder recommended for stainless steel. For how to solder, see Basic Methods: How to Solder Metal.

Steel bent. Hammering is difficult because stainless steel is very strong and resilent. Try to squeeze out bend in a vise. Or place one end of the steel piece in a vise and bend the other end by hand.

Scratched. Rub with very fine emery cloth.

Separated from another material. See household decorative accessories. If you use screws or bolts, be sure they are of stainless steel.

STAIRS

Risers deeply scarred. This happens if treads are unusually shallow. For a temporary repair, fill scars with plastic wood. For a more permanent repair, cover the risers with some material that will not scar so badly as wood: tempered hardboard, vinyl flooring, linoleum, laminated plastic. Glue to risers with appropriate glue.

Treads badly worn. Call in a carpenter.

Balusters loose. If balusters are set into treads, gently loosen them from the handrail, pull out of treads and glue with Weldwood plastic resin glue. If balusters are nailed to top of treads, drill small holes diagonally through them into the treads and then anchor with finishing nails. Fasten loose balusters to the handrail with glue.

Newel post wobbly. Additional nails and glue should strengthen it. Or screw to bottom tread with iron angles.

Stairs creak, squeak. If you can get under them, drive thin wedges (shingles) between risers and treads and into grooves of stringer. Otherwise, nail treads to risers with cement-coated finishing nails and squirt powdered graphite into other joints. (But note that graphite is messy and the treatment doesn't last forever.)

STEAM IRON, ELECTRIC

Doesn't steam. Ports are clogged. Treat with a prepared steam-iron cleaner available from housewares store, but don't expect miracles. If it doesn't work, take iron to a service shop. And henceforth use only distilled water in iron.

Doesn't heat. See iron, electric.

STEEL

Dented. If you can get at back of metal, hammer out the dent. If this is impossible, clean surface with steel wool and fill dent with plastic steel. Sand smooth when dry.

Rusted, pitted. Clean with steel wool and apply paste or liquid rust-remover. Fill pits with plastic steel. Prime with rust-inhibiting paint and apply finish paint.

Small holes. Steel-wool area around hole and edges of hole. Fill with plastic steel.

Large holes. Cut a patch that overlaps hole about ½″ on all sides. Hold in place over hole and drill a series of holes through both pieces of metal. Insert steel rivets, cut off all but about ⅛″ of ends and hammer the ends down. If hole is to be made leakproof, spread plastic steel between metal surfaces before riveting. The plastic steel alone will hold the patch in place only if the steel is not subjected to any strain.

Another way to patch holes, large or small, is by soldering. See Basic Methods: How to Solder Metal.

Steel broken. If no strain is put on broken piece, you can solder pieces together or glue with epoxy glue. But if break is under strain, have the steel welded.

Seams open. Rivet together. Or clean thoroughly and solder.

Steel bent. Depending on the thickness of the metal, you may be able to hammer out the bend. Hit sharply but do not pound. An easier method is to bend the metal in a vise.

Steel separated from other materials. Screw, bolt, or rivet them together. Or use glue (see household decorative accessories).

Joints broken in a steel wire grill (as in charcoal grills, bicycle baskets, etc.). Clean wires with steel wool. Bring them together and, if necessary, clamp with a C-clamp or with a loop of light wire. Heat with a soldering iron or torch and apply solder.

STEPLADDER

Note. Don't break your neck because of a patched-up job. Make repairs properly.

Ladder wobbly. The rivets holding the side rails to the iron angles under the top step are undoubtedly loose. Remove them by filing off the heads and replace with bolts. Brace the iron angles, if necessary, by screwing wood blocks to the bottom of the step and tight against the iron angles.

Also replace rivets or screws holding the spreader to the rails with bolts. Tighten cross braces, if any, on the back of the ladder.

Step of wood ladder broken. Loosen nut which holds the steel tie rod under the step. Cut step in two and carefully pull pieces out of mortises in side rails. If they resist, split the pieces into narrow strips. Remove nails holding the step. Cut new step out of clear white pine. Coat ends with Weldwood plastic resin glue and spread glue in the mortises. Set the step into the rails and secure with a couple of small finishing nails. Tighten tie rod.

Rail of wood ladder broken. Out of clear white pine cut a splint that overlaps both ends of the break at least 24″. Spread epoxy glue on broken edges of rail and press them together. Then screw splint to outside of rail.

Aluminum ladder comes apart. Put it back together again with aluminum — not steel — nuts and bolts. That's all there is to it.

STEPS, BRICK

Bricks broken, loose. See brick.

Iron railings loose. See porch, masonry.

STEPS, CONCRETE

For cracks, holes, roughness, see concrete.

Edges chipped, broken. Clean thoroughly. Coat edge with latex liquid that comes with latex cement. Mix latex cement to thick consistency and trowel on step. Shape properly and hold in place with boards if necessary.

Iron railings loose. See porch, masonry.

STEPS, STONE

Stones loose. See stone.

Iron railings loose. See porch, masonry.

STEPS, WOOD

Treads split, broken, weak. Replace with new boards which have been saturated with pentachlorophenol wood preservative.

Steps sagging. If they have simply pulled loose from a porch, renail them with spikes and then screw iron angles to the stringers and the porch. If the posts under the stringers have rotted out, replace with new posts saturated with pentachlorophenol wood preservative.

If the stringers are cracked or rotting, take the steps apart carefully and use the pieces as patterns for new steps. The new steps should be built, if possible, out of wood that has been pressure-treated at the mill with preservative. Otherwise, brush two coats of preservative on all boards and timbers after they have been cut to shape. Don't let bottoms of stringers touch the ground or rest directly on flat paving; raise them about 2″ on bricks or concrete so they will be above standing water and moisture and not so easily attacked by termites.

STONE

Mortar joints around stones cracked or eroding. Chip out bad mortar. Blow out crumbs with vacuum cleaner. Fill with mortar made of 1 part cement and 3 parts sand. Trowel to match surrounding joints.

Stone broken, chipped. Where it is impossible or inadvisable to use concrete mortar (as in the case of a statue), dry broken surfaces thoroughly. Spread Miracle Adhesive on one and press surfaces together firmly for at least 24 hours.

Stone ornament separated from some other material. See household decorative accessories.

Stains, efflorescence on stone. See brick.

Smoke stains. See fireplace, masonry.

STONE WALL

Collapsed. Lift off stones that have been dislodged, and rebuild. Set largest stones at the base of the wall. Arrange all stones so that joints are staggered. Support teetering stones with stone chips.

Heaved by frost. Take down broken section of wall. Dig a trench about 18″ deep under wall and fill it half way with rubble. Tamp well. This should provide the drainage necessary to prevent heaving.

STONEWARE

See earthenware.

STORM WINDOW

Pane broken. See window pane.

Adjusting arms stiff. They're undoubtedly rusted. Clean with emery cloth and apply oil.

Loose in frame, leaks cold air. Apply rubber weather stripping which has a flat nailing flange and a fat, round edge. Tack flange to edge of sash so that when sash is closed the round edge of the strip presses tight against the crack between the sash and the frame.

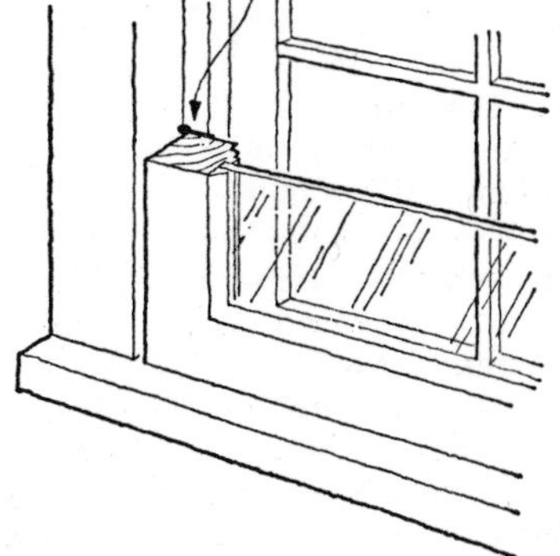

STOVE

See range, electric; or range, gas.

STRAW, WOVEN

Weave broken. Coat broken ends of straw and body of weave with a little Elmer's Glue-All. Cover glued surface with wax paper. Then clamp the break between boards. If necessary, break can be reinforced on the wrong side of the straw with cloth coated with Elmer's Glue-All.

Holes. Leave ends of broken straws jagged: they will be less obvious than if you cut them off cleanly. Cut a patch out of matching straw, coat edges with Elmer's Glue-All and paste under the hole. Cover both sides of straw with wax paper and clamp patch between boards.

A better-looking mend is made by weaving in new straw, but this is possible only on simple, coarse weaves like those used in old farm hats.

STUCCO

See exterior wall, stucco.

STUFFED ANIMAL

Seams split. Resew edges with tiny overcasting stitches.

Losing its stuffing. Coarse wool or shreddings from an old fiber rug cushion makes the best stuffing. Cram in tightly and then restitch the torn seam.

Glass eye loose or off. First try looping a small hairpin through the eyelet in the back of the eye. Pinch the bend in the hairpin closed. Put a dab of Duco cement on the back of the eye and on the hairpin wires. Stick hairpin all the way into the head. Give the cement an hour or two to dry before testing whether eye is secure. If it comes loose, remove the hairpin. Thread a needle with heavy cotton thread and poke it through from the back of the head to the eye socket. Run thread through the eyelet in the back of the eye. Then poke needle back through the head to the point you started from. Pull eye up close to the head, squeeze the head slightly, and tie a square knot in the ends of the thread so that when you release pressure on the head, the thread will be tight.

STYROFOAM

Broken. Glue pieces together with Elmer's Glue-All. This is not a very sturdy repair but will hold if you don't put strain on the joint.

Holes. Break off a piece from a scrap of styrofoam. Fill hole with Elmer's Glue-All. Press scrap into it. When glue is dry, shape the scrap with a knife.

STYRON

See plastics—general. See also interior wall, plastic tile.

SUEDE

Holes, tears. If a hole, trim it out neatly. If a tear, bring edges together neatly. Sew a patch of matching suede under the opening. If the garment is old and will not be dry cleaned, patch can be glued on with rubber cement. (Glue is dissolved by dry cleaning.)

Stains. Take garment to dry cleaner; even he probably cannot remove the stains, but he can conceal them by spray-dyeing.

SUITCASE

Leather slashed. Lift edges, spread Elmer's Glue-All underneath and smooth down.

Fabric slashed. Spread Devcon Patch glue underneath and smooth down.

Plastic slashed. Glue down with plastic-mending adhesive or patch with matching plastic and the adhesive.

Fabric of lightweight, unreinforced bag cut. Cover cut on the inside with adhesive-backed mending tape, or cut a patch out of lightweight canvas with pinking shears, coat with Devcon Patch glue and smooth over back of tear.

Leather on handle worn, torn. Sew down loose flaps of leather if possible. Otherwise, glue in place with Pliobond cement. If wire hooks in ends of handle are loose, bind lightweight wire tightly around them and glue leather over them.

Leather edge bindings worn, torn. Cut out worn spot. Apply a little Pliobond cement under ends of remaining bindings. Out of matching leather, cut a new binding to fit. Apply Pliobond cement to back of patch and to edge of suitcase. Let dry until tacky, then press binding in place.

Leather scuffed. Trim off little flaps of leather with scissors. Rub scuffed area vigorously with palm of hand. Then apply appropriate polish.

Lining loose. Paste back in place with Devcon Patch glue.

Travel labels loose, worn. Place a sponge dampened in warm water on top and weight down. Peel label off when it loosens.

SUMP PUMP

Doesn't go on. Check: Has fuse on house circuit blown? If basement is flooded and fuse box is down there, don't go near it until you shut off the house current at the meter. Is there trouble in the motor? See motor, electric. Did float fail to rise with the water level in the sump? Clean the rod on which it is mounted with steel wool and coat lightly with grease. If this doesn't correct the problem, float may have a hole in it and be waterlogged. Remove, empty, and solder hole, or cover with plastic steel; or buy a new float.

Motor working but pump not pumping. Check whether sump is filled with muck and pump intake is clogged. If these are okay, call a serviceman.

Note. Don't fool around in a sump without first turning off the electricity to the motor.

SWIMMING POOL

For problems with the pool itself see pool, concrete; pool, fiberglass; pool, plastic; pool, rubber; pool, steel.

SWIMMING POOL PUMP AND FILTER

Note. Follow manufacturer's directions for maintaining and adjusting the pool pumping system. Have pool contractor go over system every spring and call him if you have trouble—but before doing this, check and correct the following points.

Pump not working. Check whether fuse has blown.

Pump works but doesn't pump water. Stop motor and check whether it has lost its prime. If so, fill strainer with water, put on lid, and restart motor.

Pump labors, does not deliver enough water. Take out strainer, empty, and rinse. Replace in pump, fill with water, tighten lid, and start motor.

Filters clogged. Sand filters are cleaned by backwashing; earth filters by hand. Follow maker's directions.

SWING, PORCH

Creaks, squeaks. There is little you can do to stop creaking permanently. Remove rust on chains or springs with emery cloth, steel wool, and liquid rust-remover. Apply a light coating of car grease if clothing will not touch it. Otherwise keep lightly coated with oil.

Holes, tears in cushions. See cushion, bench.

Enameled steel rusted. Clean thoroughly with steel wool. Apply rust-inhibiting paint. Then apply trim and shutter paint.

SYRINGE, RUBBER

Collapses when pinched, slow to suck up water. Coat joint between nozzle and bulb with plastic rubber. If bulb is thin and cracked in one spot, spread thin layer of plastic rubber over it. If there is an actual hole, cut a patch out of rubber, roughen back and the area around the hole with sandpaper, brush rubber cement on both surfaces. When dry, apply another coat of cement to patch and press down.

TELESCOPING TUBES (as in an indoor TV antenna, camera tripod)

Jammed. If the metal has been dented, try to straighten the dent by inserting a metal rod, heavy wire or wood dowel up inside the tube. Or you can try to squeeze out the dent with pliers wrapped with adhesive tape to prevent scarring of the metal. But either job is very difficult and success is highly uncertain.

If the tubes are jammed by corrosion, saturate the joints with Liquid Wrench penetrating oil.

Bent. If you want the tubes to telescope, your only hope is to work out the bend by inserting a metal rod, etc., as above.

TELEVISION ANTENNA

Antenna leaning, loose at mounting. If antenna is mounted on chimney, tighten metal straps holding it. If one of these is broken, replace it with a new strap or with baling wire.

If antenna is clamped to wood siding, a window, or the fascia board at the eaves, remove U-shaped pipe hangers and screw them to firm wood (don't count on the ability of screws to hold in plastic wood crammed into old screw holes). Install additional pipe hangers if needed.

If antenna is bolted to masonry siding, lead anchors in the wall have probably pulled out. Replace with new anchors. If these are also loose, drive in larger screws.

If antenna is mounted on roof, it should be held upright by guy wires. If you have these, check whether they have broken or come loose. If you don't have these, attach three or four to antenna pole and to large screw eyes at edges of roof.

Antenna twisted, not aimed at station. Loosen antenna pole from brackets holding it and reorient. If antenna is badly rusted, you'll probably need to saturate brackets with Liquid Wrench penetrating oil before you can turn pole. Have some one check the picture on the TV set while you are adjusting the aim.

Antenna pole bent. You'll have to take the whole thing down and bend it on the ground. Better get a serviceman, and probably a new antenna.

Antenna rods out of position. Reset the rods and tighten bolts.

Inside antenna damaged. See telescoping rods.

Lead-in wire connections at antenna broken. Strip about ½″ of insulation from the ends of the wires, scrape with a knife and twist strands together. Clean terminals with emery cloth. Wind the wires to the right around the terminals and tighten. Then wrap cellophane electrical tape around them. If wire has been hanging loose from the antenna, strap it to pole with several strips of electrical tape.

Lead-in wire supports loose. Reset the supports in a sound surface if very loose and fill the old holes. If only slightly loose, straighten them and pack mastic into the holes around them. Use asphalt roofing compound for supports nailed or screwed into roof; caulking compound for those in siding.

Lead-in wire broken. It is best to have this replaced, but it can be spliced. Cut out broken wires, strip back insulation for a distance of about ½″ on opposing wires. Twist these together, solder, and wrap with cellophane electrical tape. See electric cord.

TELEVISION RECEIVER

Note. Don't under any circumstances try to repair a TV set. However, before calling a serviceman, there may be several points you can check and correct.

Picture has lines across it, sound is wrong. Check whether antenna lead-in is tight at terminals in back of receiver. Look for breaks in the lead-in wire, especially where it may be mashed under a door or window. Broken wires can be cut out and ends of sound wires twisted together and soldered (see electric cord).

Picture jitters, fades; sound noisy. Check electric cord and plug for a break. Repair as in electric cord.

Ghosts or shadows in picture. Check whether antenna is twisted and not aimed at station.

Picture too short. With a screwdriver, adjust the "vertical" and "height" screws on the back of the set. First mark their present positions with pencil lines, then turn right or left, keeping track of number of turns. You can do this safely while set is on.

Picture too narrow. With a screwdriver adjust the "horizontal" screw on the back of the set.

Tuning knobs loose. Tighten set screw if there is one. If not, see radio.

Wood cabinet damaged. See wood.

TENITE

See plastics—general.

TENT

Beckets (peg loops) frayed or torn loose. You can replace them with new loops made out of canvas, but they'll probably come apart quickly, too. Buy heavy belt-webbing and cut to proper length. Punch a small hole near each end. Make corresponding holes in bottom seam of tent. Insert a metal rivet through a small washer and then through the webbing and the tent seam. Place another washer over the shank. Then hammer down end of shank. The loop should be formed so that the two rivets are about 3″ apart.

Holes, tears. Dry tent. Cut patch out of matching material and glue down with Devcon Patch.

Tent leaks, though no holes are

to be seen. Erect tent in a warm place and let it dry. Brush or spray on prepared waterproofing compound available from camping supply store.

Window netting torn. Sew torn edges together with overcasting stitch.

Holes in window netting. Cut edges cleanly. Out of matching netting cut a patch at least 2″ larger in all directions than the hole. Coat patch heavily with Devcon Patch and place over hole. Press between wax paper and two boards.

Seams split. Stitch seam together on one side with running stitches. Use heavy cotton thread coated with beeswax. Then spread a thin layer of Devcon Patch glue in seam and, before this dries, stitch along other side.

Holes in floor. Make sure floor is dry, then cut a patch out of matching material, coat with Devcon Patch glue and paste over hole. If tent pole is the cause of the hole, paste down two or three layers of canvas under the pole; or after patching the hole with fabric, paste a piece of tire tube over it with Pliobond cement.

Umbrella tent spreader arms slide down pole. If pole is too slick or thumb screw too small to hold arms, drill a hole through the pole at the right height and stick a blunted nail through it every time the tent is raised.

TERMITE SHIELD

Joints open. Crimp metal together. Solder if possible. If not, seal with asphalt roofing cement.

Holes. Clean metal with steel wool and cover holes with plastic steel.

TERRA COTTA

Broken. Clean edges thoroughly and make sure they are dry. If appearance is important, coat both edges with epoxy glue and press together for 24 hours. If appearance is not too important, spread Miracle Adhesive on one edge and press pieces together firmly. Let adhesive set overnight.

Terra-cotta ornament rough on bottom, scratches surface on which it stands. Out of felt or cork cut a covering for the bottom. Apply Pliobond cement to one side of covering and let it dry. Then apply cement to covering and to bottom of object. Let dry until tacky and smooth covering down.

TERRACE, BRICK

If bricks are set in mortar, see brick.

If bricks are set in sand, see walk, brick.

TERRACE, CONCRETE

See floor, concrete.

TERRACE, STONE

See walk, stone.

TEXTOLITE

See plastics—laminated.

THERMOS BOTTLE

Liner broken. Buy replacement liner and follow manufacturer's directions for installing.

Plastic cup broken. Wash in water and dry thoroughly. Coat broken edges with plastic-mending adhesive and press together for 24 hours.

TILE, CERAMIC

Broken. If tile is loose (used as a hot mat, for example), coat broken edges with Duco cement. Let dry. Apply a second coat to one edge and press pieces together until cement sets. If tile is fixed (as in a wall, floor or table top), you may be able to conceal break with porcelain glaze. Otherwise, chip the tile out and replace it as below.

Loose or missing from wall, floor, table, etc. Remove tile. Chip out mortar joints. Clean mortar base if cement, or remove it entirely if an adhesive. Coat back of tile with Miracle Adhesive (Type M if tile is exposed to moisture) and press it into center of hole. (To hold a wall tile in a centered position, insert toothpicks around the edges.) Let the adhesive set for 24 hours or more. Then soak joints with water, remove excess from the bottoms of joints and fill joints with a commercial grout or a grout of white cement. Remove excess cement with a damp cloth.

Ornamental tile separated from some other material. See household decorative accessories.

Rust stains on tile. Rub with commercial rust-remover sold at hardware store. If this doesn't do the trick, wash with a solution of 1 part hydrochloric acid to 20 parts water and rinse immediately with clear water.

Grease stains. Wash with washing soda and let the solution stand on the stain for an hour. Then rinse thoroughly.

Nail polish on tile. Wipe off with nail-polish remover.

Tile joints stained. Scrub with a household detergent. Lingering discoloration can be removed with a scouring powder.

TILE, HOLLOW

Broken. Clean edges and dry. Apply Miracle Adhesive to one and press the pieces together firmly for 24 hours.

Tiles separated. Scrape off old concrete. Spread concrete (1 part cement to 3 parts sand) on edges of bottom tile. Press next tile into this. When concrete has set but is still workable, trim off excess. If the arrangement of the tiles permits, an easier method is to spread Miracle Adhesive on edges of bottom tile and press next tile into this.

TILE, METAL

See interior wall, plastic tile.

TILE, PLASTIC

See interior wall, plastic tile.

TIRE

Tube punctured. If hole is not visible, inflate tube and place it in a tub of deep water. Bubbles will show location of leak. Use a tire-tube patching kit. With the top of a can, roughen the rubber around the puncture. Apply rubber cement evenly to tube and let dry to tackiness. Apply a second coat of cement in same way. Remove fabric backing from patch and press on to cement. Roll flat.

Tubeless tire punctured. Use a tubeless-tire patching kit. Tire does not have to be dismounted. With pliers pull out object that punctured tire. Clean the hole with rubber plug needle (in kit) dipped in cement. Work more cement into hole with needle. Roll small end of a rubber plug that is about twice as large as the hole into needle eye. Dip plug and needle into cement and push plug into hole. Unhook needle by pulling straight out. Trim plug off ⅛″ above tread.

TOASTER, ELECTRIC

Doesn't toast. Check whether fuse on house circuit has blown. Plug a light into outlet used for toaster to see if outlet is defective. Disconnect toaster and examine cord for a break. Replace if necessary. If these measures fail, take toaster to service shop.

Toast doesn't pop up. Remove crumb tray and clean. With a vacuum cleaner blow crumbs out of inner workings. If pop-up mechanism still doesn't work, you'd better take toaster to service shop. However, you can remove outer shell by removing handles (some screws may be hidden under metal nameplates embedded in plastic handles; the nameplates are easily pried out) and unscrewing from base. Examine mechanism to see whether anything is out of place. But don't force parts.

TOBOGGAN

Bottom board broken. Unscrew the board from the cross braces and break the glue bonds. Cut the board in two immediately under one of the braces in front of the break. Angle the cut so that the front edge of the board is slanted upward toward the front of the toboggan. Cut a hickory board to the proper length and angle the back end to overlap what remains of the broken board. Glue the angled edges together with epoxy glue. Then glue and screw the old

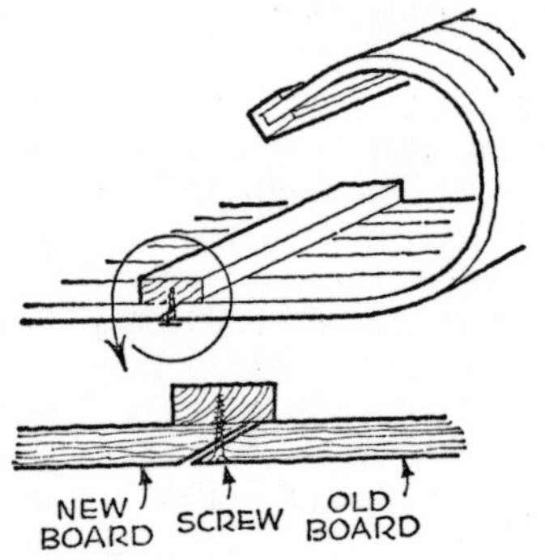

and new lengths of board to the cross braces.

TOILET

Water runs steadily into toilet. Is stopper ball dropping squarely into the outlet seat? If not, see if rod is bent and make sure the guides attached to overflow pipe are in line. If this is not the problem, replace stopper ball with a new one of the same size. Clean the edges of the outlet at the same time.

Water runs into overflow pipe. Lift the copper or plastic float ball as high as possible. If this stops the overflow, bend the float rod downward slightly to lower the

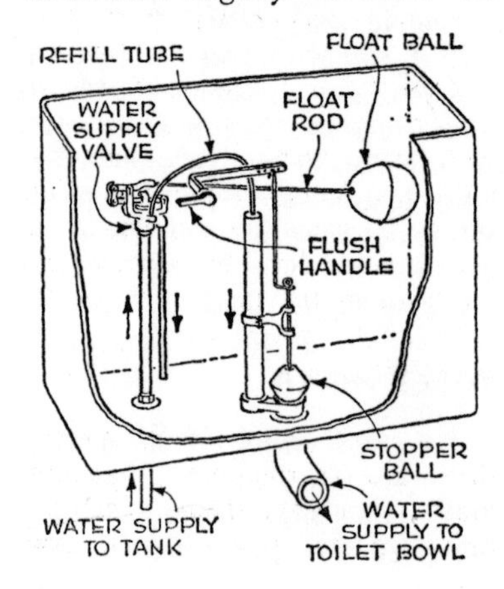

float. If overflow continues, unscrew float ball. If it is full of water, replace with a new one. If overflow still continues, release the screws that hold the float arm in place and lift out valve plunger in top of inlet pipe. Unscrew metal collar at bottom of plunger, remove the flat washer and install new one of the same size.

Tank does not fill enough. Bend float rod upward.

Drain clogged. See plumbing drains.

Tank top broken. Make sure edges are clean and dry. Coat with epoxy glue and press together.

Tank or bowl cracked. Turn off valve on inlet line and flush out all water. Then dry surface completely. Scratch crack open slightly with an ice pick. Be sure to remove all dirt. Spread epoxy glue over the crack and force it in as much as possible. Let dry 24 hours before refilling tank.

Ceramic caps covering bolts that hold toilet to floor loose or off. Clean top of bolt and cut plaster out of cap. Fill cap with patching plaster or plaster of Paris and reset it firmly over bolt.

Plastic film peeling from seat. Glue down with Elmer's Glue-All.

Tank sweats. The only way to prevent this is to fill tank by hand with warm water every time it is flushed—a laborious job. It's easier simply to catch the condensate in a pan made for the purpose and hung under the tank.

TOOLS, HAND

See axe, chisel, drill, electric drill, file (carpenter's), hammer, knife (pocket), plane (carpenter's), pliers, power tools, saw, soldering iron, wrench (pipe).

Note. The greatest enemy of all tools is rust. If it forms, rub it off with fine steel wool and then with liquid rust-remover. Wipe an oily rag over tools that are stored in a damp place.

Other common problems are broken or loose handles, dull and nicked cutting edges, clogged teeth, and stiff movement of such jointed tools as braces and wrenches. The methods for correcting these problems are obvious and generally similar to those used for the tools for which specific entries appear.

TOWEL

Edges of terry-cloth towels frayed. Trim off edges. Run two lines of machine stitches along them.

Holes, tears in terry cloth. Discard the towel or cut it into smaller towels or washcloths. Machine stitch the edges as above.

Other problems. See clothing—fabrics.

TOYS

See also ball, doll, and stuffed animal.

Note. There are so many different toys on the market that it is impossible to cover them all individually. But all are relatively easy to repair if you (1) examine the problem and the way the toy is put together; (2) have patience, and (3) follow the proper methods for fixing the different materials used. Above all, remember that the greatest problem with toys is that they are often flimsily constructed and need to be reinforced.

Plastic toys cracked, broken. Clean edges of break, apply plastic-mending adhesive and clamp together overnight. Reinforce the break with a strip of rigid plastic or wood, and glue in place with plastic-mending adhesive. Or if contours of toy prohibit use of rigid strip, try bolting aluminum flashing to back of plastic or, if worse comes to worst, glue down heavy sheet vinyl with plastic-mending adhesive.

Note. There is no adhesive that works on polyethylene, the material of which flexible plastic toys are usually made.

Plastic loose from wood or metal. Drill holes through the plastic and other material and secure with small bolts. For a neater repair, use rivets. Insert these from the plastic side and do not pound too hard on shank or you may crack the plastic.

Plastic or metal caterpillar treads come apart. Drill tiny holes through the edges of the treads that have separated. Loop fine steel wire or nylon fishing line through them and twist or tie ends together.

Dents in steel toys. If metal is thin, bend out dents with your fingers. Otherwise, hold a block of wood against the concave side of dent, and tap the other side with a hammer or wood block.

Flanged joints in steel toys broken. Toy joints are often formed by inserting a metal tab through a slot and then bending down the tab. If the tab breaks off, try cleaning the metal inside the separated pieces with steel wool, tie the pieces together with string or C-clamps, heat with a soldering iron and run in a little solder (see Basic Methods: How to Solder Metal).

If the steel pieces in the joint overlap ¼″ or more, you can, instead of soldering, drill matching holes through them and bolt together. Or drive in self-tapping screws from the outside and blunt the points with a file.

Heavy steel broken. Coat broken edges with epoxy glue and press together overnight.

Steel loose from wood. Secure with screws or, better, bolts.

Wood toys broken, split. Coat broken edges with glue and clamp together. Use Elmer's Glue-All or Weldwood plastic resin glue on toys used indoors; Elmer's waterproof glue on those used outdoors. Reinforce breaks with wiggle nails, steel mending plates (see Basic Methods: How to Fasten Wood) or by gluing on wood splints.

Joints in wood open. Pry far enough apart to scrape out old glue and spread in new glue, as above. Clamp for 24 hours. Reinforce with nails or screws.

Wood models broken. Reglue with Elmer's Glue-All or Duco cement. If gluing surfaces are very small, reinforce joint by cutting a sewing pin in two and tapping into the joint.

Tears in flexible rubber toys. Cut a patch out of a scrap piece of rubber and roughen back surface with sandpaper. Roughen area around tear. Coat both surfaces with rubber cement and let dry. Then apply a second coat of cement to patch and smooth over tear.

Hard rubber gouged, broken. Clean with gasoline and roughen with sandpaper. Spread on plastic rubber or So-Lo rubber.

Fabric in toys torn. Cut a patch out of appropriate material, coat lightly with Devcon Patch glue and paste over tear.

Wheels off toys. On such large toys as doll buggies and wagons, wheels today are held on with cap nuts which are simply hammered on. Replace missing nut with one of these or, better, drill a small hole through the axle, slip a steel washer or two on the axle, then insert a cotter pin in the hole.

On cheap small toys the axles are flattened at the ends. To make repair, push wheel back on axle, being careful not to widen the hole in the hub. Then melt a blob of solder on the end of the axle.

Wheels wobble. Pry off cap nut and slip one or more steel washers on the axle; replace wheels, and add more washers. Then replace nut or drill a hole through the axle and insert a cotter pin. The washers should fit tightly around the axle. The greater the diameter of the washers next to the wheel the better.

Steel wheels bent. You can remove these and try straightening, but it's a tough job. Try to find replacement wheels.

Wood wheels broken. Apply epoxy glue to broken edges and press together for 24 hours.

Solid or semi-pneumatic tire loose or off wheel rim. Clean tire with gasoline and roughen with sandpaper. Remove rust and dirt from wheel rim with steel wool and spread in plastic rubber. Then work tire back on rim. If rim lips are bent, hammer straight after tire is on.

TRAVERSE ROD

See curtain rod.

TRAY

Rim of gallery tray loose. If possible, clean metal and solder rim in place (see Basic Methods: How to Solder Metal). Otherwise, run a small bead of plastic steel around bottom of rim where it joins the base.

Glass in tray broken. Pry off wood or hardboard back. Replace glass. Reglue back with Elmer's Glue-All.

TRELLIS

See fence, wood. Repairs are the same.

TRICYCLE

See bicycle.

TROUSER HANGER

Trousers fall out. Stick strips of felt to inside surfaces of the wood cuff-holders with Elmer's Glue-All. If hanger still doesn't close tightly enough, bend the heavy wires inward.

Wires pull out of cuff-holders. Coat wires with epoxy glue and set into the holes in the wood.

TRUNK

Lock bent. This is very difficult to straighten but try to do so with pliers. If this doesn't work, pull away trunk lining, and file heads off rivets holding lock. Remove lock and straighten it in a vise and by hammering. Then rivet back on the trunk.

Leather handles broken. Remove trunk lining and file heads off rivets holding the end caps. Remove caps and handle. Cut heavy webbing belt to proper length and whip ends with thread. Then make a hole in both ends and rivet or bolt the webbing to the trunk. Re-rivet end caps or try sticking them down with epoxy glue.

Metal corners pulled off. Glue down with epoxy glue.

Lining torn. Stick back in place with Devcon Patch glue.

TYPEWRITER

Keys work stiffly. With a toothbrush, loosen eraser crumbs in the key slots. Then blow out crumbs and dust with a vacuum cleaner hose. Run a very little sewing machine oil into key slots and work keys.

Carriage moves sluggishly. Put a drop of light oil on either end of the rod or bar on which carriage glides. Work carriage back and forth.

Letter head on key loose. You can fix this temporarily by raising key half way and supporting it there. With a small pair of pliers, carefully position head. Be careful not to mar the letters. Hold with pliers and heat one side of head with soldering iron briefly. Remove heat but not pliers and let solder harden.

Key sticks at ribbon slot. Check on which side of slot key is binding; then bend key head slightly to other side. Often if you just wiggle key back and forth several times it will straighten out.

UMBRELLA

Tears. Cut a small matching patch and paste to underside of umbrella with Devcon Patch glue. Use as little of the glue as possible.

Fabric torn from the end of a steel bow. Resew the seam if it has ripped. Then sew the fabric to the tip of the bow. It may be advisable also to glue it to the tip. Use Pliobond cement and apply to the fabric and the tip; let dry until tacky, and then stick fabric down.

Fabric needs to be replaced. Replacement covers with instructions for applying them on the frame are available from mail-order houses. But it's easier to go to an umbrella repair shop.

Bows bent. Umbrella bows are small U-shaped strips. When bent, the sides bend inward or outward. To prevent breaking the bow as you bend it straight by hand you must also bend the sides back to their proper positions with pliers. The whole job must be done very gradually: straighten the bow a bit, then bend the sides a bit until finally the job is done.

Bows broken. Better let an expert take over. However, it is sometimes possible to join the broken pieces with a metal splint. Use a 1″ to 1½″ length of baling wire or a finishing nail and glue this into the channel in the bow with epoxy glue.

Handle loose. If this is a perennial problem, remove handle and coat hole in it with epoxy glue. Replace on shaft and let glue dry at least 24 hours.

Upper catch won't hold. Take umbrella to a repair shop.

URETHANE FOAM

Torn. Apply plastic-mending adhesive to one edge and press torn pieces together.

VACUUM CLEANER

Doesn't work. Disconnect and examine cord for a break. Check whether plug is broken. Make necessary repairs (see electric cord). If this doesn't work, take vacuum to service shop.

Suddenly stops after making rattling noise. Whatever caused the rattle (a nail or safety pin, for example) is jammed in the fan. Disconnect vacuum, disassemble enough to get at fan, and loosen it by turning. Object should fall out.

Doesn't pick up dirt. Remove threads wound around brush. Check whether outlet from machine into bag is clogged and poke out lint and dirt with a stiff wire. Check whether hose is similarly clogged and clean with a long wire.

Hole in bag. If bag is plastic, use a plastic-mending adhesive kit. Cut plastic patch so it overlaps hole about ½″. Cover one side with plastic adhesive. Stick over hole on inside of bag. If bag is cloth, cover hole on inside with adhesive-backed mending tape or press-on mending tape.

Hole in hose. If hose is plastic, seal small holes with plastic-mending adhesive. If hole is large, use plastic patch and plastic adhesive as above. If hose is covered with fabric, cut a patch out of matching material. Coat one side of patch and area around hole with Devcon Patch glue. Stick on patch and let dry before using vacuum.

Hose loose from metal tube. This is a fairly common problem with new vacuum cleaners which have hoses made out of plastic over a flexible metal coil. If plastic sleeve on end of hose is separated from the hose, coat end of hose with plastic-mending adhesive and screw into the sleeve. Let glue dry overnight. If plastic sleeve is loose from metal tube, wrap ¼″ adhesive tape around end of tube to form a ridge; then force sleeve over this.

Tubes battered at ends, won't hold together or hold on cleaning tools. Straighten ends with pliers. Check whether the metal clips that are sometimes used to secure the joints are catching properly. If these measures don't work, about the only thing you can do is bind the tubes permanently together with cellophane electrical tape or adhesive tape.

VARNISHED SURFACE

Minor scratches. Rub with the meat of a walnut or similarly oily nut, or with floor paste wax.

Larger scratches. These can be filled by rubbing with a wax stick made for use on furniture. Or you can touch up the scratches with matching oil stain applied with a small artist's brush.

The alternative is to sprinkle rottenstone, available from a paint store, on the scratch and rub with a cloth dipped in salad oil or sewing-machine oil. Work with the grain. This will take off quite a lot of the finish, and it may be necessary to refinish with oil stain. But if you haven't cut through the varnish to the wood, several applications of paste wax should pretty well hide the blemish.

Varnish rough, gummy. This may happen if the varnish is very old or has not been applied under the proper conditions. The best answer is to strip the surface with paint-remover. Steel-wool the undersurface. Then apply new varnish (see Basic Methods: How to Paint).

Water spots. First try rubbing spot with cigaret ashes and a cloth dipped in salad oil or sewing-machine oil. If this doesn't work, put spirits of camphor on a cloth and daub on spot. Let dry for about 30 minutes. Then rub on rottenstone with cloth dipped in oil. Remove residue with benzine.

Heat marks. Wipe spot with camphorated oil and then dry quickly. If surface is rough, rub with very fine steel wool. If this doesn't work, rub with rotten stone and a cloth dipped in salad oil.

Alcohol spots. Rub with rottenstone and a cloth dipped in salad oil.

Paint spots. Paint-remover will play havoc with the finish. About the only thing you can do is scrape off the paint with the point of a sharp knife. Then, if surface is damaged, rub it with rottenstone and oil as above.

Nail polish on varnish. Don't apply nail-polish remover or other lacquer thinner. Scrape off with a knife like a paint spot (see above).

Candle wax on varnish. Remove as much as possible with your fingers, then scrape off the rest with a dull table knife. Wipe residue off quickly with benzine.

Crayon or lipstick marks. Rub with Jubilee cleaning wax.

VASE

Leaking cracks. If vase is metal, clean surface with steel wool and cover crack on the inside with plastic steel. If vase is pottery or translucent glass, pour melted paraffin into it and slosh around to cover the sides as well as the bottom. If vase is clear glass, you can try coating crack on the inside with epoxy glue, but don't count too much on this.

Broken. See entry for material of which vase is made.

VELOCIPEDE

See bicycle.

VENEER

Loose. Carefully bend veneer away from its base and scrape out old glue. Apply Weldwood plastic resin glue or Elmer's waterproof glue and press veneer back in place. Cover with wax paper, then a piece of wood. Clamp or weight. Wipe off glue that oozes out from under veneer.

Broken or missing. Buy new veneer of matching wood. With very sharp knife, cut out broken veneer in a rectangle or diamond. Be sure cuts are clean and straight. Scrape out old glue. Cut new veneer to fit hole exactly. Apply Weldwood plastic resin glue or Elmer's waterproof glue and set patch in place. Cover with wax paper and weight down for 24 hours. Then sand patch level with surrounding veneer and apply matching stain.

Blistered. If wood is stiff and brittle, cover with damp rags until it becomes more flexible. Slash blister with a sharp knife, cutting with the grain. Lift edges carefully and squirt or spread Weldwood plastic resin glue or Elmer's waterproof glue underneath. Press down. If edges overlap, trim one to match the other. Wipe off excess glue, cover with wax paper and weight down.

Scratched, dented, etc. See furniture, wood.

VENETIAN BLIND

Tapes broken. Take down blind. Remove the raising cords, then slide out slats and remove the tapes (which are tacked to the top and bottom boards in wood blinds; clamped in place in metal blinds). Buy new tapes at department or variety store. Cut to right length and attach to top of blind. Then rehang blind and slide slats into tapes and attach tapes to bottom board. Knot cords at one end and slip other end up through the bottom board, the slats and top board. Then run cords over pulleys and down through the hole in which cord catch is located. Adjust tension on cords so that blind does not tilt when raised.

Wood slat broken. If break runs with grain, coat the edges with epoxy glue and press together. Then with epoxy glue stick a patch cut from thin aluminum or a tin can to the back of the slat over the joint. Clamp with C-clamps until dry.

If break is across the grain or if you don't like the patched-up repair above, loosen tapes and cords from the bottom of the blind and take out the broken slat. Replace with a new one, or if blind is too long anyway, simply shorten it by one slat.

Metal slat bent. Straighten it by hand and with pliers (cover the jaws of the pliers with adhesive tape so you don't mar the finish on the slat). If slat cannot be straightened decently, remove and replace it as above.

Cord catch doesn't hold, blind sags. Take down blind, scrape rust from catch and oil. While blind is down, clean and oil other moving parts, too.

VINYL

Tears in vinyl fabric. Bring torn edges together and overlap if possible. Coat with plastic-mending adhesive and let dry overnight.

Holes in vinyl fabric. Use plastic-mending adhesive kit, which contains a vinyl patch; or cut a patch out of matching vinyl. Clean surface around hole. Apply plastic-mending adhesive to edges of patch and press over hole.

Breaks in rigid (or reasonably rigid) vinyl. Clean edges and apply plastic-mending adhesive to one. Press pieces together overnight. If glued edges are thin, reinforce the joint by gluing a scrap of vinyl or other rigid plastic over it.

Problems with vinyl floors. See floor, vinyl.

VINYL-ASBESTOS TILE

See floor, vinyl-asbestos tile.

VULCANIZED FIBERBOARD (like that on trunks, laundry mailing boxes)

Broken. Cut a patch out of vulcanized fiberboard, roughen one side with sandpaper. Roughen area around tear. Apply epoxy glue to patch and press together.

An alternative is to cut a patch out of thin aluminum flashing, hold it back of tear and drill small holes through the two materials. Then insert aluminum rivets.

WADERS

Holes, tears. See tire (tube punctured). Clean surface and rub with sandpaper. Cut a patch out of matching material. Apply a thin coat of plastic rubber to both surfaces and smooth down the patch over the hole.

WAFFLE IRON, ELECTRIC

Doesn't heat. Check whether fuse on house circuit has blown. Plug a light into outlet used for waffle iron to see whether outlet is defective. Then disconnect waffle iron and examine cord for breaks. Replace it if necessary. If these measures fail, take iron to service shop.

WALK, BRICK

Cracks in mortar joints. See brick.

Bricks set in sand heaved, sunken or broken. Lift out brick and make new base of sand. Tamp smooth. Set in brick and fill around it with more sand. If bricks heave or sink frequently, sand base is of insufficient depth. Remove all bricks in the area, dig out soil and provide a cushion of sand or hard cinders 3″ or 4″ deep.

WALK, CONCRETE

Water stands in low spots. If walk is laid in sections, try raising the troublesome section with a crowbar and filling underneath with gravel. If water collects in middle of walk, clean surface thoroughly and trowel on latex cement. If depression is more than ⅛″ deep, apply cement in two or more coats. Note that patch will not match surrounding surface.

Crack between walk and house foundations. Scrape out crack and let dry (use a torch if necessary). Fill with asphalt roofing cement. If crack is very wide and roofing cement would be unsightly, fill crack to within 1″ of top with roofing cement and strands of manila rope. When cement has hardened, fill crack the rest of the way with mortar made of 1 part Portland cement and 3 parts sand.

Other problems. See floor, concrete.

WALK, STONE

Cracks in mortar joints between stones. Chip out broken and weak mortar with a cold chisel. Blow out crumbs with vacuum cleaner. Pack in mortar made of 1 part cement and 3 parts sand.

Stone loose. Lift it out. Chip away mortar joints around edges and chip away top of mortar bed to a depth of 1″ below old level. Clean out crumbs and dirt. Saturate mortar bed overnight with water, then let dry until no standing water remains. Brush on a soupy grout of cement. Then immediately spread on mortar bed a new layer of mortar made of 1 part cement and 3 parts sand. Set in stone and level it with surrounding surface. Fill in around edges with more mortar. Keep covered for about 48 hours with damp burlap.

Stones set in sand heaved or sunken. See walk, brick.

WALL

See exterior wall or interior wall. Also retaining wall or stone wall.

WALLET

Seams ripped. You can resew them. Or if wallet is leather, apply a thin coat of Pliobond cement to both edges. Let dry until tacky and press edges together. On plastic wallets, use plastic-mending adhesive.

Leather or plastic worn through at fold. Out of thin matching or complementary material cut a strip that will overlap the sides of the holes and will wrap over the top and bottom edges of the wallet about ¼″. Glue up and down the fold and at top and bottom on the inside with appropriate glue (see above).

Ornamental metal corners off. Coat the groove in the metal corner with Duco cement, place on corner of wallet and crimp lightly.

WALLPAPER

Loose. Lift carefully (wet with water if very stiff). Spread thin wallpaper paste underneath. Smooth down with clean, damp rag.

Blistered, bulged. Soak with water until paper is soft. Cut across blister with a very sharp razor blade. Lift edges carefully and spread thin wallpaper paste underneath. Smooth down with a clean, damp rag. If edges overlap, you can trim them or let them overlap.

Tears, holes. Tear a patch out of a leftover scrap (torn edges are less noticeable than cut edges). Smear thin wallpaper paste on the back. Position patch to match pattern and smooth down over tear.

Grease stains on non-washable paper. Make a stiff paste of dry starch and carbon tetrachloride. Spread a ½″ layer on stain and let dry. Then brush off.

Staining of non-washable paper can be prevented by covering it with a transparent protective coating available from paint or wallpaper dealer.

Stains on washable paper. Wipe off with mild soapsuds or detergent.

Crayon marks on washable paper. Remove with Jubilee cleaning wax.

WARM AIR DUCT

Leaks at joints. Make sure duct is straight. If sagging, loop wire around it, straighten and attach wire to joists overhead. Seal joints with asbestos cement.

WASHCLOTH

See towel; also clothing–fabrics.

WASHING MACHINE

Note. Call a serviceman if machine doesn't work properly, but before doing so check and correct points noted below.

Doesn't work. Check: Is it plugged in? Has fuse blown? Has a garment been thrown out of the basket? Some machines have a tendency to do this, but you can often remove the garment by disconnecting the machine, removing entire top and reaching down under basket.

Doesn't empty. Check if a garment has been thrown out of basket. See above.

Oversudses. Check: Did you use too much detergent or a new kind? Follow directions in instruction book or let suds settle and then pump out.

Water comes in cold. Probably because you've overdrawn supply elsewhere in house. But check whether inlet valves are turned on. Maybe you should move up water-heater thermostat setting. Maybe you need a larger water heater.

Clothes not clean. Check: Are you using enough detergent? Is water hot enough?

Agitator frozen on post. If you can't remove cap that holds it on, call a serviceman. Henceforth, remove cap every two weeks, lift out agitator, clean post, and apply vaseline to screw threads under cap.

Rust spots on top, especially around lid hinges. Scrape with a knife and clean with emery cloth till metal shines. Touch up with epoxy resin sold for porcelain repairs.

WASTEBASKET

Paper or fabric covering torn or loose. Glue with Elmer's Glue-All.

Leather covering torn or loose. Coat back of leather and base with Pliobond cement. Let dry and apply another coat. When this is tacky, smooth the leather down.

Top binding badly torn. Replace with binding cut from adhesive-backed mending tape.

Plastic basket cracked. Coat cracked edges with plastic-mending adhesive and clamp together for 24 hours.

Fancy perforated metal strip broken from solid metal below. This will never look the same, but you can mend the basket pretty well by sanding off paint on inside of strip and metal below it. Out of coarse metal window screen cloth cut a strip 1″ to 1½″ wide and long enough to cover the break. Spread a thin coat of plastic steel on basket and embed mesh in it. Do not add additional plastic steel unless mend seems weak when patch dries.

WATER HEATER

Leaks. See water tank.

Doesn't work. Call a serviceman. But if you have a gas water heater and the pilot light is out, you can proceed as follows: First shut off the A valve, which is the main gas valve to the burner, and the B pilot valve. Wait five minutes. Then turn on B valve and ignite with a match. Then turn on the A valve.

Note. Instructions for lighting pilot lights are printed on a tag attached to heater. Don't lose these.

Water too hot or too cold. Call a serviceman if you have a storage-type heater. If it's an indirect take-off heater, change the opening on the mixing valve.

Not delivering enough hot water. Chances are heater is clogged with scale. Call a serviceman. It may also be advisable to install a water softener.

Sediment in hot water. Open valve in side of heater and drain until water runs clear.

Rust in hot water. Either the tank is corroding or something is wrong with your main water supply. Call a serviceman.

Gas heater smells. Shut off main gas control valve at once and call a serviceman. Don't look for leaks with a lighted match.

Gas heater's flue pipe corroded, out of line. See furnace flue.

WATER PUMP

Note. It is not overly difficult to keep a water pump and pressure system which are installed in a pump house or basement operating properly if you have the manufacturer's instruction manual. But there are many repairs which call for an expert.

Doesn't operate. Check whether fuse has blown. Check whether pump can be turned by hand. Consult instruction book. If you can't get pump going, call a serviceman.

Motor slow, overheating, sparking. See motor, electric.

Pump operates but produces no water. Check whether water level in well has dropped too low. Strainer at bottom of well may be clogged. Difficulty may also be in pump itself. Call a serviceman.

Pump noisy. Check oil in crankcase; be sure it is at proper level. Check whether water level in well has dropped too low. Be sure pump pulley is tight on shaft and that belt is tight.

Pump leaks around piston rod at stuffing box. Tighten nut just enough to stop drip. If leak persists, unscrew nut and carefully dig out old packing material with a wire. Replace with new packing supplied by pump maker.

Tank waterlogged. This happens when the air cushion in the tank is too small. The result is to make the pump turn on and off frequently. If you have an automatic air control, the situation can be corrected by removing the valve core in the air valve and replacing with a new one of the same type (automobile tire valves won't work). If this doesn't do the trick, pump air through the valve into the tank with a tire pump. If trouble keeps on, call a serviceman.

If your system does not have an automatic air control, there is what looks like an ordinary tire valve on the pump. Remove the cap. If the valve core is okay, it will now suck in air as the pump operates. When proper air cushion is restored (it takes a day or so), replace cap. If the valve core doesn't suck in air, replace it with a new core. If this still doesn't work, drain the system entirely by turning off the pump, opening a valve or pipe on the outlet side of the tank to let in air, and opening the valve at the bottom of the tank to let out water. When tank is empty, close valves and refill.

Tank air-bound. When a tank has too large an air cushion water flows from the faucets in violent bursts. To remedy situation, drain system entirely as above and then refill.

WATER TANK

Leaks. Draw off water to below the hole. Clean metal thoroughly with steel wool. Force plastic steel into hole and spread out over surrounding surface. Let dry completely before refilling with water.

A slightly more reliable repair can be made with self-tapping screws and expansion bolts produced specifically for plugging holes in tanks and large pipes (but not all hardware stores carry these). To use one of the screws, simply cut a gasket about twice the size of the screw head out of a tire tube, and coat it on both sides with iron cement. Stick the screw through the center of the patch, then drive it into the hole by turning its head with a wrench. To use the special bolt, drill a ⅜" hole in the center of the leak. Insert bolt and screw up on it. As you do this, a split-metal "nut" on the bolt expands and clamps tight against the inside of the tank. A neoprene gasket under the head of the bolt simultaneously draws tight against the outside of the hole.

Air-bound or waterlogged. See water pump.

WATERING CAN

Holes in galvanized can. Remove rust from around hole with steel wool and spread on plastic steel.

Seams in copper can open. Clean thoroughly inside and out with steel wool. Bring edges together. Then apply solder (see Basic Methods: How to Solder Metal).

End of spout collapsed. Depending on the size of the spout, open it as much as possible with a screwdriver or nail. Then, to shape the opening properly, tap in a round of hardwood (such as a broomstick or dowel) which has been sharpened slightly at the end.

Sprinkler head clogged. Remove from can and scrape the inside of the head with a screwdriver. Then open the holes by inserting a stiff wire from the outside.

WEATHER STRIPPING

Metal stripping vibrates noisily when wind blows. With a putty knife bend the unattached edge of the strip outward so that it presses more tightly against the door or window.

WHEELS

See toys and bicycle.

WICKER

Broken. Coat break with Weldwood plastic resin glue or Elmer's waterproof glue. Apply glue to area around break. Cover wicker on both sides with wax paper and then clamp the broken piece between boards for 24 hours. Break can be further reinforced with wire woven through surrounding wicker.

WINDOW, AWNING

Window stiff or stuck. Lubricate operator and adjusting arms with powdered graphite and remove any paint on them. If window still works badly, you may need a new operator. Call in carpenter.

Leaks at top of window frame. See window, double-hung.

Other problems. See door. Solutions are similar.

WINDOW, CASEMENT

Window stiff. Lubricate adjusting arm and make sure it is free of paint. If window has a rotary operator, squirt powdered graphite into joint at base of handle. Then open window and squirt more graphite into back of operator and on to sliding track.

Air leaks around edges of window. If windows are metal, install rubber stripping that is slotted to fit over the edges of the frame. A flange laps over the window edges and prevents air from entering. Flexible metal weatherstripping is better but should be installed by an expert. If windows are wood, tack one edge of metal stripping to the frame and bend up the other edge so that it presses against the edges of the sash. The tacked edge should face outward for out-swinging casements so that it won't interfere with the closing of the window.

Water leaks at top or sides of window frame. See window, double-hung.

Other problems. See door.

WINDOW, DOUBLE-HUNG

Window sticks. Check whether it is painted shut. Run point of a sharp knife carefully around edge of sash. If necessary, drive a thin putty knife between sash and stop beads.

If sticking results from swelling of wood, rub paraffin or beeswax on the stiles. Or spray stiles with a dry lubricant.

If this still doesn't work, pry up stop beads and move them away from the window.

Sash cord broken or stretched. Pry off inside stop bead on one side of sash and remove lower sash. Unscrew top of pocket cover in the stile and take out sash weight. Cut off cord. Push new cord over pulley at top of window frame and run it down through slot in frame. Tie it securely to sash weight, replace weight in frame and pull it up to the pulley. Set sash on window sill and pull cord down 3″ below hole in edge of sash. Knot cord at this point and wedge knot in hole. Replace window in frame and work it up and down. Adjust length of cord. Then replace pocket cover and stop bead.

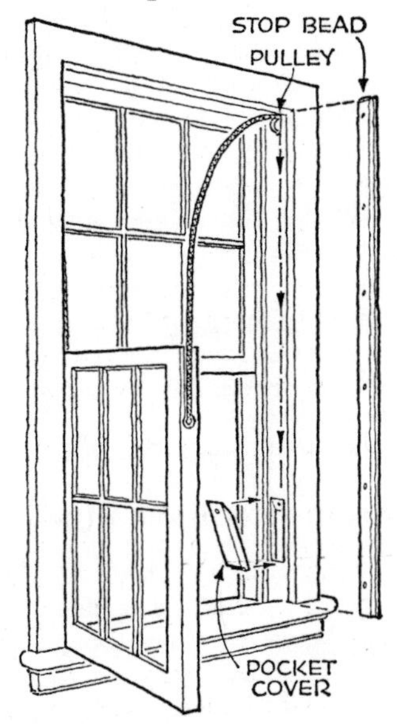

If sash cord on upper sash is broken, repair is made in same way. To remove sash it is necessary first to remove bottom sash as above and then to pry up the parting strip between the two sashes.

Note. Sash chain can be used instead of cord. It won't stretch.

Air leaks around edges of window. Install weather stripping. Metal stripping is best and also permanent, but installation is difficult. Installation of rubber or felt stripping, on the other hand, is simple. Just nail to the frame so that the edge presses firmly against the sash. Use aluminum nails spaced every 2″. The strips go on the inside of the bottom sash, outside of the top sash.

Water leaks at sides of window frame. Squeeze caulking compound into the cracks and smooth down flush with the siding.

Water leaks at top of window frame. Clean out old caulking compound between window frame and siding. Force in new compound. If siding is of any material other than masonry and if window is not flashed, cut a strip of aluminum or copper flashing 4″ longer than width of window. Center over window frame and force it up under siding as far as possible. Bend

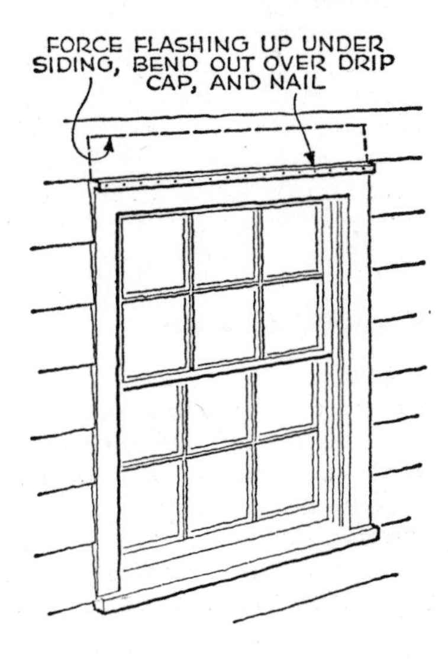

metal at base of siding and then bend down over top of window frame. Nail to the front of the frame.

WINDOW, JALOUSIE

Air, water enter through louvers. Despite manufacturers' claims, this is inevitable. There is nothing you can do that will not spoil appearance of window. But check whether hinges are working properly and allow louvers to close all the way.

Stiff. Clean crank and closing mechanism on sides. Apply light oil and work louvers up and down.

WINDOW, SLIDING

Window sticks. Check whether it is painted shut. Run point of sharp knife around edge of sash to break paint film. Rub stiles with paraffin or beeswax or spray them with dry lubricant.

Leaks at top or sides of window frame. See window, double-hung.

WINDOW BOX

Holes in metal box. With steel wool clean metal until it is bright. Then cover hole with plastic steel. To prevent recurrence of rusting, coat inside of box with liquid neoprene or asphalt roofing cement. To make sure drainage is adequate, drill additional holes in bottom.

Wood rotting. See plant tub.

WINDOW PANE

Broken. Crack out glass. Carefully cut out old putty. All of it must be removed so that wood is bare. Then coat wood lightly with linseed oil or lead and oil paint so that putty will stick. Have new pane cut 1/16" to 1/8" narrower and shorter than opening. Spread a thin bed of putty evenly on the rabbets. Press pane firmly into place and tap in glazier's points around the edges. Space points about 4" apart. Spread thick layer of putty on rabbets with a putty knife. Then hold knife at an angle against the glass and the outside edge of the rabbet, and press putty into place with a smooth, even stroke that starts at one corner of the opening and runs to the next. Let putty dry several days before painting.

Broken panes in metal windows are handled the same way. But the glass is held in place by special wire clips instead of glazier's points and special glazing compound available from hardware store is used instead of putty.

Bullet holes in windows. There is no remedy but until pane is replaced you can keep out air by gradually filling hole with Duco cement.

WINDOW SHADE

Won't wind up properly. Pull shade down two-thirds. Remove roller from brackets and roll up shade by hand. Replace roller in brackets. Shade should now roll up properly, but if it doesn't, repeat process.

Snaps up violently when raised. Raise shade to top. Remove roller from brackets. Unroll shade by hand half its length. Replace in brackets. Repeat procedure if shade is still too tight.

Won't catch when rolled down. Remove roller from brackets. Clean and oil ratchets on the flat rotating pin.

Roller falls out of brackets. Remove bracket from one side of window and move it in toward window a fraction of an inch. If brackets are mounted inside the window frame, insert cardboard or wood shims underneath one of the brackets.

Fabric torn. Cover tear with adhesive-backed cloth mending tape.

Bindings broken on bamboo or split wood shades. Unroll shade on floor and remove broken bindings. Cut a new cotton cord about three times the length of the shade and fold it in two equal lengths. Loop it around bottom wood strip and tie with a square knot; then loop it around next strip and tie, and so on to the top of the shade.

WOOD

Finish marred. See lacquered surface, painted surface, shellacked surface, varnished surface, as case may be.

Burns, dents. See furniture, wood.

Holes in painted wood. If there is backing behind the wood (as in house siding, for example), brush linseed oil into hole and fill with putty. Paint when surface is hard. If there is not backing behind the wood (as in a box), tack a scrap of thin aluminum behind the hole and fill with putty as above. Or for a neater repair, cut the hole to a geometrical shape with a coping saw. Be sure sides of hole are straight. Then cut a plug of wood to fit, and glue it into the hole with Weldwood plastic resin glue or Elmer's waterproof glue.

Holes in stained wood. Treat as above, but use plastic wood instead of putty. Mix the wood with stain before applying it; it will not take stain when it dries.

Gouges in painted wood. If the gouge has paint in it, fill with spackle, sand smooth when dry, and apply paint. If the gouge does not have paint in it, brush linseed oil on the bare wood and fill gouge with putty. Paint when surface hardens.

Gouges in stained wood. Mix matching stain into plastic wood, smooth into gouge and sand when dry. Stick shellac can be used as an alternative (see furniture, wood). For a neater repair, whittle a strip of matching wood to fit in the hole. Soak it in stain matching the damaged wood and let dry overnight. Then glue it into gouge with Weldwood plastic resin glue or Elmer's waterproof glue. Let excess glue fill cracks around the patch. When glue dries, sand the patch smooth.

Wood split. Coat edges of split with Weldwood plastic resin glue or Elmer's waterproof glue and clamp together. If necessary, reinforce with nails, screws, or wiggle nails.

If wood siding is split and edges cannot be brought together, coat the edges with linseed oil and then fill split with putty.

Wood broken across the grain. Coat edges with epoxy glue and press together firmly overnight.

Wood rotting. If rot is widespread, wood should be replaced. But if rot is just setting in, dig out the soft wood with a knife and chisel. Saturate surfaces with pentachlorophenol wood preservative (zinc or copper naphthanate can also be used). Let dry. Then fill holes with plastic wood.

Rotten wood can also be treated with Calignum (see boat, wood), but this material is quite expensive.

Knots loose. Either remove knot

and fill hole with putty or push knot out, coat edges with glue, and reset knot in the hole.

Wood warped. See furniture–table (top or leaf warped).

Joints in wood loose, broken. Rejoin with glue and/or metal fasteners.

Wood separated from another material. Refasten with screws or bolts. Or use appropriate glue (see household decorative accessories).

Sawed edges rough, soak up paint. Wrap sandpaper around a block of wood and sand edges as smooth as possible. Roughness that remains can be eliminated by spreading on plastic wood.

Stains. These are very difficult to remove because of absorbency of wood. First try wiping off the stain with turpentine or benzine. Then sand. If this doesn't work, bleach the spot with a commercial bleach according to manufacturer's directions. But don't count on the results.

WOOD BOWL

Cracked. If bowl is not used for salad, force epoxy glue into crack from both sides. If bowl is used for salad (in which case wood may be too oil soaked for glue to adhere), cut out crack in a V on the inside of the bowl and pack in plastic wood. Smooth down firmly. Then force epoxy glue into crack from the outside.

Worn, marred. Fill gouges with plastic wood after sanding them thoroughly. Obliterate scratches and general roughness by sanding.

WORLD GLOBE

Split at seam. If globe is made of cardboard, coat edges with Elmer's Glue-All and press together. Reinforce with cellophane tape if necessary. If globe is metal, bring halves together and put tiny dabs of plastic steel across the joint at three or four points.

WRENCH, PIPE

Teeth dull, rounded. Clamp wrench in a vise and deepen grooves and sharpen teeth with a small triangular metal file.

WROUGHT IRON

Joint separated. Try soldering (see Basic Methods: How to Solder Metal) but it is better to have the joint welded.

Pitted. Clean pits with steel wool and smooth in plastic steel.

Rusted. Clean with a wire brush, steel wool and liquid rust-remover. Apply a rust-inhibiting primer and finish paint.

ZIPPER

Jammed. Use Dritz zipper-repair kit available at the Five and Ten. With the tool in the kit or a screwdriver, pry open the narrow end of the jaws of the old zipper and remove it. Open new slider by holding the end of the bottom jaw and bending back the pull tab. Place open slider at the bottom of the zipper and pinch the jaws closed by bending the pull tab flat. You're in business.

Teeth of zipper missing. A few isolated missing teeth usually don't make much difference. But if several in a row are gone, rip the entire zipper from the garment and replace with a new one.

Section 2

BASIC METHODS

HOW TO FASTEN WOOD WITH NAILS, SCREWS, AND OTHER METAL FASTENERS

Nails are the easiest fasteners to use. Common nails with large flat heads are for rough work. Box nails also have large heads but are thinner and help to prevent splitting of wood. Finishing nails have small heads that are easily countersunk below the surface of the wood.

In addition to these basic nails, there are a number of others with greater holding power. Some are coated with rosin or cement; some have spiral shanks; some have ring-grooved shanks. These are used as noted in the mending section.

The worst drawback of nails is that they tend to split the wood into which they are driven. This can be prevented to some extent by blunting the points with a hammer. A much more reliable method—especially when nailing in oak or yellow pine—is to drill holes slightly smaller than the nails almost through the wood.

Screws. A screwed joint is stronger than a nailed joint and can be easily taken apart. To facilitate driving a screw, drill a hole for it first. Use flat-head screws if you want the head to be flush with the surrounding surface. (In hard wood it is usually necessary to drill a shallow hole into which the screw head can be countersunk; but in soft wood the head usually countersinks itself as you turn the screwdriver.) Oval-head screws project slightly above the surface while round-head screws are entirely exposed.

Bolts are used mainly for joining metal but may be used in wood in cases where nails or screws won't hold or if the joined wood is frequently disassembled and reassembled. To use bolts, drill a hole the size of the shank all the way through the wood. Before screwing on the nut, insert a flat metal washer to protect the wood and then a lock washer to prevent loosening of the nut.

Wiggle nails, also known as corrugated fasteners, are used for joints that are subject to little strain. Hammer them into wood slowly, with light taps; and to avoid splitting the wood, do not run them parallel with the grain.

Scotch fasteners are a substitute for wiggle nails. They are not as strong but are easier to use and less likely to split the wood.

Flat metal mending plates are known by a number of names depending on the design. Screwed to the wood, they make a strong joint but add nothing to its attractiveness.

Joints. Most of the joints used by professional carpenters are difficult to make. But there are plenty of others that you can handle. Their strength varies as noted below. But the use of glue in addition to metal fasteners will make even the weakest sturdy.

Butt joints are among the easiest to make but are not very strong. The end of the piece to be butted must be cut off perfectly square. Joining is done in the ways shown.

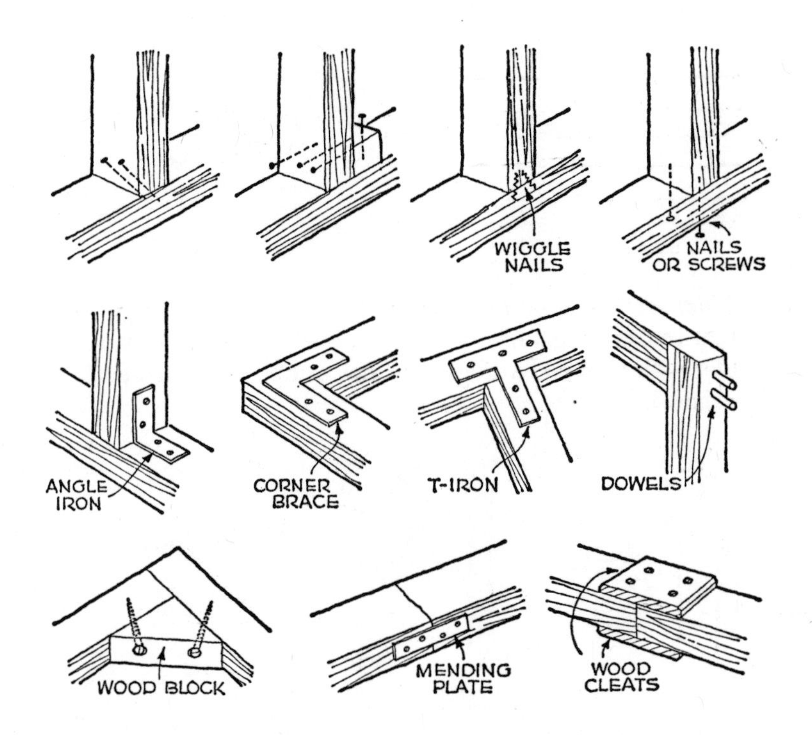

Lapped joints are another easy-to-make type. The simple laps, however, are not likely to hold too well because they depend for strength entirely on the screws or nails driven through the two pieces. Laps in which part of the wood is cut away are much stronger. (See drawings on next page.)

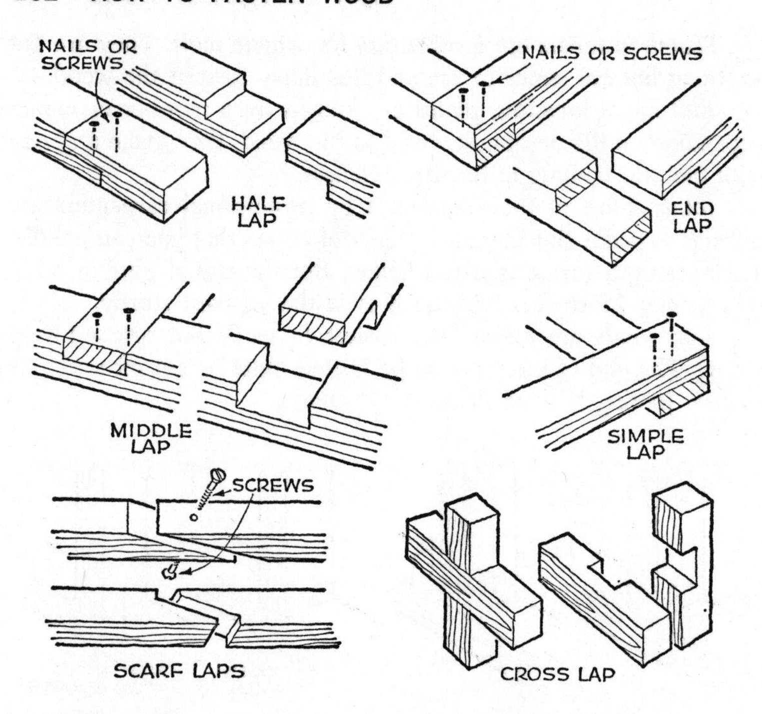

Miter joints can be made accurately only if you have a miter-box that controls the angle of the cuts. Such joints are usually held together with glue and a single nail but can be strengthened in the ways shown.

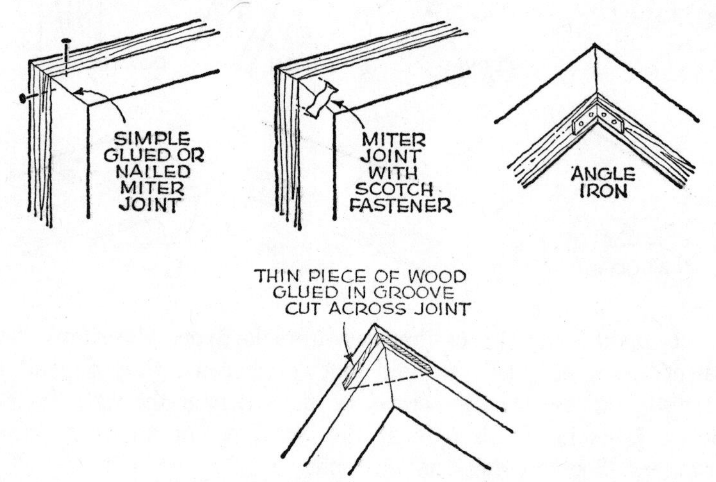

The dado joint is made with saw and chisel. Even without special fasteners it is considerably stronger than most butt joints.

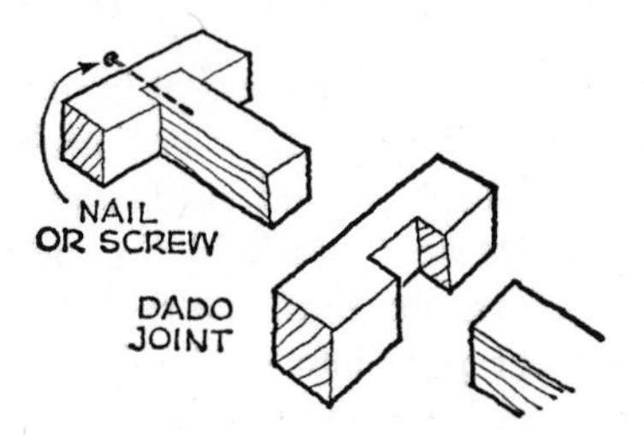

HOW TO SOLDER METAL

Soldering is an easy way to mend metals permanently. Small soldering jobs are best done with an electric soldering iron of the conventional type or of the faster gun type. Large jobs are done with a torch (a conventional gasoline blowtorch or the more convenient propane torch). The tips of soldering irons must be kept smooth, clean, and tinned (coated with a thin layer of solder). Torch tips must also be kept clean and undamaged if they are to give a steady blue flame of the proper size and shape.

Solder is a mixture of tin and lead. It is available in the form of wire, bars, or paste. Wire solder may be solid solder or contain a core of acid or rosin flux. Bar solder is solid. Paste solder comes mixed with acid flux.

Whenever solid solder is used, a flux which cleans the metal must first be applied to the metal. This is available as a liquid or paste. Rosin flux is used only in making electrical connections and on terne metal. Acid flux is used for all other work. Galvanized iron and stainless steel require especially strong acid fluxes.

Aluminum is soldered without fluxing, but a special solder called Chemalloy is required.

Here is the step-by-step procedure for soldering:

1. If the object to be soldered contains a liquid or gas, empty it completely.

2. Clean the metal with steel wool until it shines brightly.

3. Apply flux to the cleaned surface if the solder does not contain flux.

4. Heat the metal until it is hot enough to melt the solder applied to it. Except in the case of lead and pewter, the solder should always be melted by the metal being soldered—not by the soldering

iron or torch. If the metal is not heated sufficiently, the melted solder looks dull, granular, and rough. It should flow and form a smooth, bright film.

5. To join two pieces of metal (except in plumbing work), it is advisable to tin (flow a film of solder on) each piece separately. Then place tinned surface to tinned surface and apply heat until the solder melts. Remove heat and hold the metal pieces together with a screwdriver, pliers, etc. until the solder hardens.

6. To solder copper pipe into a plumbing fitting, clean both pipe and fitting and brush on an acid flux. Insert pipe into fitting and apply heat to the joint. Then touch solid solder to the joint. It will be drawn by capillarity into the joint and seal it.

7. When acid flux is used, wash off the residue thoroughly with water after the metal has cooled.

HOW TO FASTEN METAL WITH BOLTS, RIVETS, ETC.

In addition to joining pieces of metal by soldering and, to a very limited extent, by gluing, you can often do the job with the following metal fasteners:

Bolts. The most commonly used types are machine bolts, which have square or hexagonal heads that are gripped with a wrench, and stove bolts, which have rounded, slotted heads for a screwdriver. To use bolts, drill holes just slightly larger than the threaded shank. Slip on lock washers before screwing on the nuts.

Self-tapping screws are threaded right up to the head. They are used primarily to join thin sheets of metal which are exposed only on one side (for example, the back of an automatic washing machine is attached to the side flanges with self-tapping screws). To use the screws, first drill holes slightly smaller than the widest diameter of the screw threads. Then just screw into place.

Rivets. Steel, copper, and aluminum rivets are available at hardware stores in various sizes. They are used to make neat, unobtrusive, permanent joints. To use, drill through the pieces of metal to be joined a hole the size of the rivet shank. Insert the rivet and place it head down on a hard metal surface. Clip off all but about 1/8″ of the exposed shank. Then hammer down the shank with light blows so that it overlaps the hole. Do not hammer so hard that the rivet is completely flattened. It should have a rounded contour.

Cotter pins are used to hold together metal pieces which may be frequently disassembled or which move. The hole for the pin should be just slightly larger than the shank. Insert the pin and bend the two halves of the shank in opposite directions.

HOW TO GLUE THINGS TOGETHER

Gluing is about the easiest way there is to mend most things. But selecting the right glue for a given job is difficult because (1) so many different types and brands are on the market; (2) many essentially dissimilar glues can be used for the same purposes; (3) the materials of which glues are made are often not listed on the packages.

At the risk of being accused of partiality toward certain types and brands of glue, I have here attempted to simplify matters by recommending only a few basic glues and by identifying them either by their generic name (when this is commonly shown on packages) or by one specific brand name.

Epoxy glue. The newest, strongest, and most expensive of all glues, epoxies are highly resistant to moisture and temperature, can be used on porous and non-porous materials such as wood, glass, metal, plastics. As a rule, the glue comes in two tubes. To use, squeeze out equal strips of Part 1 and Part 2 on aluminum foil. Mix together thoroughly until the color is uniform. Apply a thin coat to both of the surfaces to be joined and press together for two hours or more. Clamping is not essential but makes for a neater joint. *Note:* Do not mix Part 1 of one brand of epoxy with Part 2 of another brand, or vice versa.

Weldwood plastic resin glue. A strong, moisture-resistant urea resin glue, this is primarily used on wood but can also be used on most porous and semi-porous materials of non-mineral composition. To use, pour the powder into a glass container, add a little cold water and mix to a heavy paste. Then add more water and mix to the consistency of heavy cream. Brush glue on both surfaces and clamp pieces together within a few minutes. Let dry overnight before removing clamps.

Elmer's waterproof glue. This is a waterproof resorcinol glue used on wood and other porous materials. It is particularly recommended for outdoor use. The glue comes in two parts—a liquid and a powder. Mix in the proportions recommended by the manufacturer. Add the powder to the liquid and stir well. Brush on both surfaces and clamp together overnight in a room temperature of 70°F. or higher.

Elmer's Glue-All. This is a ready-to-use, white polyvinyl resin glue that dries clear. It is used on wood, paper, cloth, and other porous materials, but will break down if soaked in water or exposed to high heat. To use, simply apply it to one surface and clamp pieces together for two hours.

Duco cement. A cellulose cement, this is excellent on china and glass, can also be used on wood and other porous materials. It cannot withstand too much contact with water and breaks down under heat. To use on non-porous materials, spread a thin coat on both surfaces and press together until the glue sets. On porous materials, apply a thin coat to both surfaces. Let dry. Then apply a second coat and press together.

Rubber cement. Rubber cement can be used on both porous and non-porous surfaces, is especially recommended when the joint is subject to flexing. It has good resistance to water. For the strongest joint, apply cement to both surfaces and let dry. Then apply a second coat to one surface and press pieces together at once.

Pliobond cement is a special type of rubber cement that adheres well to most materials but is especially useful for bonding flexible materials. Apply it to both of the surfaces to be glued, let dry until tacky and then press the surfaces together and hold under pressure for 15 minutes.

Miracle Adhesive. This is a black, waterproof glue that is used on tile, glass, metal, concrete, brick. Apply it to one surface and immediately press the two objects together with a twisting motion. Allow to set for several hours.

Plastic-mending adhesive. This is a waterproof glue that can be used on many kinds of plastics as well as on china, wood, and leather. Spread on both surfaces to be joined and clamp the pieces together overnight.

Devcon Patch glue. This is a white glue that is used on all fabrics and leather. It is water- and heat-resistant. To use, spread a thin coat on one surface, smooth pieces together and let dry.

Resilient flooring adhesives. Selection of the proper adhesive for laying linoleum, vinyl, rubber, asphalt, vinyl-asbestos, and cork depends not only on the type of resilient flooring but also on the condition and location of the subfloor. Consult your flooring dealer.

Plastic steel and *plastic aluminum.* These are better used as fillers than for joining materials. However, they do form a reasonably strong, waterproof bond between two metals. To use them, simply spread on one surface and clamp the edges to be joined for about three hours.

The rules for using glue are generally similar, no matter which one you are working with:

1. Scrape off old glue from the article to be mended.
2. Remove dirt, dust, oil, etc. from the surfaces.
3. Sand or plane wood surfaces smooth.
4. When gluing glass, china, pottery and the like, decide which glue you should use—an epoxy or Duco cement. The epoxy makes a much stronger joint and should be used if the object is to be washed and/or heated. However, if the object is not to be washed or heated, I prefer Duco cement for two reasons: First, it is easier to remove the excess from the surface, and even if it isn't removed entirely, it is not particularly noticeable because of its transparency. Second, there are many joints that are so small or so shaped that you cannot clamp them. Duco cement dries fast enough to make it feasible for you to hold the joint together by hand. Epoxy, however, takes a couple of hours to dry.
5. Apply glue in thin coats and spread it over the entire area.
6. If a patch is to be applied, round the corners of the patch slightly. They are not so likely to come loose as square corners.
7. Align surfaces to be glued and press together. In most cases, clamping is then called for. Use C-clamps where possible; they are easy to handle and apply strong pressure. But tourniquets, weights, and other methods may have to be used instead.
8. To prevent glue that squeezes out from a joint from sticking to an adjacent surface, wipe off as much as possible; then lay wax paper between the glued surface and the one you have to protect.
9. If you try to glue a tight-fitting dowel into a hole, the glue collects at the bottom of the hole and prevents the dowel from being inserted all the way. To solve this problem, flatten the dowel very slightly on one side with a plane. This permits the excess glue to be squeezed out of the hole as the dowel is driven in.
10. Remember that glue needs air to dry rapidly. So if you are gluing large flat surfaces or using glue in a small, deep hole, don't expect it to dry within a few hours. You may have to wait a couple of days before putting any strain on the joint.

HOW TO MIX AND HANDLE CONCRETE

Several types of ready-mixed concrete are available at building supply stores. These are very convenient to use although somewhat more expensive than homemade mixes. If you are not sure which type you need, tell the dealer how you plan to use it.

If you mix your own concrete, take pains to measure accurately. The proportions of the various mixes commonly used are given in the mending section.

Cement, sand, aggregate, and lime to be used must be clean and free of vegetable matter. Cement is usable as long as it can be crumbled in the hand easily. If old cement is lumpy, screen it.

Ordinary Portland cement can be used for all work. But in cases where the concrete is exposed to freezing and thawing or salt action (as on a driveway or walk) it is advisable to use cement containing an air-entraining agent. This is designated Type IA Portland cement.

Latex cement is a new kind of cement that is mixed with a chemical instead of water. It is used primarily for leveling uneven surfaces since it can be troweled on in very thin layers.

In Portland cement mortar, use coarse, sharp sand—not fine stuff that is almost dusty. Do not use sea sand unless it has been thoroughly washed in fresh water.

Coarse aggregate, when used, should include stones from 1/4" up to 1 1/2" diameter.

Mix concrete in clean containers or on a clean, flat platform of wood. Spread sand out evenly and cover it with cement. Mix until it is a uniform color. Then add lime or aggregate and mix until they are evenly distributed in the mixture.

Form a hollow in the center of the mix and add water slowly, mixing all the time. The batch should be uniformly damp—smooth, plastic, and sticky when you work it with a trowel. It should not be runny or crumbly.

The mortar must be used within a half hour. Do not add water if it becomes stiff.

In placing concrete, pack it thoroughly to eliminate voids. Slice into it with a spade, trowel, or mason's trowel and then press down and smooth off.

If a rough surface is desired on a patch, finish off the concrete

—after it has become quite stiff—with a wood float. For a smooth finish use a steel trowel.

After concrete has set, cover it with damp burlap and keep this damp and in place for two to five days.

Concrete can be used in freezing weather, but it requires special attention. Either put off your work until the temperature rises or call in a mason.

If concrete is to be colored, use dry powder pigments made for the purpose. Mix these with the cement before adding the cement to the sand and other ingredients. To determine how much pigment to use, make up sample batches. Remember that concrete will dry lighter than it looks when damp.

HOW TO MAKE BASIC SEWING STITCHES

Back stitch. This is the strongest hand stitch. Make a short, straight stitch through the fabric, double back, and start the second stitch in the middle of the first. The stitches underneath are 1/8″ to 1/4″ long; those on top, made by doubling back, are half that length.

Basting stitch. This is a temporary stitch used to hold fabric in position until permanent stitches are put in. The stitches are 1/4″ to 1/2″ long; they do not have to be even.

Blanket stitch. This is a decorative stitch used for making thread loops and edging heavy materials. Hold the thread at the left. Take a stitch upwards through the fabric, then bring the thread down through the thread you are holding; take another stitch upwards and down through the thread; etc.

Chain stitch. This is a decorative stitch. Insert needle from the reverse side of fabric, form a loop and hold it, stick needle back through fabric at the starting point; bring needle out through fabric and through the bottom end of the loop; form another loop; etc.

Diagonal basting. This is slightly stronger than the ordinary basting stitch and is sometimes left in permanently. It is particularly useful when you are working with slippery material. The diagonal stitches are made on top of the material and may be up to 4″ long. The short stitches are underneath and are up to 3/4″ long.

Herringbone stitch. This is primarily a decorative stitch but has strength and is used for mending sails. Starting at your left, make a slanting stitch upwards; then on the reverse side of the fabric

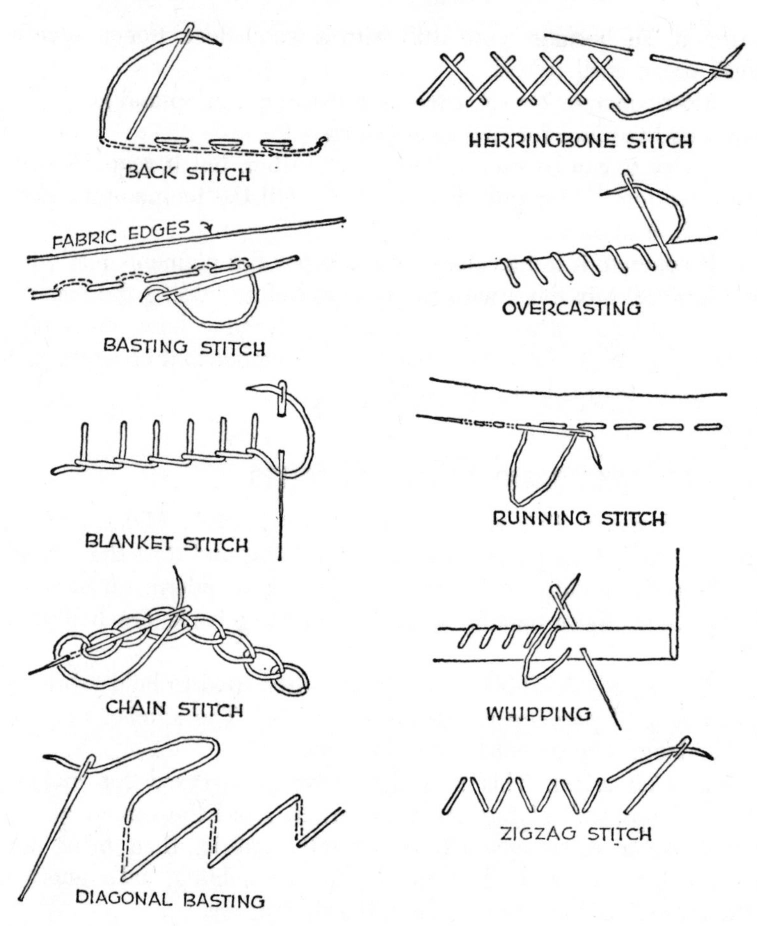

make a short stitch backwards; then make a slanting stitch downward across the first stitch; then make a short stitch backwards and make another slanting stitch upwards.

Overcasting. This stitch is used to prevent raveling of fabric edges. The stitches loop diagonally around the edge and extend about ¼″ into the fabric. Do not pull the thread up tight or you may pucker the material.

Running stitch. Most common of all permanent stitches, this is best made by running the needle through the fabric several times, pulling the needle through, then repeating. The shorter the stitches the better.

Whipping. This is similar to overcasting but the stitches are not so deep. The purpose is to hold down a fabric edge that has been turned under.

Zigzag stitch. This is a strong, decorative stitch used for applying lace, applique work, etc. Each stitch goes at an angle to the one before it. Zigzagging is best done on the sewing machine with a zigzagger.

HOW TO SUPPORT THINGS ON WALLS THAT WILL NOT RECEIVE OR HOLD NAILS AND SCREWS

On masonry walls. Use masonry nails if the object to be supported is not heavy. The specially hardened nails can be hammered directly into mortar joints, concrete blocks, and cinder blocks.

Lead anchors are stronger and more reliable. Drill a hole into any type of masonry surface with a carbide-tipped drill. Tap in a lead anchor the same size as the hole. Then insert a screw of the size recommended for the anchor used. The screw, of course, is first passed through the object to be supported.

Rawl plugs are used like lead anchors, do the same job and are equally reliable. Made of fiber, they require slightly smaller holes.

Miracle anchor bolts or nails are used primarily when other supporting means are difficult to use or when you install a considerable number of anchor points (as when applying wood furring strips to a basement wall). Simply butter the large, flat, perforated head of the bolt or nail with Miracle Adhesive and stick it to the wall. When the adhesive sets, the object to be supported is drilled to receive the bolt or nail, slipped over the anchor and fastened down.

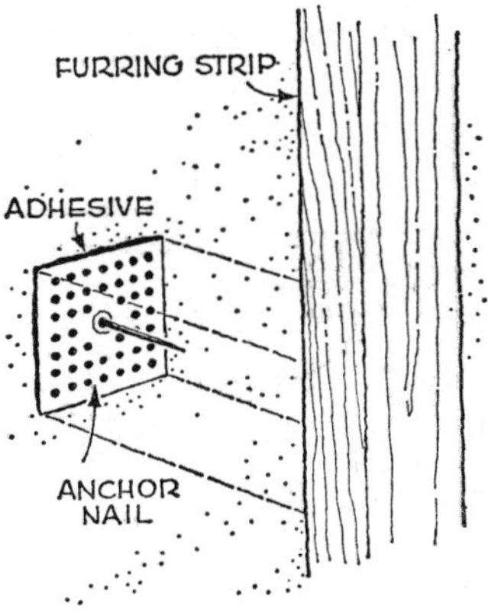

On ceramic tile walls. Use Miracle anchor bolts or nails.

If you are installing towel bars or coat hooks, you can also use the self-attaching type which comes with a capsule of adhesive. Just puncture the capsule, spread the adhesive on the back of the hanger and press the hanger to the wall for two minutes.

On plaster, gypsum board, composition board, hardboard, hollow tile, and other hollow walls. Spring-wing toggle bolts can be used on any wall of this type. Drill through the wall a hole just large enough to admit the spring-wing nut. Insert the bolt through the object to be supported and screw on the nut. Then push nut and bolt through the hole in the wall and tighten the bolt. As you do this, the wings of the nut open against the back of the wall.

A variation of the spring-wing bolt is a conventional toggle bolt that is installed in the same way. The wings, however, are in one piece and pivot at the center. The advantage of this bolt is that you do not have to drill such a large hole in the wall. However, the bolts are not so widely available.

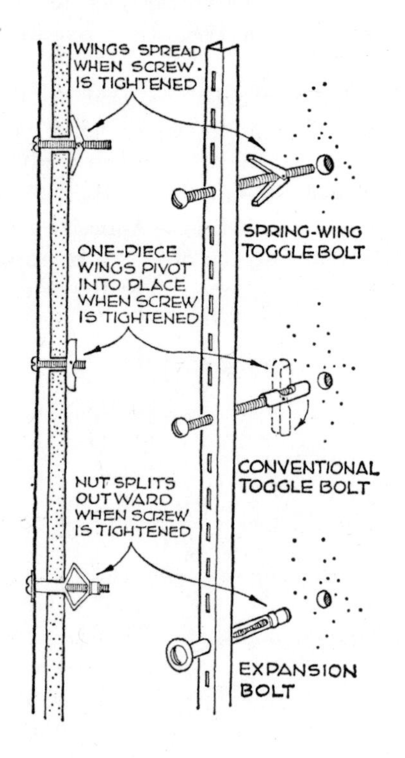

Expansion bolt hangers are best in walls with thin surfaces. The shank of the anchoring "nut" should be no longer than the thickness of the wall surface. The hangers are installed like spring-wing toggle bolts. As you screw up on the bolt, the bottom of the nut splits outward and presses against the back of the wall.

HOW TO CHECK OUT ELECTRICAL APPLIANCES

Electrical appliances are pretty complicated gadgets and difficult to repair. They are also hazardous to repair because you may either get a shock in the process or cause a fire later.

Nevertheless, before you rush out for a serviceman, there are several obvious checks to make:

1. Is the appliance plugged in and turned on? It's surprising how often people call a serviceman without determining this.

2. Are the prongs on the end of the cord plug loose in the outlet? Bend them outward slightly and try plugging in again.

3. Is the outlet into which the appliance is plugged operative? To check this, simply plug a light into it. If the light doesn't go on, the outlet may need to be replaced (see electric outlet).

4. Has the fuse blown on the circuit into which the appliance is plugged? If it has, the little window on the back will be clouded. To replace it, turn off the house current at the meter. Then screw out the fuse and replace with one of exactly the same amperage (this is marked on the tip). Don't use a penny in place of a fuse.

If you have circuit breakers instead of fuses, the breaker handle on the inoperative circuit will be tripped. All you have to do is push it back on again to restore current. (You don't have to shut off the entire house current.)

If when you put in a new fuse (or reset the circuit breaker) it blows again at once, that is a signal that the circuit is overloaded or has a short. An overload is easy to identify. Just disconnect one or more of the appliances that are plugged into the circuit. If the next fuse you install doesn't blow, then you know that you simply were trying to operate too many appliances at the same time.

A short in a circuit is more difficult to spot. You can safely assume, however, that it is in the appliance which doesn't work. So disconnect the appliance and don't reconnect it until you have located the problem.

5. Is the plug loose from the end of the appliance cord? Discon-

nect it and make sure that the bare ends of the wires are screwed down tightly inside the plug (see electric cord). Of course, if the plug is molded on to the cord, you can't do this. But trouble rarely occurs inside such a plug.

6. Is the appliance cord broken? If the cord is of the detachable type, substitute another one for it. If the appliance then works, you know the original cord is defective. If the cord is not detachable, unplug it from the wall outlet and examine it carefully. If you find a break, either make the necessary repairs or replace the cord entirely (see electric cord).

7. Is a built-in type of cord disconnected from the terminals in the appliance? Sometimes it is easy to open up the appliance and check this; more often it is not.

If the appliance still doesn't work after you have taken these steps, it is now advisable to call in a serviceman or take the appliance to him. But if you feel like exploring further, be sure to disconnect the appliance before you proceed.

There are several other things you should know about electrical appliances:

Many minor troubles can be prevented or corrected if you have the instruction books that come with all appliances. Never throw these away. Keep them together in some convenient place.

Keep appliances clean and free of dust. They will work a lot better.

Don't oil appliance motors unless the manufacturers recommend it. Follow their directions exactly.

If an appliance doesn't run at what you think should be the right speed or if it doesn't heat properly, your house wiring may not be adequate. But sometimes the slowdown occurs because there is a voltage drop in the utility's power lines and you are not getting the normal amount of power. (In this case it usually doesn't continue for long.) Both conditions should be checked out by an electrical contractor.

HOW TO PAINT

Since personal experience influences one's thoughts and actions, it is inevitable that my own experience in painting and repainting colors what is written here. I make no apologies for what may seem to be arbitrary opinions. If you want to argue with them or take the opinion of your paint dealer or some one experienced in painting, that's up to you.

Removing old finish. Of course it is not always necessary to do this. On the other hand, it is necessary if you want to replace a paint finish with a natural finish; if the old finish is badly scarred or eroding; if the old finish is too thick, or if the old finish is of a type which cannot be covered.

First, scrape off as much of the finish as you can with a putty knife, paint scraper and pocketknife. Don't work too hard at this; just take off the loose film.

Don't burn off the remaining finish with a torch. It's too dangerous. Electric removers are safer, although even they can cause the paint film to flame up. They are especially useful in removing paint on siding and exterior trim. Just move the tool slowly over the surface and strip off the paint with a putty knife after it.

Liquid removers are best in most jobs. The water washaway type is preferred by many people because, after it softens the finish, you just remove the sludge with a wet cloth. But I have found this type less effective than the others. I prefer the flammable benzol type; the non-flammable type, however, is safer and very good. In any case, the paste removers are easiest to use on vertical surfaces and work as well as the thin liquids on horizontal surfaces.

When using paint-remover, always work in a well-ventilated place. Wear gloves. It's advisable also to wear goggles.

Follow manufacturer's directions. Flow on the remover with an old paintbrush and don't brush back over it. Let stand for 15 minutes or so until finish is soft. Make a test scraping. If finish comes up easily, strip down the entire surface On stubborn areas, apply more paint-remover. Do the scraping with a putty knife, paint scraper or pocketknife. If the old finish is thin and the surfaces are contoured, use coarse rags, steel wool, and a toothbrush. Complete the job by washing the surface with benzine.

While paint-removers are useful for most jobs, there are better methods for others:

Whitewash and kalsomine come off with warm water. Casein paint comes off with warm water to which household ammonia is added.

Floor finishes should be removed by sanding with electric floor sanders.

On ornamental metal use simply a scraper, knife, stiff wire

brush, even a cold chisel. These won't remove all the paint, but liquid removers are too time-consuming.

Penetrating stains can be removed only by sanding, planing or bleaching with a commercial bleach.

Preparing surfaces. When the old finish is removed, fill imperfections in the wood. Then smooth the entire surface with sandpaper.

If old finish does not have to be removed (as on a wall), wash the surface with a mild solution of washing soda or household detergent, then rinse with clear water. Fill holes and cracks with spackle, plastic wood, etc. (for the appropriate filler for a given material, see the mending section). When this is dry, sand smooth. Then, if spackle or patching plaster were used, prime the patches with paint. Prime knots in wood with shellac or aluminum paint.

If the painted surface is very shiny (a hard gloss enamel, for example), roughen with sandpaper.

Painting tools to use and how to use them. Whether you use a brush, roller, or spray gun (or spray can) depends on the contours of the surface, the area and accessibility, and the finish desired.

A brush is the best all-round painting tool. It can be used to apply any type of paint on any type of surface and to achieve any type of finish. A roller is much faster, but its use is pretty well limited to large surfaces and it leaves a slightly stippled finish; furthermore it is very difficult to clean if used with anything other than water-based paint. A spray gun, when properly used, is extremely fast and leaves an almost perfectly smooth paint surface, but the fine mist it produces is a nuisance. A spray can has similar advantages and disadvantages. I recommend that you use sprayers only for painting intricate surfaces (wicker chairs and shutters, for example), for applying lacquer, and for refinishing kitchen cabinets where an extremely flat finish is desired.

Buy the most expensive brush you can afford. It flows the paint on better, doesn't lose its bristles, lasts longer. If you're starting with a new brush, shake out the loose bristles, then suspend the brush in linseed oil for 12 hours so the paint will not cling so tightly in the bristles. Squeeze out the oil with a stick, and spin the handle between your palms to remove the last drops.

Dip the brush only halfway into the paint and slap off the excess on the inside of the can (don't scrape it across the rim). Apply paint with light, short strokes using only the ends of the bristles. Brush back and forth; then smooth the paint with cross strokes; then, to eliminate brush marks almost entirely, smooth out again in the direction you started.

Paint should be brushed on. Enamel, varnish, and lacquer are applied with a somewhat fuller brush and flowed on.

Use short-nap rollers for most jobs; long-nap rollers when painting rough surfaces (stucco or concrete, for instance). Do not overload the roller when filling with paint. Start rolling on paint a slight distance from the previously painted area and work towards that. Roll lightly back and forth—in any direction—but finish by rolling all strokes in one direction.

Instead of buying a spray gun, rent one. Tell the dealer what you are going to paint and have him give you the correct nozzle. Mix the paint thoroughly and strain through cheesecloth or wire screening. Thin it according to dealer's directions.

Before starting to spray, cover everything that is not to be painted with canvas, newspaper, masking tape. Wear a mask—preferably a respirator—when painting.

Spraying is done with a full arm motion. Hold the gun nozzle 6″ from the surface and keep it pointed toward it at right angles. Start your stroke before pulling the trigger and release trigger before reaching the end of the stroke. Always keep the gun moving to avoid building up paint in one spot. Generally it is advisable to spray from side to side, then top to bottom. Overlap spray patterns about one-quarter to one-half.

Painting sequences. If you paint things in logical sequence you will save time, do a better job.

Always start by removing hardware—door knobs, catches, light switch plates, curtain rods, etc. Cover areas you don't want to paint.

In a room, paint the ceiling first, then the walls, then the woodwork.

On a ceiling, start in a corner and work across the width of the room (not the length) to the other corner. Then come back to the wall at which you started and paint another strip across the room. Make each strip only as wide as your arm can reach. Work fast so that edges of first strip are still wet when you paint the second strip (otherwise the overlap cannot be smoothed out).

On a wall, start at the ceiling and paint down to the baseboard. Paint in narrow strips. Don't stop work until entire wall has been painted from corner to corner.

On a paneled door, paint the molded edges around the panels

first, then the panels, then the edges of the door, then the horizontal rails and finally the vertical stiles.

On a window, paint the mullions first, then the frame.

On the exterior of the house, paint the siding first and then the trim (except when you are painting the peak of a tall house, when it is easier to paint siding and trim at the same time). Follow the sun around the house; don't paint in its hot rays.

On chairs and tables, paint the bottoms first, then the top.

On chests and cabinets, paint from top to bottom—the interior first, then the sides, then the front.

What paint to use where. Many modern paints have excellent coverage and are sold for "one-coat" application. But two coats do a better job. For the first coat use a primer or undercoater of the type recommended for use with the final finish.

Most paints and clear finishes are easy to apply if you use the right tools and prepare the surface properly. But two present problems.

Lacquer is tricky because it dries so rapidly. It must be flowed on with a full brush in one quick stroke that leaves an even film. Strokes should overlap very little and you shouldn't brush over a covered surface unless the lacquer has sagged. Spraying is easier.

Another problem with lacquer is that it wrecks other finishes on which it is applied. Therefore, do not use lacquer if you cannot positively identify the original finish as lacquer.

Varnish is somewhat annoying in another way. Because it dries slowly, it picks up dust from the air. In refinishing furniture, therefore, work in a clean, draftless room and, as an extra precaution, it is advisable to hang a tent of newspapers over the piece before you go to work.

SURFACE	PAINT TO USE
Aluminum	Zinc chromate primer followed by any house paint.
Automobiles	Rust-inhibitor followed by auto enamel.
Basement walls	
Masonry	Exterior latex paint, 2 coats.
Gypsum board	Interior latex paint, 2 coats.
Plywood, wood	For a clear finish, apply oil stain followed by wax or dull varnish. For a paint finish, apply primer followed by alkyd paint. For a paint finish on fir plywood, apply white Firzite followed by alkyd paint.

SURFACE	PAINT TO USE
Boats	
Bottoms	2 or 3 coats of antifouling marine paint.
Topsides, wood decks	Marine undercoater followed by 2 coats of marine paint. For a clear finish, apply 2 or 3 coats of spar varnish (if you start with bare wood, apply a marine wood-sealer first).
Canvas decks	Non-skid deck paint, 2 or 3 coats.
Canvas	Canvas paint (but don't use this on decks—only awnings, beach umbrellas, and the like).
Ceilings	Latex paint
Exterior trim, doors, windows	Trim-and-shutter paint, 2 coats (1 often does the trick if trim was previously painted).
Exterior walls	
Wood	For a paint finish, apply 2 coats of alkyd-reinforced oil paint. Use a breather type of paint if condensation is a problem. For a natural finish, apply a penetrating sealer.
Masonry	Exterior latex or vinyl-base paint, 2 coats.
Asbestos cement	Exterior latex paint, 2 coats.
Fences	
Wood	Exterior oil paint or trim-and-shutter paint.
Metal	See iron.
Floors	
Wood	For a clear finish, apply 2 coats of penetrating floor-sealer, then wax. For a paint finish, apply 2 coats of porch enamel.
Concrete	Apply 2 coats of porch enamel.
Furniture, children's	See toys.
Furniture, indoor	For a clear finish, fill open-grained woods, such as oak, with a paste filler of the selected wood color. On all woods, apply 1 coat of oil stain, then two coats of varnish. Sand first coat lightly before applying second. Rub down final coat with very fine steel wool. Follow this, if you wish, by rubbing with rottenstone and linseed oil. Then apply wax. For a paint finish, apply undercoater and gloss enamel.
Furniture, outdoor	For a paint finish, apply trim-and-shutter paint. For a natural finish, apply penetrating sealer as for exterior walls.
Galvanized iron	Zinc dust primer followed by any house paint.

SURFACE	PAINT TO USE
Interior trim, doors, windows	For a paint finish, apply primer followed by enamel. Use a gloss enamel in bathrooms. For a clear finish, apply oil stain followed by dull varnish.
Interior walls	
Gypsum board, plaster, masonry	2 coats latex paint. Use gloss enamel in bathrooms.
Plywood, wood	For a clear finish, apply oil stain followed by wax or dull varnish. For a paint finish, apply primer followed by alkyd paint. For a paint finish on fir plywood, apply white Firzite followed by alkyd paint.
Iron	Apply Rust-Oleum 769 Damp-Proof Red Primer. Follow with trim-and-shutter paint if iron is outdoors; semi-gloss or glass enamel indoors.
Machinery	Rust-inhibitor followed by a machine-and-implement enamel.
Porches, steps, decks	2 coats of porch enamel or deck paint.
Radiators	Rust-inhibitor (if radiator is rusted) followed by 2 coats of oil or alkyd paint. Do not finish with metallic paint.
Screens, window	For a clear finish, 2 coats of spar varnish. Or use screen paint.
Sports equipment, outdoor	
Wood	For a clear finish, stain (if desired) followed by 2 coats of spar varnish. For a paint finish, 2 coats of trim-and-shutter paint.
Steel	See iron.
Steel	See iron.
Toys	Never use exterior paints. For a paint finish, apply undercoater followed by gloss enamel. For a clear finish, apply stain (if desired) followed by 2 coats of varnish or shellac.

Cleaning up after the job. Remove spatters of water-based paint with water; of other types of paint with turpentine.

Wash brushes and rollers used with water-based paint under a running stream of water. Clean out pan used for roller painting at the same time.

Rinse brushes used with other paints in turpentine or Varnaline, then slosh up and down in paintbrush cleaner. Loosen paint in center of brush with your thumb. Rinse again in cleaner. Twirl brush between the palms of your hand. Hang to dry. Store brushes flat.

To revitalize an old brush, soak it in brush cleaner for a day or two. Work it up and down occasionally and scrape out paint as it loosens with a splinter of wood. As cleaner becomes fouled with the paint, strain it through cheesecloth into another container. Keep soaking brush until bristles are clean.

Clean rims of paint cans with a rag before putting on lid. Don't hammer lid down. Step on it firmly.

HOW TO CUT GLASS

It costs so little extra to have glass cut for you that I recommend you do it that way. However, if you want to do the job yourself, you can very easily (but only on single-thick glass like that used in small windowpanes).

Wash the sheet of glass with soapy water. Place it on a clean, firm surface. Use a wood yardstick as your straight edge. Hold glass cutter, slots down, between your first and second fingers with your thumb under the handle. Hold cutter straight up and down and, starting 1/8" from edge of glass farthest from you, press it firmly to glass. Then draw it in a straight, continuous stroke with even pressure along the straight edge toward you.

To break glass, clasp it at end of cut between the fingers of your two hands. Hold firmly on either side of line. Snap quickly downward (away from cut). Another way to break glass is to hold one of the cut ends off the table several inches and tap directly underneath the cut with the end of the glass-cutter handle. To break off a narrow strip of glass, hold it in one hand, slip cutter slot over the edge and snap downward. If uneven edges are left after breaking the glass, you can break them off with the glass-cutter slots or with pliers.

To cut glass in a perfect circle requires a special cutter which turns around a spindle. Cut the circle first. Then cut straight lines from the circle to the edges of the sheet. Break out the waste glass in sections.

HOW TO PREVENT CORROSION

Corrosion—the eating away of metal that occurs when the metal is exposed to oxygen and moisture—is the cause of millions upon millions of repair jobs every year. One authority has estimated that it costs the people in the United States alone about eight billion dollars annually. The corrosion of things you own contributes to the bill.

Obviously, if you don't want to keep on shelling out money and making repairs (which are often difficult or impossible), you should try to prevent the metals in your home, automobile, boat, etc. from corroding. Here, quickly, are some of the things you can do:

In the plumbing system. If your water is very corrosive, install a water conditioner on the supply line where it enters the house. Consult your plumber.

Install insulating joints between pipes of different metals.

If your water pressure is very high, install a pressure-reducing valve on the main supply line. This will cut down water hammer; and that, in turn, will help iron pipe to retain its protective inside coating of rust.

Insulate pipes to prevent sweating and resultant corrosion.

Install a water heater with a solid copper, aluminum or, best of all, copper-silicon (Everdur) tank. Or install a magnesium rod in a steel or glass-lined tank (this is effective in protecting tanks in some parts of the country but not all).

Use Monel instead of brass linkages in toilet tanks.

Use Monel screws to hold washers on faucets.

Don't try to save money on faucets, shower heads, and other bathroom fittings. Only the expensive ones are built to withstand very corrosive waters.

In the heating system. Stop leaks in hot-water and steam lines and radiators. Do not drain the boiler unless your plumber advises it. Water that has been heated time and again loses the oxygen that causes corrosion. Fresh water brings in oxygen.

If you have a gas burner (which produces large amounts of water), install tile-lined or aluminum flues. And put a Tee connection in the base of the stack so that excessive amounts of condensate can drain through the bottom of the Tee instead of collecting in the horizontal runs of the flue.

Drop an inhibitor, such as borax, into the fuel oil tank to prevent corrosion by the moisture that condenses in the tank. Consult your fuel-oil dealer about this.

Outside the house. Keep "tin" roofs, galvanized iron gutters and leaders painted.

Separate aluminum flashing from the mortar in chimney joints with asphalt roofing compound.

Paint aluminum gutters on the inside.

Don't buy cheap aluminum screens, windows, doors if you live near the ocean. Look for quality seal of the Aluminum Architectural Manufacturers' Assn.

Nail siding with aluminum nails. If you use steel nails, countersink the heads and cover with putty.

Paint or varnish window and door screens every year.

In automobiles. Apply undercoater.

Install the best mufflers and exhaust pipes you can buy.

Wash car—especially the undersides—often during the winter when salt is used on the roads.

Avoid short, start-and-stop rides. The condensation produced by combustion of the fuel does not have time to evaporate. Result: the cylinder walls corrode.

Stop leaks in radiators. Every time you add water you add oxygen, which causes corrosion.

Keep battery cables clean and coated with vaseline at the terminals.

In boats. Install Everdur, stainless steel or Monel fastenings and fittings (but not on aluminum or steel boats).

Don't let one type of metal touch another. Insulate them with rubber or neoprene.

Install tinned Everdur or tinned copper fuel and water tanks.

Install copper or Everdur fuel and water lines.

Install copper mufflers and exhaust lines.

To protect steel and aluminum hulls and other underwater steel components from salt water, attach Special High-Grade zinc anodes directly to them. Also recommended are zinc-cadmium-aluminum anodes.

Tools. Dry off thoroughly every time you use them outdoors or near water. Store in a dry place. Rub occasionally with an oily rag.

When storing power mowers and similar equipment, clean

thoroughly, remove rust, touch up chipped paint, rub an oily rag over bare metal. Remove spark plug and squirt a little oil into hole; then turn engine over two or three times by hand or with the starter cord. This will prevent rusting of cylinders, pistons, and valves.

Toys, sports equipment. Keep in a dry place if possible.

Keep painted.

Miscellany. Paint insides of garbage cans with asphalt roofing cement. Paint under the bottom, too.

Don't use dip cleaners on silver plate.

Dry lid hinges on automatic washing machines after every use.

Don't use steel wool or strong detergents on cast-iron utensils.

Install weatherproof electric outlets, switches, etc. outdoors. For good measure, paint them with liquid neoprene.

HOW TO STOP CONDENSATION

You can't see condensation—water vapor—except when it collects on your windows. But it is likely to be the cause of—

rotting timbers in the attic
rotting joists in the floor over a crawl space
rotting sills in a crawl space
blistered and peeling paint on the outside walls of a wood house
falling plaster
stained and loose wallpaper

There are four ways to stop this invisible menace.

1. Reduce humidity in the house. You can do this by improving housekeeping practices (for instance, cover pots on the stove; use as little water as possible when mopping floors). But you should also equip sinks, lavatories, tubs, and showers with mixing faucets so that you will not saturate the air with steam. Cover the ground in unexcavated areas under the house with 55-lb. roofing felt laid with 2″ lapped joints or with heavy polyethylene film.

2. Improve ventilation. You probably have a ventilating fan in the kitchen. Install one in the laundry, too. And consider putting fans in the bathrooms.

Increase the size of screened ventilating openings under the roof and in all unexcavated areas, or install additional openings. This is a job which calls for an expert who fully understands the rules for sizing ventilators. (If you can't find such, write to the Superintendent of Documents in Washington for the House & Home Finance Agency's booklet, "Condensation Control.")

3. Install vapor barriers in all outside walls, floors over crawl spaces and top-floor ceilings (or roof). The purpose of these is to prevent condensation from seeping out of your rooms into wall, roof and underfloor cavities. In an existing house, the easiest way to install the barriers is to paint the walls and ceilings on the inside with two coats of oil, alkyd or rubber-base paint and to cover wood floors with varnish.

4. Insulate the house. This will raise the surface temperature of walls, ceilings, and floors and prevent water vapor from condensing on them. Note, however, that if you don't have vapor barriers, insulation should not be installed, because it may actually increase the danger of condensation forming in the wall, etc., cavities.

HOW TO COPE WITH TERMITES

Suppose you discover that the sills and other wood members in the lower part of your house are "rotten." If there is no evidence that moisture is causing the damage, you must suspect termites. They are now found in every state except Alaska.

How to tell if you have termites. Here are four ways:

1. Termites look like ants but have thick waists and four wings of equal size. Ants have pinched-in waists and the wings are of different size.

2. When termites swarm out of the ground—usually in the spring—they lose their wings. You may find these in little piles on the ground.

3. Termites build small tunnels of earth on foundation walls.

4. Termite damage to wood is not always visible. But if you find that a piece of wood is soft enough for you to stick an ice pick in deeply, tear off the outer layer. If termites have been at work, you will find tunnels running with the grain and littered with small gray specks.

How to get rid of termites. The following steps are essential:

1. Scrape termite tubes off the foundation walls. Fill holes and cracks in walls with concrete or asphalt roofing compound.

2. Remove wood, paper and other cellulose material from

around and under house. It even pays to dig up the soil and remove the debris you find.

3. Don't let any wood part of the house touch the ground. Raise on concrete blocks or piers.

4. If your basement or crawl space is damp, take steps to get rid of the dampness. Pipe roof water away from the house. Slope the ground away from the house. Waterproof the foundation walls. Install larger ventilators in crawl spaces. Some of these things you can do yourself; some require the services of a mason.

5. Treat the soil under and around the house with chlordane, dieldrin, or aldrin. This is a simple enough job but requires arduous digging and crawling into cramped, hard-to-get-at places. You'll be better off to call in a pest-control firm.

6. Whenever you have to replace a sill or other wood structural member, use pressure-treated wood (wood that has been impregnated with a preservative under pressure). Brush additional preservative (pentachlorophenol, zinc or copper naphthanate) on all cut or bored surfaces.

GLOSSARY OF TERMS AS USED IN THIS BOOK

Aerator. A device on the end of a faucet which introduces air into the water and thus breaks up the hard flow. This is done by a system of tiny screens inside a screw-on cap.

Angle iron. An L-shaped piece of rigid steel used for joining and bracing the corners of doors, windows, etc.

Auger. A plumber's boring tool resembling a long coiled spring with a claw at the tip and a handle to crank it.

Bail. The wire handle on a bucket.

Becket. One of the loops by which the edges of a tent are fastened to the ground.

Bevel. To cut the square edges of, say, a board at an angle. A bevel is also an angled surface.

Batten. A strip, usually of wood, fastened lengthwise over a crack between adjacent materials.

Bulkhead. The outside basement door which is installed above the steps leading down from the yard into the basement.

Butt. To bring together. In a wood floor, for example, the wood strips are butted together.

Caulk. To fill and seal a crack with some plastic material such as putty or caulking compound.

C-clamp. A clamp shaped like the letter C. Small C-clamps are made of steel; large ones of wood and steel.

Chuck. On a drill, the sleeve which tightens around a bit and holds it on the brace.

Coarse aggregate. The clean stones of varying size used in some concrete mixes.

Cold chisel. A heavy steel chisel used for cutting stone, brick, metal, etc.

Commutator. The round, segmented copper collar on the shaft of some electric motors.

Compression faucet. The most common type of faucet, though now being displaced. It can be identified by the rubber or composition washer screwed on the end of the faucet spindle.

Cotter pin. A device used to join two things (usually made of metal). The pin has a ring-like head and two parallel prongs which are bent to the side after the pin is installed.

Countersink. To drive beneath the surface. Nails are countersunk with a steel punch. Screws are countersunk by drilling a shallow hole large enough to receive the screw head. The nail or screw heads are then covered with spackle, putty, etc.

Disc sander. An electric drill converted to use as a sander by inserting in the chuck a round, flat, sandpaper-covered disc in place of the drill bit.

Dowel. A straight, round pin, usually of wood but sometimes of metal, which is inserted in opposite holes in two materials that are to be joined together.

Eccentric. A device which revolves in an unusual pattern.

Efflorescence. The crusty, whitish stains that appear on masonry surfaces.

Escutcheon. A more or less ornamental covering plate, such as the plate behind a doorknob.

Fascia. The outward-facing board under eaves and cornices.

Ferrule. A ring of metal used to strengthen and hold together a tool head and handle.

Finial. The ornamental top on lamps, bedposts, etc.

Finishing nail. A slender nail with a small head that is easily countersunk.

Flange. A projecting edge or rim which holds a thing in place. At the bottom of an official U.S. mailbox, for instance, there are four flanges which fit around the board on which the mailbox sits.

Flashing. The sheet material, usually metal, used to prevent leaks at joints in the roof and exterior walls.

Flux. Liquid or paste material used to clean metal that is to be soldered. It assures that the solder will adhere tightly to the metal.

Friction tape. Black, fabric, sticky tape, sometimes called tire tape.

Furring strip. A strip, usually of wood, which separates and permits the easy joining of one flat surface to another. For example, when gypsum board is to be applied over a basement wall, wood furring strips are first attached to the wall and the gypsum board is nailed to these.

Gasket. A device made of more or less flexible material which seals a joint. On a water pump, for example, gaskets are used to seal the joints between sections of the suction chamber.

Gate valve. A plumbing valve that controls the water flow by means of a metal tongue which screws in and out of the body of the valve.

Gland nut. The metal nut which holds stuffing material, called a gland, in place. The gland prevents water leakage around a propeller shaft or a piston rod in a water pump.

Glazier's point. A small, triangular piece of metal used to hold a windowpane securely.

Grout. A soupy mixture usually of Portland cement and water used either to fill small joints (as in a ceramic tile floor) or to ensure the adherence of a stiffer mortar.

Gypsum. A mineral used for making plaster or the rigid, paper-covered boards used in place of plaster.

Jamb. One of the pieces forming the sides of a doorway or window opening.

Joist. One of the timbers supporting a floor.

Lath. The base to which plaster is applied. In modern construction the lath is commonly a flexible roll of perforated steel. Wood laths are thin strips of unfinished wood which, in walls, are nailed parallel to one another across the studs.

Lead anchor. A cylinder of lead which is tapped into a hole in masonry or plaster to hold a screw.

Louver. One of the slanted strips of wood, metal or glass set in a frame that is designed to admit air but not water. The word is also used to describe the entire ventilating device; an attic louver, for example.

Miter. To cut at an angle other than 90°. As a noun, the word means the acutely angled joint formed by two pieces of material that are fitted together, as at the corners of a picture frame.

Mortar joint. The cement-filled joint between bricks, stones, concrete blocks, etc.

Mortise. A hole or recess into which something fits. For example, a hinge is set into a mortise in a door jamb.

Mullion. A wood or metal strip which divides one windowpane from another. Mullions are more properly called muntins, but the latter word is disappearing from common use.

Neoprene. A special type of rubber.

Packing nut. The large nut which holds flexible stuffing material in place around the stem of a faucet.

Placket. An opening or slit in a garment. For instance, a skirt has a placket at the waistline to permit putting it on and it may have plackets at the hemline to provide ease of movement.

Plumber's friend. A bell-shaped rubber device with a wood handle. It is used to dislodge stoppages in plumbing drains.

Pumice. A fine abrasive powder used for rubbing down materials to obtain a smooth finish.

Quarter round. A strip of wood which, viewed end on, forms one quarter of a circle.

Rabbet. A groove in the edge or face of a piece of wood, metal, etc. For example, mullions are rabbeted to receive panes of glass.

Rail. One of the horizontal members of which a door is made.

Ratchet. The device which engages a toothed or cogged wheel and either makes it turn or prevents it from turning.

Riser. The vertical part of a step.

Rottenstone. A fine abrasive powder used for rubbing down materials to obtain a very smooth finish. It is slightly less coarse than pumice.

Rouge. A very, very fine red abrasive powder.

Scale. The rough material deposit that forms on surfaces in the presence of some waters.

Self-tapping screw. A screw used in metal work.

Shank. The leg or part of a device by which it is connected to another device.

Sheathing. The boards or panels nailed to the outside of studs or rafters to form a base for the finish siding or roofing material.

Shim. A thin piece of wood, metal, stone, cardboard, etc. which is inserted under or behind something in order to make it level or to move it outward or upward.

Siding. The outside covering of the walls of a building.

Spackle. A type of plaster for filling holes, cracks and dents (usually fairly small) in plaster, gypsum board, painted wood, etc. Ordinary spackle is a dry powder which is mixed with water, but there is now available a pre-mixed vinyl-base spackle.

Spline. A thin strip of wood or metal. In a screen, a spline is laid over the screencloth and the two are pushed into a slot in the frame to hold the screencloth tightly in place.

Spreader. A metal gadget used to brace wobbly chairs and tables. It consists of a central turnbuckle to which four wires are attached. The wires, in turn, are attached to the chair or table legs. A better known type of spreader is the wheeled cart used to spread fertilizer and grass seed.

Stile. The vertical pieces that form the sides of a door or window. Compare with "rail".

Stop bead. One of the strips against which a door rests when it is closed tight, or which holds a window sash in its frame.

Stop valve. A plumbing valve which controls the water flow by means of a flat washer which can be turned tight against a valve seat. It is the type most commonly found in homes (on the supply lines leading to lavatories and toilets, for instance).

Strike plate. The metal device which is screwed to a door jamb and engages the latch when the door is closed.

Stringer. The saw-toothed timbers to which stair treads and risers are attached.

Stud. One of the upright timbers in a wall. These are usually 2″ by 4″ and are spaced 16″ on centers.

Stuffing box. The small chamber around a propeller shaft or water pump piston rod. It is stuffed with flexible material, sometimes called a gland, which prevents water leakage around the shaft or rod.

Tang. The slender, pointed end of a knife, fork, file, etc. which fits into the handle of the implement.

Tenon. The thing which fits into a mortise.

Terne. Steel coated with lead and tin. Thin terne sheets are used on roofs.

Toggle bolt. A bolt used for fastening something to a surface when the back of the surface is inaccessible. For example, toggle bolts might be used to bolt a heavy mirror to a plaster wall.

Turnbuckle. A device used to join and tighten two threaded rods. The rods are threaded in opposite directions so that when you turn the turnbuckle to the right it simultaneously draws the rods toward each other and when you turn to the left it pushes the rods apart.

Valve seat. The surface inside the body of a faucet on which the washer is seated when the faucet is turned off.

Whiting. A mineral used in putty.

Wiggle nail. Colloquial name for a corrugated metal fastener—a small strip of corrugated metal with sharp points along one side.

INDEX